LIZ EDMUNDS

HERE ARE NOTES FROM HAPPY FOOD NANNY FAMILIES:

"We are sick of cereal!" When I heard those words from my kids I knew I needed help with dinner. The Food Nanny gave me realistic recipes and a plan that actually works for my family. The concept is a no-frills approach to getting dinner on the table and to getting the family talking. The great thing is you are already buying the food, now you get to use it instead of throwing it away because you're not organized! I love the Food Nanny Meal Plan.

Debbie Worthen

For anyone without the always-organized, magazine-cover family, this book is for you. As a mother with two young children and a husband working long hours in the hospital, I had all but given up on consistent family dinnertime. It took tremendous energy each day to plan a recipe, purchase the ingredients, cook the meal, and then have it on the table perfectly timed for our busy family. It seemed I was at the grocery store almost on a daily basis. Picking up take-out that could be reheated as needed became an increasingly attractive option. Liz's message has brought my family back to the dinner table together and saved me hours each day in the process. It has now been five years since I have been following her easy and straight forward weekly meal plans, including her tips on making grocery shopping more organized and effective. My family loves her recipes, and her books are a permanent fixture on my counter-top cookbook stand. It is far more than a collection of delicious, easy-to-follow recipes, but rather a brilliant formula for family success! The time spent around the dinner table is the highlight of the day for all of us. No kitchen is complete without this cookbook!

Jenny Preece

Back when I was first introduced to the Food Nanny Plan I was very over weight. I knew that I needed to change things in my life. With the help of exercise, eating right/portion control, and planning meals out I knew I was well on my way. After a month and half I was down 20 lbs. and over the space of six months I had lost 60 lbs. I feel a huge factor to my weight loss was Liz's two-week meal plan. Not only did this stop me from eating out, but it allowed me to see that I could cook for my family healthy and delicious meals. I had tried dieting. I had tried weight loss cookbooks. None of them taught me how to plan and cook meals that I liked. I didn't want to give up the foods that I loved and I didn't want to cut my calories to 500 a day. The Food Nanny is so easy to follow; it has many suggestions of substitutions to make the meal lighter, and even gives easy advice as to what sides to serve with the meal. Obviously losing weight takes time, commitment, and exercise, but I feel like The Food Nanny set me on the right path, taught me how to plan, and gave me confidence to cook. I have now reached my goal weight, however, The Food Nanny meal plan and recipes continue to be our family routine!

Kara Jenkins

I first met Liz 3 years ago when my twin daughters were starting to eat solid foods. She came to my home and taught me how to help my children enjoy a variety of foods right from the start. I have shared that knowledge with many friends and family members who have wondered why my children will eat anything I cook. The Food Nanny cookbook is my favorite source for recipes, and Liz's Nanny Plan has helped me simplify my life because I know in advance what I'm fixing for dinner each day. The Food Nanny really has rescued dinner at our house.

Jennifer Ross

My first encounter with Liz Edmunds was at Deseret Book 5 years ago when she was debuting her first Food Nanny Cookbook. Her enthusiasm over family dinnertime was contagious, her samples were delicious, and I bought autographed copies for myself and all 5 of my daughters. Since then, I have been privileged to attend many of Liz's classes, and have been inspired by her personal attention to nutrition and family togetherness in many venues, including her own kitchen. She has transformed the way my family thinks of dinnertime and has given us the tools to simplify and truly enjoy cooking again.

Eileen Swenson

My daughter's success with The Food Nanny made me want to try it myself. I had one son left at home that we hardly saw. He was a senior in H.S. busy with sports and other activities after school, and just never came home. I was determined that cooking dinner on a consistent basis would bring him home. I designed a meal plan with all the foods that we loved and craved the most. The Food Nanny said, "Cook and they would come home!" That is exactly what I did. The first couple of nights he did not come home, but I encouraged him to do so and pleaded with him to join us for dinner. On the third night he called and asked, "Mom are you really cooking dinner tonight?" I said yes, and dinner would be at 6:00 p.m. as promised.
I had not been cooking dinner because of crazy schedules, including my own. We wanted to spend more time together and especially to get to know our son before he left for college. We spent the most memorable year getting to know each other, all because I was cooking and putting on a consistent family dinnertime. My two sons eventually did a tour in Iraq and I was so grateful for the time we were able to spend together at the dinner table. Thanks, Food Nanny for your meal plan and yummy recipes!

Donna Christensen

Liz has spent her life traveling the world, and has brought to all of our tables tried and true recipes from Italy to Thailand. Before knowing Liz and using her inspired meal plan method and recipes, dinner was not something any of us looked forward to in our home. We ate out a lot! Now we can't wait to get dinner on the table, and I love making it! It has changed everything! The meal plan simplifies dinnertime, cooking and shopping, and the recipes will truly become your favorites.

Natalie Kirkham

This book is dedicaded to families all over the world.
May sitting together at the dinner table,
with good food and good conversation,
become the foundation for each new day.

Xo The Food Nanny!!!

A MESSAGE FROM THE FOOD NANNY

Since my first book came out 5 years ago, I have had the opportunity to visit many of you in your hometowns. I love people, so this has been a wonderful experience for me. In my presentation, I talk about how to make dinnertime happen in your lives no matter what your situation or budget. I have a system that really works. It is a meal plan that I have been living and teaching for over 30 years. For me, it has become a way of life. I have gone into homes and "Rescued Dinner" on my reality TV show called, The Food Nanny, on BYUtv. We traveled to London, Italy, Greece, and Turkey just to cook and talk with different families about how important dinner is in their culture, and how they make it happen. I have been taught new recipes by some of the best chefs in the world. And, of course, I have also gone into homes here in America to help families that are struggling to get back to the dinner table.

No matter where we live, we all want the same thing: we want our families to stay close. Getting together as a family at dinnertime is the connection we need in our homes on a consistent basis to keep our families strong. President Reagan said, "All great change in America begins at the dinner table." How right he was. This is where we teach family values, share dreams of past, present and future. This is where we learn the art of conversation. My Food Nanny conversation starters have proven to be a big help to families when it is hard for family members to get a conversation started. Dinnertime keeps us close, well fed and happy.

See you at dinner.

Xo The Food Nanny

MAKE MEAL PLANNING SIMPLE WITH A FEW EASY RULES

My theme nights saved me!

MONDAY **COMFORT FOOD**
TUESDAY **ITALIAN NIGHT**
WEDNESDAY **FMB NIGHT**
THURSDAY **MEXICAN NIGHT**
FRIDAY **PIZZA NIGHT**
SATURDAY **GRILL NIGHT**
SUNDAY **TRADITIONS**

These are themes that worked for our family. If these themes don't work for you, choose ones that will. Remember, the hardest part about cooking dinner is trying to figure out what to cook. Having a theme for each night will make planning easy and fun at the same time.

THE RULES THAT CHANGED MY LIFE

1. Don't eat red meat on back to back nights.
2. Eat no meat at all (meatless dishes) at least 1 to 2 times a week.
3. Eat fresh fish at least once a week, preferably 2 nights a week.

1. Don't eat red meat back to back. Why? I learned over 30 years ago that eating red meat back to back on a regular basis could clog up our systems...There is controversy on that today but I still adhere to that rule. Over 40 years of cooking meals for my family has proven to me that eating more veggies, greens, whole grains and fruit, with slimmer portions of meat is healthier. It is moderation in everything that is the rule here. Common sense would tell us to eat all things in moderation and eat a great variety of food. Whether red meat clogs up your system or not, I believe that smaller portions are best. I also believe that small portions of red meat are essential to our diet.

2. What do I mean by eating Meatless meals? We do not need to eat some kind of meat every night for dinner. There are those that consider fish to be meat and those that don't consider fish to be meat. I like to think of fish as not eating meat. It is nice to eat meatless a couple of nights a week, and for me fish would be included in meatless. In both of my books, I have delicious meatless meals to choose from for every night of the week.

3. Introducing fresh fish into your family's diet is essential. In many parts of the world, families are eating fresh fish every night. Many nutritionalists recommend serving fresh fish at least two nights per week. I have tried to incorporate at least once a week into my personal meal plan.

FOOD NANNY Additional Rules

1. Make a 2-week meal plan.
2. Make a grocery list at the same time you create your menu, and then go shopping.
3. Apply Portion Control.
4. Plan 2 to 3 vegetables with most meals.
5. Incorporate whole grains into your diet, offer fresh or bottled fruit often.
6. Make a planned dessert one night a week.

When I sit down once every two weeks the rules listed above are the rules I follow. It makes planning so easy. Let me talk briefly about each one of the rules I have mentioned above.

1. I learned through trial and error that a 2-week meal plan was perfect. I tried a one week plan for a time but found that it was not long enough in-between planning. I tried a month plan. That was too much food to buy and too much to think about in 10-15 minutes. I tried 2 weeks. That became my ideal.

2. Creating a grocery list at the same time while planning your menu gets two necessary steps done at once. It is easy. When you get good at it all you will need is about 10-15 minutes to create both, especially if you have the recipes right in front of you. Make your plan, create a grocery list and do one main shopping every 2 weeks. You may have to go back for more essentials like fresh fruit, veggies or milk.

3. Portion Control is probably the Number 1 most important rule when it comes to eating. I learned this as a child. Teach kids and adults to take smaller amounts on their plates. Eating until we are comfortable and satisfied and not full or stuffed is eating with Portion Control. If you can get this practice down you will never have a weight problem, ever. You will avoid going up and down in weight. Diets don't work long term. Eating with portion control does. I have been doing it my entire life and have taught portion control to my family from the beginning. When you eat out, share your food or eat half of it and take the other half home. Realize also that when you do eat out you are consuming most likely 30 - 50% more calories on the exact same dish you would cook at home. Why? Because you have control over the butter, cream and cheese.

4. Eating Vegetables on a daily basis is so important to our diet. I get most of my vegetables at dinner. There are a few exceptions. If I am making pancakes for dinner, I am not eating vegetables with my pancakes. I don't always have veggies on my pizza. But on a consistent basis I am eating plenty of veggies. I made sure to have at least 2 to 3 veggies on the table when my kids were growing up. I knew that they would find at least one or two veggies that they enjoyed eating. I made sure that the side dishes were more important than the meat. I used fresh veggies, frozen and canned.

5. Whole Grains. Everyone knows that eating plenty of veggies, fresh fruits and whole grains makes for a great diet. With whole grains we get more nutritional value than calories.

6. Make a planned dessert one night a week. I made a planned dessert on Monday Night. Everyone looked forward to it. I had other sugar treats often during the week such as homemade cookies, a birthday cake, or a pan of brownies for example. I found that if you deny kids of all sugar treats they would find it someplace else. Nothing is wrong with a few cookies, or a small piece of cake or pie once in awhile. We were big on chocolate malts, in small little glasses. Teach your children to eat desserts in small portions. This is so important. Share desserts when you go out to eat. Teaching these few principles when it comes to desserts will keep your family healthy and really happy!

HERE IS HOW YOU GET STARTED

1. Use my Nanny Plan template and Shopping List page 330-331.

2. Get out my cookbooks and other recipes that you love.

3. I say to cook 5 nights a week. Take 2 days off. It is nice to eat out or order-in food a couple of nights a week. That gives us a break and makes life enjoyable. However, when I was raising my family, I was on a budget and could not eat out 2 times a week, so I always planned for the entire 2 weeks. If I happened to go out, no problem, I saved that meal and incorporated it into my next 2-week plan. If a night got crazy and I got off my plan, no problem. The next night I picked right back up. Homemade waffles or grilled cheese sandwiches were my crazy day go-to meals.

4. Start with Comfort Food Night. Look through the recipes. Choose a meal. Write the name of the recipe you have chosen in Comfort Food Night. Then write in the ingredients you will need on your shopping list. If you choose meat then you will need to pick your sides. Sides will include plenty of veggies, a starch such as potatoes, rice, quinoa, pasta, salad etc.…write down your side dishes. Now go over and write down on your grocery list what you will need. Don't serve a starch and bread with every meal. Sometimes just a starch. Sometimes just bread. Sometimes both. Often, meat and a salad, or meat and veggies. Leftovers are fine, but not every other night. (I will give you a 2-week sample menu for you to follow along on page 12.)

5. Choose something for the next meal either meatless or a meat that you didn't have the night before. Make sure to include fish in your menu plan. (If your family cannot eat fish, then choose meatless). Just make sure that the star of your meal will be plenty of veggies, or salad greens along with whatever meat you are serving. As you create your menu you will see that you are getting this great variety of food. Red meat, poultry, no meat, plenty of veggies, fruit, salads, breads.

This menu plan has kept my family and me healthy for 3 decades. It has made cooking fun and easy.

BUDGET FRIENDLY

Most people report back to me that they **save 50%** on their food budgets by using my plan. Too often we go to the store and buy food that will end up wasting because we don't have a plan. **Don't go to the store hungry.** If you do, you will also end up buying food that will waste, or you will buy prepared food that you could have made homemade for half the cost.

If you don't cook on a regular basis your pantry is empty and when you do decide to cook, say lasagna, you have nothing so it seems really expensive to cook a meal. No spices, no canned tomatoes, no cheese etc....so the lasagna ends up costing $40 to make. When you cook often, you start to **build a pantry.** When you see lasagna noodles on sale buy 2 of them, etc. If you used ricotta cheese, for example, in preparing another dish and you have some left over choose another meal with ricotta cheese in the next 2 weeks. You will be surprised at the ingredients you start to build as you cook and bake more. Often I would go to the store and find many items on my list on sale, it was such a pleasant surprise. Try it, I know it will happen for you as well.

I know people who look in the paper and see **what's on sale** and then build their menu around sale items. Buy generic items instead of name brands. Often you can save $$ **clipping coupons** if you like doing that. If you have the money, **buy in bulk**, which costs much more up front, but then lasts a long time as it saves you money.

Depending on my budget I did all of these things
at different times in my life.
Whatever season of life you are in make it work for you.

thefoodnanny

SHOPPING LIST

mm/dd/yy - mm/dd/yy

PRODUCE
- Potatoes - 5 lbs.
- Red Potatoes - 4
- Onions - 3
- Carrots - 2 lb
- Rosemary -
- Green Onio
- Celery -
- Tomat
- Parsl
- Len
- L

FISH/MEAT
- Boneless/Skinless
- Chicken - 8 pieces
- - 2 lbs.

CANNED GOODS
- Peaches - 1 can
- Tomato sauce - 1 8oz. can

DAIRY
- Butter - 2 lbs.
- Unsalted Butter - 1 lb.
- Sour Cream - 1 large
- Milk - 2 gallons
- Cheddar Cheese - 8oz.
- Parmesan Cheese - 8 oz.
- ggs - 2 doz.
- Cheese -

FROZEN
- Peas - 16 oz.

OTHER GROCERIES
- All Purpose Flour
- Whole Wheat Flour
- Brown Sugar
- Powdered Milk
- Quick oats
- Olive oil
- Vegetable oil
- Cooking wine
- Cider Vinegar
- Balsamic Vinegar
- Honey
- ayonnaise
- ut butter

thefoodnanny

mm/dd/yy - mm/dd/yy

NANNY PLA

MON	TUES	WED	THURS	FRI	SAT	SUN
Comfort Food	Italian Night	FMB Night	Mexican Night	Pizza Night	Grill Night	Traditions
Shepard's Pie with Chicken, Zucchini The Queen of Chocolate Cup Cakes	Authentic Ragu with Fuselli, Salad - butter lettuce, tomatoes, red onion, olive oil, balsamic vinegar French Baguettes	Macadamia Nut Crusted Fish, Rice Steamed broccoli, Cauliflower, carrots	Chicken Taquitos, Food Nanny Lime Rice	Little Italy Pizza	Easy Grilled Teriyaki chicken Grilled Lemony Potatoes, Fresh green beans and carrots, steamed	Rosemary Lamb Cho Parmesan Noodles, Zucchini, fried carrots, baked Homemade Crescent Rolls

MON	TUES	WED	THURS	FRI	SAT	SUN
Comfort Food	Italian Night	FMB Night	Mexican Night	Pizza Night	Grill Night	Traditions
Bangkok Stir Fry, Almond Cake with Fresh Rosemary Cream	Ravioli with Sage in Butter Sauce, Salad - Butter lettuce, tomatoes, red onion, olive oil, balsamic vinegar Warm Artisan Bread	Flap Jacks with Oats and Whole Wheat, Butter and Syrup Peaches- fresh or canned	Beef Enchilada Dinner, Salad - Butter lettuce, tomatoes, red onion, olive oil, avocado, balsamic vinegar	Fabulous Thai Chicken Pizza	Grilled Balsamic Honey Glazed Salmon, Creamy Grilled Potatoes, Bruschetta	Brilliant Oven BBQ Chicken, Mashed Potatoes Corn on Cob Steamed Broccoli Homemade Crescent Rolls

OTES:

Liz Edmunds

THEF

NANNY PLAN AND SHOPPING LIST

*Here is an example Nanny Plan and Shopping List so you get the idea of how I would make a typical 2-week meal plan.
I have listed all of the items that would be needed to carry out this meal plan, so you get the idea.*

NANNY 2-Week Meal Plan
NANNY SHOPPING LIST

Someone has to be in charge:
I tell women that statistics tell us that women still own dinnertime and we do. Women are still responsible for the nurturing and health of the family. Moms just need to make dinnertime happen. The word dinnertime comes with a lot of meaning. It does not mean just throwing any kind of food together and letting everyone know that dinner is cooked when they want to eat it. Dinnertime is a way of life. Family members respect that time. Parents or caretakers realize that this time is critical. This is where we come together at the end of the day to catch up with one another. Preparing the food should involve all family members. If you live in the house, everyone is expected to be at the table. Everyone. Even a teenager who doesn't feel like eating, or a sibling who is angry with another family member.

Adults are required to catch as many dinnertimes as possible during the week.
I learned early on that you can't wait for everyone to be home for the dinner hour to motivate you to cook. You cook for the people who are there. The latecomers will come home and they will have a plate waiting for them. Set a dinner hour time and get everyone to commit to being there as often as possible. Someone has to be in charge of making a menu plan, shopping for the food and putting it away. You can share responsibility in cooking the meals. As long as the recipe is handy, even kids 12 and older can have a night assigned to them. Years ago I had visions of taking kids off the streets and turning them into chefs in their own homes.
I soon realized that would never happen unless a caretaker paid for the food and gave them a plan. With a plan, kids of all ages are cooking and doing something worth while after school.

Leaning how to cook is so vital to this generation because it is becoming a lost art. Learn to make your own "fast food" at home. And what I call fast food at home would be something like great Bruschetta, an omelet, a Frittata, a piece of fresh fish, a piece of broiled meat, or salad. Leftover chili and corn bread. Sometimes making healthy food takes longer than 30 minutes and that is not a bad thing. Just plan for it and make the necessary adjustments.

TAKING TIME

Cooking for 1 or 2 people:
Take time to plan, prepare, and sit down, even if it means eating alone. It is well worth the effort. Often lately, I have found myself sitting down to something yummy with a good book. A good book is company as well. Everyone needs to enjoy a meaningful dinnertime. You get a chance to restore yourself and that is benefit enough. Simple but thoughtfully chosen meals are almost always more nutritious and more satisfying than grazing your way through a miscellaneous assortment of foods. Don't stress about exactly what foods need to be included in the meal.

Remember **enjoyment** is just as much a part of it. I often suggest to those who are cooking for just themselves to invite someone in to eat with you a couple of nights a week. Take leftovers to a needy friend in your building or neighborhood. Plan to take leftovers to work with you and share with your co-workers. Making a pan of brownies, eating a couple and then taking the rest to work is a win-win. Just learn to **share food** so that you too can eat well.

Learn that taking time to take care of just you is worth it as well. Part of eating healthy is having a cozy place to eat. Get a small table just for two. **Make it inviting.** Let that space call you. I have a little table where I often eat lunch in a window that is just right for one or two people. It calls me everyday for lunch when I am alone. Create spaces that are all your own that make life fun and **rewarding.**

You owe it to yourself to nourish and nurture yourself with a nice meal.

MOVING FORWARD

More people are **home cooking** now and wanting to know more about where our food is coming from. Three out of four adults are not getting half the required daily serving of fruits and vegetables. Many of the vitamins that we need on a daily basis can come from the food we eat. We want to process our own food. We need to get away from processed food. I find often while going into people's homes they have a freezer full of **processed food** that they live on daily. I stay away from those kinds of foods. They have their place and time but not everyday. There are ways to save time when cooking your own food, like taking advantage of our freezers more. Double the sauce and freeze half for next week's dinner. Double the soup and freeze half for dinner in the next 2 weeks. **Freeze leftover** mashed potatoes, warm them for dinner the next week.

We can become more **time efficient** and at the same time help our environment with using less gas and electricity. We are "greener" than ever, which means becoming more efficient. **"Clean Eating"** simply means eating as close to natural as possible. Such as throwing in a few raw almonds into a salad. We are a decade of getting back to basics. More room for animals to graze and less spraying harmful products. **"Localvore"** is a new name here in America. It means buying food at a farmer's market within 100 miles of your own home. In my hometown we have a small cheese factory. The owners have shipped in special cows from Switzerland and they have won the best tasting Smoked White Cheddar in the world. It is wonderful! All the cheese they offer is fabulous. Almost everyone I run into has something new to say about food products being developed in their **hometowns.**

More than ever we are more aware of **fresh produce.** Some of our most **nutritious greens** include kale, cauliflower greens, chard, beet greens, arugula, spinach and broccoli. Here are the hard-core facts about **organic** vs. local. From the 1st day to the 3rd day of being picked you get 100 % of the **nutritional value.** You loose ⅓ nutritional value after 3 days, and then ⅔ nutritional value after 6 days. So it is important that we buy local and as **fresh as possible**.

KAMUT

After the first edition of this book was published, I found an ancient grain that stood out amongst all others. That grain is Kamut. I now only use, Kamut - All Purpose White Flour in all of the recipes found in this book. It is superior to all other brands of flour in protein content, antioxidants, minerals, vitamins and other nutritional benefits. This delicious flour will change everything you cook for the better! You can order this flour on line at *thefoodnanny.com*

Another post-publication discovery was French sea salt. Produced in Guerande, France, this salt is the finest in the world. The taste is superior to any other salt that I have ever used. Like Kamut flour, I now only use this brand of salt in all the recipes in this book. This flavorful sea salt will change everything you cook for the better! You can order this salt on line at *thefoodnanny.com*

Publisher Food Nanny LLC

Edmunds, Liz.
The Food Nanny Rescues Dinner Again!!! XO With all new recipes and my meal plan that works to help save family dinnertime!

Includes index.
ISBN: 978-1-4675-7510-2

Printed in China by Toppan Printing Company

Editor: Ann Luther
Design, production and Photography: Michelle Lee Freeborn
Graphic design: Mara Spangaro

First Edition Copyright 2013

the foodnanny RESCUES DINNER again! xo

Comfort Food

The hardest part about dinner is trying to figure out what to cook!
That's where I come in. Mondays are usually very busy and can be overwhelming as the new week begins. We set the example for our children with a comforting meal on the table to get the week started. My Theme Nights will save you time and time again! Monday is Comfort Food Night. For example, just think of your favorite comfort foods or use my recipes to get started. I have 9 recipes in this chapter that will take you under 30 minutes to prepare. You will find some of my favorite picks like "Chicken Curry in 30 Minutes" that is so easy and yummy!
"Shepard's Pie" that is an all American favorite. "Ultimate Mac and Cheese" will melt in your mouth. And make sure to serve plenty of veggies with every meal.
It is so important to be able to cook your own food, save money, and eat fast food or processed food less often.
Teaching our children how to cook and bond around the dinner table is as important as it is for them to learn how to read or write. Dinner is the most natural setting in the day where we have the opportunity to communicate with our families.
Turn all electronics off and just concentrate on learning how to communicate as a family. This is where children learn to talk with adults. This is also where we share our passions with each other and discuss family values and teach table manners.
Nothing can take the place of the family dinner table! See you at dinner.

The Food Nanny. xo

MONDAY
COMFORT FOOD

Meatless TOMATO BASIL CREAM SOUP

Serves 4
Time: 15-20 minutes

½ yellow onion, minced
1 Tablespoon olive oil
1 clove garlic, minced
1 Tablespoon flour
2 14.5 oz. cans small diced tomatoes
1 cup chicken broth
½ cup heavy cream
Coarse salt
Fresh ground black pepper to taste
2 Tablespoon fresh basil, chopped
Parmesan cheese, grated

1. In a medium size saucepan, sauté the onion in olive oil until soft. Add garlic and flour and stir for 30 seconds. Add tomatoes with juice and chicken broth. Bring to a boil, turn the heat down to low and cook for 5 min.
2. Blend tomato mixture in blender or an immersion blender.
3. Return tomato mixture to the saucepan, add cream, stir until cream is blended. Heat until almost boiling. Season with coarse salt, ground black pepper and fresh basil.
4. Serve topped with grated Parmesan cheese.

Serve with: Food Nanny French Baguettes page 242 or your favorite sandwich.

Variation: Use Mozzarella cheese in place of Parmesan. Use 8 fresh tomatoes, diced in place of canned.

There's not a better comfort food than homemade tomato soup and a toasted cheese sandwich on a cold winter night! You're gonna love it!!

CONVERSATION STARTER:

How much did things cost when you were a child?

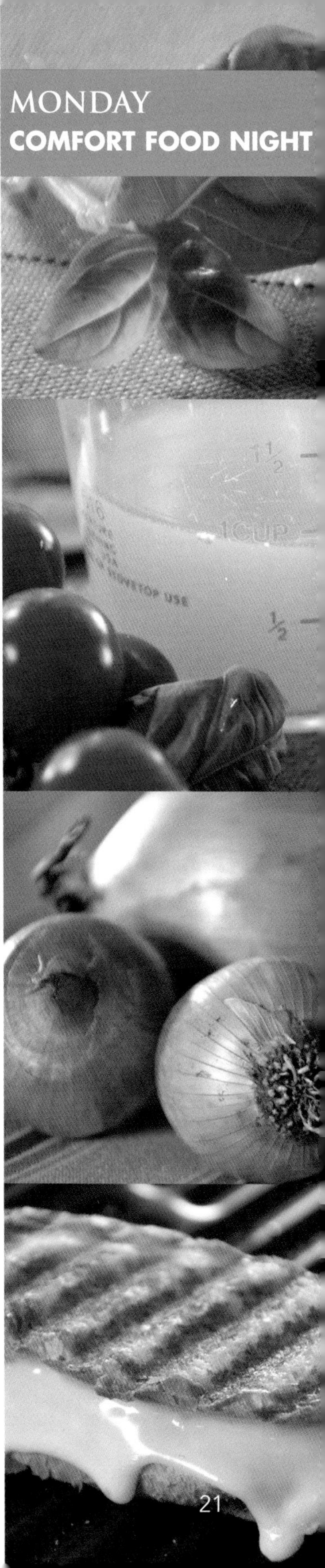

MONDAY
COMFORT FOOD NIGHT

CHICKEN TENDERS WITH GREEN CHILI SAUCE

Serves 4
Time: 1 hour

Plan Ahead: Prepare the rice up to 1 day ahead.

8 chicken tenders*
Coarse salt
Fresh ground black pepper
Rubbed sage *(sage rubbed between your fingers to almost powder)*
Cumin
Steak seasoning or another favorite "dry" seasoning
1 Tablespoon olive oil
2 teaspoons butter
⅓ cup cream
1 4 oz. can mild diced green chilies
2 Tablespoons cream cheese

Brown Rice:
1 cup brown rice
2½ cups chicken broth
1 Tablespoon butter

CONVERSATION STARTER:
How do you feel you fit into the family?

Prepare the Brown Rice:
Bring rice, chicken broth and butter to a boil. Reduce heat, cover with tight fitting lid. Simmer 45 min. Allow to rest for 5 min. Cooking times may vary.

Prepare the Chicken Tenders:

1. Wipe off the chicken tenders with a wet paper towel. Place the tenders on clean paper towels and sprinkle each one with the following in order given: coarse salt, fresh ground black pepper, rubbed sage, cumin and steak seasoning on both sides.
2. In a medium fry pan over medium heat add olive oil and butter until it just starts to sizzle.
3. Place the chicken tenders in the pan and sear about 3 min. per side. Turn the heat down to low.
4. Add cream. Cook for 1 min. Mix in the diced chilies. Dot little pieces of cream cheese around the chicken and chili sauce. Cover. Continue to cook over low heat for 15 min.
5. Serve immediately over Brown Rice.

Serve with: Brown Rice, broccoli, cauliflower, or fresh peas.
Other options: quinoa, white rice.

Variations: *Chicken Tenders – cut your own tenders from boneless/skinless chicken breasts by cutting 2-inch long strips. Use Half and Half in place of cream. Use small boneless/skinless chicken breasts.

*Cynthia was my inspiration for this recipe.
I came home and made my version of it and my family absolutely loves it. If you enjoy mild green chilies, you are going to love this recipe.
It is quick - dinner is on the table in no time! xo*

BRAZILIAN MEAT SAUCE WITH RICE & FRIES

Serves 6
Time: 1 hour

Plan Ahead: Rice can be prepared the day before.

1 lb. lean ground beef
½ yellow onion, diced
3 cloves fresh garlic, minced
½ teaspoon each: oregano, marjoram and cumin
1 fresh tomato, diced
1 8oz. can tomato sauce
1½ cups beef broth
1½ cups petite frozen peas
1½ Tablespoons white vinegar
½ cup red wine (can be cooking wine)
Coarse salt to taste
Ground black pepper to taste
2 cups long grain white rice
4 cups water
6 medium Russet potatoes, peeled
Sunflower or olive oil for frying

1. In a medium fry pan on low heat sauté the ground beef, onions and garlic. When onions and garlic are soft and the meat is browned, push the meat to one side and spoon out excess grease.
2. Add oregano, marjoram and cumin. Stir. Continue browning meat for 3 min.
3. Add tomato, tomato sauce, beef broth, peas, vinegar, wine, salt and pepper. (If the sauce looks too thick, add ½ cup water.) Cook 35 to 45 min. on medium low heat until most of the liquid has evaporated.
4. While the meat sauce cooks, place the rice and 4 cups of water in 2 qt. sauce pan. Bring the water and rice to a full boil. Cover and turn heat down to low. Simmer 25 min. or until liquid is gone and the rice is tender.
5. While the rice and the meat sauce are simmering, peel the potatoes. Cut the potatoes into ¼ inch wide strips (like french fries). Wash them well and dry completely on paper towels.
6. In medium sized fry pan pour enough sunflower or olive oil to fill the pan half-way. Heat oil on medium high heat until hot.
7. Safety Tip: Be careful not to have small children at your feet while frying the french fries. When the oil is ready carefully add the potatoes and start frying.
8. Maintain the heat for at least 15-20 min. at medium high. Turn the potatoes with tongs or a long fork. When the fries turn very light brown turn the heat up to high and continue frying for another 5 min. or so. Drain on paper towels. Lightly salt.
9. All three of these steps - meat sauce, rice and french fries - will come together about the same time. Serve the meat and peas over the rice with the fries on the side.

Serve with: Corn on the cob; Brussel Sprouts; Chiogga beets (red and white stripped beets).

Variations: Substitute corn or green beans for the peas. Use brown or black rice instead of white.

You cannot get anything like this in a restaurant.
Elaine was born and raised in Brazil.
This was a meal she grew up on. The first time I ate this meal it was the homemade fries that made it special.
Elaine cooks only from scratch.
This meal is very easy on the budget and everyone loves it.
Try it out!!

Meatless
BANGKOK STIR-FRY

Serves 4
Time: 20 minutes

Plan Ahead:
Prepare all the vegetables.

1 large carrot, peeled, cut in rounds ½ inch thick, then cut in half
1 small head broccoli, each flower bud cut into 3-4 small pieces, no stems
1 small head cauliflower, each flower bud cut into 3-4 small pieces, no stems
2 Tablespoons olive oil
3 large cloves garlic, minced
12 fresh snap peas, snap tops and pull string along both sides, snap bottom, discard
7 small, white button mushrooms, cut in half
1 heaping teaspoon oyster sauce (found in Asian food section of your grocery)
1 teaspoon soy sauce
½ teaspoon fish sauce (found in Asian food section of your grocery)
⅛ teaspoon salt
1½ teaspoons sugar
Fresh bean sprouts - small hand full (optional)
2 cups Jasmine Rice, cooked
2 boneless skinless chicken breasts (optional)

If using chicken breasts:
Cut the breast into strips ½ inch wide, then cut strips into ½ inch cubes. Add 2 teaspoons soy sauce, mix together, and set-aside until ready to stir-fry.

1. In a saucepan, bring 3 cups water to boil. Add carrots, and boil 2 min. Add broccoli and cauliflower together. Boil 4 min.
2. Pour vegetables into a colander and rinse with cold water. The vegetables will still be a bit crunchy. Set aside.
3. Using an electric skillet (set at 350°), wok, or frying pan, heat 2 Tablespoons olive oil. (Tip: You will know when your oil is hot enough if you drop in a small piece of bread and it fries quickly to a light brown color.)
4. Add minced garlic, stirring until it is light brown in color. (If adding chicken, do it now and cook chicken cubes until light brown.) Add carrots, broccoli, and cauliflower in skillet, stir and cover with lid. Cook 1 min.
5. Add peas and mushrooms. Stir. Cover and cook 1 min. Add oyster sauce, soy sauce, fish sauce, and salt. Stir. Replace lid. Cook for 30 seconds.
6. Add sugar. If adding bean sprouts, add them now. Stir and cover. Cook 1 min.
7. Remove from heat and serve immediately with Jasmine Rice.

Variation: Add ½ pound, cleaned and deveined, small shrimp with the bean sprouts at the very end. You can also substitute pork in place of the chicken.

Finally a true stir-fry!
Katie is living in Bangkok and her cook, Sue Nan, has taught us how to make this wonderful stir-fry that takes just minutes to prepare. It is so delicious and so healthy. I hope you will all enjoy this special stir-fry.
This is real comfort food when you are hungry for veggies and rice.

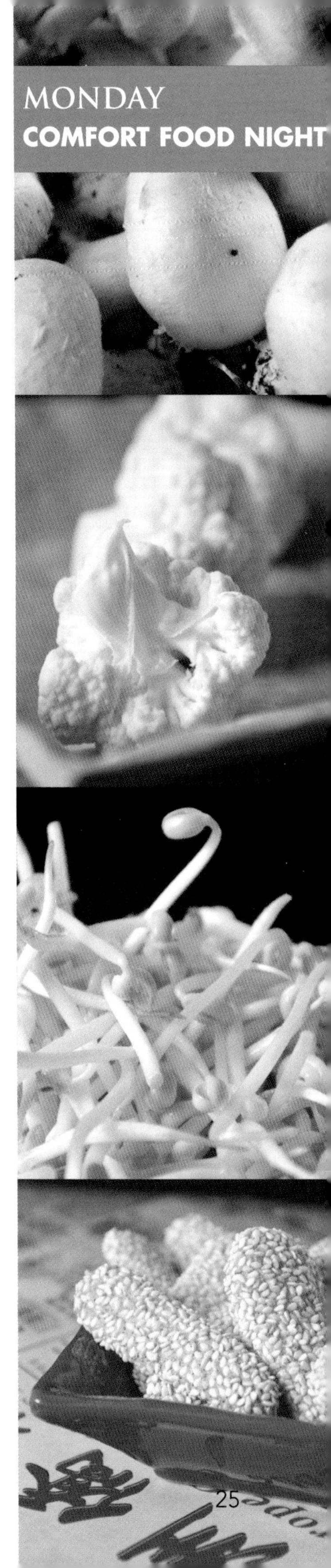

FRIED SWEET AND SOUR EGG ROLLS

Makes 21 Egg Rolls
Time: 40 minutes

Plan Ahead: Make the sauce up to 2 days ahead.

Prepare the sauce first:
¾ cup sugar
2 Tablespoons corn starch
½ cup white vinegar
½ cup water
½ cup pineapple juice
1½ teaspoons soy sauce

For the Egg Rolls:
1 1 lb. package egg roll wraps. (A thin square sheet of dough in the vegetable section at your grocery store.)
4 small boneless/skinless chicken breasts, diced
½ yellow onion, minced
1 Tablespoon olive oil
Coarse salt
Ground black pepper
3 cloves garlic, minced
2 14 oz. bags coleslaw - produce section of your store. (Shredded cabbage and carrots combined)
½ cup teriyaki sauce
¼ cup soy sauce
Sunflower oil or canola oil for frying

Prepare the sauce first:
In a small saucepan mix the sugar and corn starch. Add the vinegar, water, pineapple juice and soy sauce. Stir to combine and bring to a boil over medium high heat until thickened. Remove from heat. Cover to keep warm.
Prepare the Egg Rolls:
1. In a large soup pot, heat 1 Tablespoon olive oil over medium high heat. Sauté diced chicken and minced onion until chicken is cooked and the onion is tender.
2. Season with coarse salt and ground black pepper to taste. Add minced garlic and cook for 1 min. Add 2 bags of coleslaw, teriyaki sauce and soy sauce. Mix all together. Cover and simmer for 5 to 7 min. Drain off and discard most of the juice through a strainer. Let the filling cool down a bit.
3. One at a time put 3 Tablespoons mixture onto each wrap. Roll as directed on the package. Lay on wax paper or foil until ready to fry.
4. Add ¼ inch oil to your frying pan. Fry the rolls when the oil temperature reaches 350° or fry over low to medium heat until the rolls are light brown.
5. Lay on paper towels to remove excess oil. Place on a platter. Serve immediately with warm sauce.

Serve with: Jasmine Rice. Fried Rice. Fresh green beans or broccoli.

Variations: Fry in Peanut Oil. Shred your own cabbage and carrots. For the vinegar – use half rice vinegar and half apple cider.
Bake in oven: Heat oven to 400°. Place rolls on a baking sheet coated with cooking spray. Lightly brush the tops with olive oil and bake until golden brown, 12 min.

I have never used an easier recipe to make Homemade Sweet and Sour Egg Rolls. I got this from the cutest Spanish girl! My husband and I absolutely love these. Everyone does. They are easy and so fast to make. We never knew what to make on New Year's Eve until we got this recipe!! xo

CHICKEN RICE CASSEROLE WITH ALMONDS

Serves 6
Time: 1 hour

Plan Ahead: Prepare white sauce 1 day ahead. May be frozen. Cook the rice 1 day ahead.

The White Sauce:

2 Tablespoons butter
1 Tablespoon olive oil
3 Tablespoons yellow onion, minced
3 Tablespoons red or green bell pepper, minced
3 Tablespoons celery, chopped fine
1 garlic clove, minced (garlic optional)
¼ cup flour
1½ cups milk
½ teaspoon coarse salt
¼ teaspoon fresh ground pepper

The Casserole:

2 cups long grain rice, cooked
6 oz. fresh white mushrooms, sliced
1 teaspoon butter
1 teaspoon olive oil
2 boneless/skinless chicken breasts, chopped
1 Tablespoon olive oil
1 cup mayonnaise
4 oz. water chestnuts, sliced thin (optional)
½ cup milk
½ teaspoon salt
½ cup slivered almonds
Paprika

The White Sauce:

1. In a small saucepan melt butter with 1 teaspoon olive oil. Sauté the onion, bell pepper, celery and garlic over low heat until soft.
2. In a small bowl whisk the flour and milk together. Pour this into the vegetables, stirring constantly until the mixture bubbles and thickens. Season to taste with coarse salt and ground black pepper. Set aside.

The Casserole:

1. Cook rice on top of the stove or in a rice cooker. Measure out one cup of rice and add 2 cups water. Bring to a boil, turn down the heat and cover the pan; simmer for 25 min.
2. Clean off the mushrooms with a wet paper towel. Sauté the mushrooms in butter and olive oil until light brown. Set aside.
3. Set the oven to 350°. Sauté the chopped chicken in olive oil until cooked through. Set aside.
4. In a medium size bowl add: cooked rice, sautéed mushrooms, cooked chicken, mayonnaise, water chestnuts, milk, salt and white sauce. Mix thoroughly.
5. Pour into a buttered 9x13 casserole and garnish with slivered almonds on top. Sprinkle generously with paprika. Bake 30 min.

Serve with: Fresh or frozen peas, broccoli, asparagus or zucchini. Hot Rolls.

Variations: Use canned mushrooms. Substitute 2 cans cream of celery soup for white sauce.

The first time I ate this casserole was at Mrs. "L's" home, the Vice Principal of our school. I thought "Oh my, this dish was so elegant." Mrs. L served this with frozen peas, which we had only on occasion in our home. I remember sitting by her fireplace, a 17-year- old, all dressed up. The evening was magical. That has been my goal every since. I wanted to entertain like her - elegant but cozy. I still have her recipe hand written.

SHEPHERD'S PIE WITH CHICKEN

Serves 4-6
Time: About 50 minutes

Plan Ahead: Prepare the chicken. Use left-over mashed or baked potatoes.

6 medium Russet potatoes - about 2 pounds
½ stick butter (¼ cup)
¼ cup sour cream
¼ cup mayonnaise
2 teaspoons minced green onions (optional)
¼ cup milk
½ cup cheddar cheese; or pepper jack cheese
3 boneless/skinless chicken breasts, cut into small pieces
2 Tablespoons olive oil
1 small yellow onion, chopped
1 Tablespoon olive oil
1 large carrot, peeled and chopped
2 Tablespoons butter
2 Tablespoons flour
1¼ cups chicken broth
¼ teaspoon cayenne
½ cup frozen peas
Chopped parsley to taste
1 Tablespoon fresh tarragon or rosemary, chopped
¼ teaspoon paprika
1½ cup fresh breadcrumbs (3 pieces of sandwich bread)
4 Tablespoons melted butter

1. Peel the potatoes and cut into 1 inch squares. In a medium size sauce pan fill the pan with enough water to just cover the potatoes and bring to a boil over medium high heat. Add salt and pepper. Turn the heat down and boil until tender.
2. Drain the potatoes. Add the butter, sour cream, mayonnaise, green onions and milk. Mix with an electric mixer until smooth. Stir in shredded cheddar cheese. Season with coarse salt and ground black pepper.
3. Wipe off the chicken breasts with wet paper towels. Cut the chicken into 2 inch pieces. In a medium size fry pan over low heat, fry onion in olive oil until almost caramelized, stirring regularly, then add the chicken. Season generously with coarse salt, fresh ground black pepper and cayenne.
4. Add 1 additional Tablespoon olive oil and fry the chicken and the carrot together for 3 to 4 min.
5. In a small saucepan, melt 2 Tablespoons butter and add 2 Tablespoons flour. Stir until bubbly. Add chicken broth. Whisk together and bring to a boil until thickened. Stir in the peas. Stir this sauce into the chicken and veggies.
6. Add chopped parsley, rosemary or tarragon and paprika. Season to taste with coarse salt and fresh ground black pepper.
7. Butter a 9x13 in. baking dish. Put a layer of chicken and veggies on the bottom of the pan. Add a layer of mashed potato on the top. Repeat.
8. Mix the breadcrumbs with the butter and spread over the top of the casserole. Dot with a few pieces of extra butter. Bake at 400° for 25 min.

Serve with: Green & yellow zucchini; Swiss chard; spinach; 2 Basic Salads page 258.

Variations: May use ground lamb or hamburger - make sure to drain off the grease from the lamb or hamburger. Use beef broth in place of chicken broth. Use baked potatoes, peel and mash. You can freeze left-over mashed potatoes for up to 2 weeks. Make a double batch and freeze half. Add 1 Teaspoon dried rosemary or tarragon.

This long-time familiar dish to all cooks is making a come back here in the U.S. I like it best made with chicken. Good food always comes around again. I love this recipe of mine! xo

SAVORY LAMB CHOPS

Serves 2
Time: 30 minutes

- 4 lamb chops, 1 to 1½ inches thick
- ¼ cup flour
- 2 Tablespoons olive oil
- 2 Tablespoons unsalted butter
- 4 cloves garlic, peeled; smash each clove with the back of a knife
- 4 small bay leaves
- ¼ teaspoon dried thyme
- Coarse salt and fresh ground black pepper
- 1 Tablespoon red wine vinegar
- ¼ cup chicken stock
- 2 Tablespoons cold butter

1. Season flour with course salt and ground black pepper. Roll the chops in the seasoned flour once. Make sure you coat the sides.
2. Heat the olive oil and butter in a medium size stainless or non-stick skillet over medium heat. When the oil and butter start to sizzle add the chops. Brown on all sides about 10 min.
3. Add whole garlic cloves to the pan. Place a bay leaf on top of each lamb chop. Add thyme, coarse salt and fresh ground black pepper to taste. Cover. Continue cooking over low heat 20 min.
4. Transfer chops to a serving platter and cover to keep warm.
5. Add vinegar to the remaining garlic, bay leaves and drippings in the pan. Cook over medium high heat until most of the vinegar has evaporated.
6. Add the chicken stock and continue to cook down until desired consistency. Adjust seasoning: add more coarse salt and fresh ground pepper if needed.
7. Turn the heat down to simmer and add 2 Tablespoons cold butter. Stir.
8. Pour the sauce over the lamb chops and place a smashed clove of garlic and a bay leaf on top of each. Remove the bay leaf before you eat; but eat the garlic because it's yummy.

Serve with: Steamed red potatoes, drizzled with a little melted butter and sprinkled with parsley or Linguini with Parmesan cheese page 227. Carrots with tarragon and butter. *Food Nanny Baguettes* page 242 or any hard, crusty bread. Red Jalapeno or regular Mint Jelly.

Variations: Veal.

When making a nice sauce to go with your meat don't use an iron skillet. Your sauce will become muddy. Always use a stainless or non-stick pan. This recipe tastes so good if you love lamb like we do. It is good enough to serve to your Boss and his wife!! I have been making this for years...

CONVERSATION STARTER:

What are your talents? Your weaknesses?

Meatless RACLETTE

Serves 4
Time: 20 minutes

12 extra small Yukon Gold potatoes, washed not peeled
1 pound Raclette cheese, cut into thin slices
12 Cornichons pickles, French style, extra fine
12 cocktail onions, (found in a jar at the grocery store)
Paprika
Food Nanny French Baguettes and Butter

1. Preheat oven to 375°. Steam the potatoes until tender about 5 min. Season with a little coarse salt. Cover. Keep warm. While the potatoes are steaming prepare the cheese.
2. In a shallow baking dish place one-half of the cheese slices overlapping them slightly.
3. Bake the cheese in oven until it is just melted and smooth - 4 to 6 min. Remove from oven. Place hot dish on serving platter or wooden serving board to make serving easy while keeping the cheese hot.
4. Sprinkle cheese with paprika. Arrange half the potatoes, onions and dill pickles around the hot Raclette. Serve at once.
5. Let each person take what they want. Repeat the process with the rest of the cheese and vegetables as needed.

Serve with: Fondue forks, *Baguettes and butter.*

This is one of my go-to Comfort Foods.

OLD SCHOOL HAMBURGER STEW

Serves 6
Time: About 1 hour

1 medium yellow onion, minced
1 Tablespoon olive oil
1 lb. lean ground beef
2 teaspoons cumin
4-6 cups canned beef broth (can substitute beef bouillon cubes reconstituted with water)
¼ cup ketchup
1 8 oz. can tomato sauce
1 fresh tomato, chopped
1 teaspoon steak sauce
1 teaspoon Worcestershire Sauce
1½ Tablespoons white vinegar
1½ teaspoon salt
½ teaspoon black pepper
3 medium carrots, peeled and chopped fine
4 small red or Yukon Gold potatoes, peeled and diced
3 stalks celery, chopped fine

1. In a large pot sauté the minced onion in olive oil for 3 min. Add the ground beef - don't break it up too much - cook until browned. Drain off excess fat. Add the cumin. Brown for 3 more min.
2. Add the beef broth and all remaining ingredients. Simmer another 30 min. until the vegetables are tender.

Serve with: Blueberry Muffins, Blueberry Lemon Scones page 99 or Food Nanny Crescent Rolls page 249.

Variations: Use ground turkey.

Steve's Mom Lida made this meal once a week in the 1950's. Her kids looked forward to the Blueberry muffins hot right out of the oven! Who doesn't love blueberry muffins! It made the meal very memorable. I am still making this meal for Steve!

CHEESY CHICKEN WITH FRESH SPINACH

Serves 4
Time: 25 minutes preparation
Total time: 1 hour 15 minutes

Plan Ahead: prepare chicken breasts. Wrap them individually and freeze until needed; or keep in fridge up to 1 day.

2 large boneless/skinless chicken breasts
4 Tablespoons cream cheese, softened
Garlic salt to taste
Lemon Pepper to taste
1 cup fresh spinach
¾ cup mozzarella cheese, grated
½ cup fresh breadcrumbs (1 slice sandwich bread)
2 Tablespoons melted butter

CONVERSATION STARTER:

Who is the best cook in our family?

1. Pound chicken breasts between 2 plastic bags with a mallet - as flat as they can go without tearing so you can easily roll them up.
2. Lay them out on waxed paper. "Frost" each piece of chicken with 2 Tablespoons softened cream cheese. Sprinkle with garlic salt and lemon pepper to taste.
3. Place the spinach leaves in a single layer on top of cream cheese. Sprinkle on half the mozzarella cheese. Roll up very tightly. At this point you could roll in plastic wrap and keep in refrigerator until ready to complete the dinner, or even freeze up to a week. If frozen, thaw before baking.
4. Place on small baking sheet lined with parchment paper. Sprinkle with remaining grated cheese.
5. Mix breadcrumbs with melted butter and sprinkle over the chicken.
6. Bake at 350° for 35-45 min. or until the juice runs clear.
7. Let rest 10 min. Slice in 1-inch pieces to serve.

Serve with: Baked potatoes, rice, quinoa or fettuccini noodles. Winter squash, yellow zucchini or broccoli. Liz's Crescent Dinner Rolls page 249.

Variation: Use arugula in place of spinach. Use Borsin (a soft French cheese) in place of the cream cheese. Use tiny, fresh mozzarella balls - they melt really fast!

You can make 100 of these chicken breasts, bake them on baking sheets and have it work out beautifully for a large dinner party. Thanks, Debbie, for showing me how easy this is to do for a crowd.

MONDAY
COMFORT FOOD NIGHT

LEMON CHICKEN WITH BUTTER SAUCE

Serves 4
Time: 20 minutes

Plan Ahead: Clarify the butter.

4 small boneless/skinless chicken breasts
Coarse salt
Fresh ground black pepper
¼ cup flour
1½ Tablespoons unsalted butter or clarified butter. * See below.
1 Tablespoon olive oil
2 Tablespoons fresh lemon juice
2 Tablespoons unsalted butter
1 Tablespoon minced fresh parsley or 1 teaspoon dried

** To clarify butter follow these simple directions:*
Melt one stick butter in a small saucepan. Bring it to a slow boil. After the bubbling ceases, before the butter darkens and burns, pour the clear yellow butter through a small sieve or simply remove the foam with a spoon. I keep mine in a small jar with a lid. I use it when I really want the butter taste to come through.

1. With a wet paper towel wipe off the chicken breasts. Cut away any extra fat. Season with coarse salt and fresh ground black pepper on both sides. Place the flour in a small shallow bowl. Lightly dip the chicken into the flour and shake off any excess. Set the chicken onto a fresh paper towel or plate and set aside.
2. In a medium size skillet place the unsalted or clarified butter and olive oil. Set aside.
3. In a small bowl, put the lemon juice. Set aside.
4. Heat the skillet containing the butter and olive oil to medium until it almost starts to sizzle. Lay the chicken in the pan. Sauté the chicken until you start to see it turn white along the edges about 3 min. or until light brown. Turn over and continue sautéing for another 3 min. Cook until the chicken springs back when touched. Remove from heat and place the chicken on a serving plate and cover.
5. Quickly swirl the last 2 Tablespoons butter into the drippings until melted. With a spoon, drizzle each piece of chicken with a little fresh lemon juice and pour on the hot butter sauce. Sprinkle with fresh parsley and serve immediately.

Serve with: Couscous, rice pilaf, quinoa or Linguine with Parmesan cheese page 227.

Variations: For a true butter taste you must clarify the butter first. Prepare clarified butter in advance. It will keep for months in the refrigerator or freezer covered.

Make sure your side dishes are all ready to go and your table is set when this chicken is finished. It is best eaten hot. I love my version of this delicious, fast easy recipe. I hope you will love it as much as I do. The best Lemon Chicken I have ever tasted was in Beijing, China. I would have paid for the recipe!

FOOD NANNY CHICKEN SOUP

Serves: 2
Time: 20 minutes

Plan Ahead: Prepare chicken ahead and freeze it.

1 chicken breast, bone in or boneless/skinless
1½ Tablespoons butter or olive oil
3 Tablespoons onion, minced
2 Tablespoons celery, chopped
1 carrot, peeled and sliced thin
4 cups water, or use the broth from cooking the chicken
5 chicken bullion cubes or 5 teaspoons chicken flavored bouillon
½ cup frozen peas
½ teaspoon salt
Fresh ground black pepper, to taste

Dumplings:
½ cup flour
1 teaspoon baking powder
¼ teaspoon salt
¼ cup milk
1 Tablespoon olive oil or 1 Tablespoon melted butter

1. In a small saucepan bring one chicken breast and water to a boil with just enough water to cover the chicken. When it boils turn the heat down to low and cook over low heat for 10 min. Cover, turn the heat off and let steam for 10 min.
2. In a small saucepan heat 1½ Tablespoons butter. Add onion, celery and sliced carrot. Sauté until the onion is soft. Add 4 cups water and bouillon cubes or chicken flavored bouillon. Bring to a boil, turn down the heat and simmer until carrots are tender.
3. Tear the chicken into pieces with your hands. Add it to the onion, celery and carrot. Add frozen peas. Sprinkle with coarse salt and fresh ground black pepper to taste. When the peas are cooked and the soup is heated through but not boiling, remove from heat and serve immediately.

Serve with: Liz's Crescent Dinner Rolls page 249. French Baguettes page 242. Can serve soup over mashed potatoes.

Variations: Add ½ cup cooked rice to the soup. Or add the rice with the carrots. Let it cook 5 min. longer. Or add 4 oz. noodles when you add the water. You can use leftover chicken.

Make it even tastier by making homemade dumplings:
1. In a small bowl combine the flour, baking powder and salt. Stir together.
2. Mix the milk and oil together in a liquid measuring cup and pour this over the flour mixture. Mix just until moistened.
3. Bring the soup to a boil. Using a teaspoon, drop the dumplings one by one on top of the chicken and vegetables. Start from the outside of the pan and work in. Makes about 10 teaspoon-size dumplings.
4. Cover tightly with a lid and turn the heat down to simmer, but still boiling. Simmer for 15 min. Serve in bowls.

This soup is so versatile!! Make this chicken soup when you have a cold. Take this dinner to someone who is at home sick. We make it a lot with dumplings because we can't get enough dumplings. It was the first real recipe I ever made up. We poured it over mashed potatoes and the next night just added more broth and served the same meal with rice or noodles, and hot bread and butter. Kids love it. It is a comfort food like no other!

CHICKEN CURRY IN 30 MINUTES

Serves 4
Time: 30 minutes

Plan Ahead: Rice can be made a day ahead.

Start the rice before you start on the curry.

Rice:
Place the following ingredients in a saucepan or rice cooker.

1 cup Jasmine or Basmati rice
½ teaspoon salt
1 Tablespoon olive oil
2¼ cups water

Chicken Curry:

6 chicken thighs
1 cup yellow onion, chopped
4 cloves garlic, minced
1 Tablespoon fresh ginger, minced
½ teaspoon ground turmeric
¼ teaspoon ground coriander
1 14 oz. can coconut milk
½ cup chicken stock
1 can chickpeas or garbanzo beans, drained
¼ bunch fresh cilantro, chopped
3 teaspoons curry powder
2 teaspoons fresh jalapeno pepper, minced, seeds removed or leave seeds in for more spice

1. Cut most of the chicken off the bone, into bite size pieces, leaving some skin on a couple of pieces.
2. Place the chicken pieces and bones in a large pot on top of the stove. Turn the heat to high. Brown meat well, turning often.
3. When meat is brown, turn heat down to medium, add onions and cook for 3 min. Add fresh garlic, ginger, turmeric and coriander. Stir for another couple minutes to heat through.
4. Add coconut milk, chicken stock and drained chickpeas. Turn heat down to simmer, cover and cook 8 to 10 min. Remove from heat.
5. Remove the chicken pieces and bones. Let rest a minute to cool, then tear chicken off the bones and add to the pan. Discard all bones. Remove any chicken skin that is floating on top and discard.
6. Add the cilantro, curry powder and fresh jalapeno. Heat again. Check seasoning. Adjust curry and jalapeno. Add salt and pepper to taste. Serve over cooked rice.

Serve with: Fresh zucchini sliced thin, skin on, and fresh cabbage, sliced thin. Sauté the zucchini and the cabbage in a medium size pan with 1 Tablespoon olive oil and ¼ cup sliced yellow onion over low heat until the vegetables start to turn brown. Salt and pepper to taste.

I will never forget the Abernathy family who shared this recipe with me. She didn't measure anything but could tell me how her dear friend from India would come over and make this quick dinner. I perfected this recipe for my family and I know it will become one of your favorites. It is wonderful.

Meatless ULTIMATE MAC & CHEESE

Serves 6
Time: 30 minutes

½ cup (1 stick) butter or black truffle butter
1 (3-oz.) package cream cheese
¼ cup heavy cream
1¾ cups Half & Half
1 teaspoon garlic powder
½ cup Parmesan cheese, grated
Salt and ground black pepper, to taste
2 cups Penne pasta
1½ cup white cheddar cheese, grated
1 cup Asiago cheese, grated

Topping:
1 cup crushed Ritz crackers (about 25 crackers)
¼ cup melted butter

1. Melt butter in a medium saucepan over low heat. Mix in the cream cheese.
2. Stir in heavy cream, Half & Half, garlic powder, Parmesan cheese, salt and pepper. Bring to a boil. Decrease heat and simmer 10 to 15 min. stirring often.
3. Cook the pasta and drain. Add prepared sauce, cheddar cheese and Asiago cheese to the pasta. Mix well.
4. Pour into an 8x8 inch baking pan. Mix together Ritz crackers and melted butter and sprinkle over the top. Bake at 350° for 15 min. or until bubbly.

Serve with: Mixed vegetables.

Variations: Add chopped jalapenos. For a drier mac and cheese, use a 9 x 13 casserole dish and cook for 15 min. May also broil the cracker topping after baking for a crunchier texture.

*Sally and I tried to make
the ultimate Mac and Cheese at home.
Sally said, "Liz,
start with your Alfredo sauce recipe!!"
It was perfect. Next we added Asiago.
The four cheeses really made it
the Ultimate Mac and Cheese.
The best Sally and I have ever eaten!*

CONVERSATION STARTER:
What was the craziest or most embarrassing thing that has happened to you?

Italian Night

It was in Italy that I learned that there are no rules when it comes to cooking!
You can prepare quick pasta with as few ingredients as olive oil, fresh tomatoes,
garlic, onion, pasta water, pasta and Parmesan cheese.
Now that's my kind of cooking.
Sometimes less is more, and in Italy that is exactly what you find.
You find less on pizzas, less in their salads, less ingredients in real Italian
homemade sauces. Olive Oil is Italian's most important ingredient-it's heart
healthy, has natural antioxidants, and a relatively high cooking temperature,
which is great for pan frying or searing.
I always have a "finishing" olive oil – which is extra virgin olive oil and comes from
the first cold press. It is also best if it is not refined. The more fresh the olive oil
the more peppery the taste. That is my favorite! I use this olive oil for special needs
like drizzling on pizza or a salad or into a special sauce.
I use it sparingly and treasure every drop of it.
In this chapter, you will find authentic recipes that I learned by cooking with some
of the best cooks in Italy – Mario, Marzia, Michelle, Vittorio and Raffaella.
Look for Raffaella's Pasta, Authentic Ragu, Ravioli with Sage Butter Sauce,
Bruschetta and Cacio E Pepe. I also have my own yummy Romano Chicken with
Beurre Blanc, Chicken Parmesan, and American Lasagna.
Italian Night never tasted so good!

Prego. Xo

TUESDAY
ITALIAN NIGHT

Meatless

eatless

RAVIOLI WITH SAGE IN BUTTER SAUCE

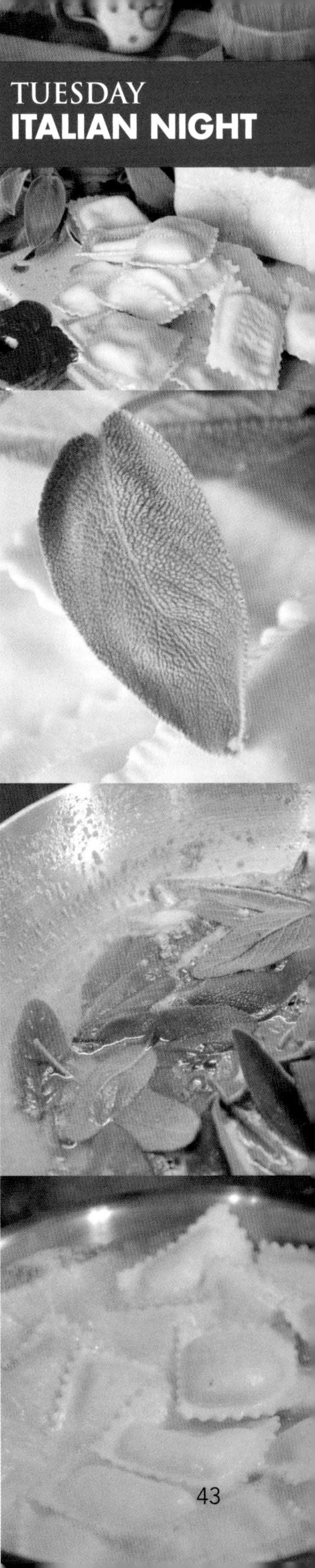

Serves 2
Time: 10 minutes

Plan Ahead: Buy 9 oz. prepared, fresh or frozen Spinach Ricotta Cheese Ravioli.

9 oz. about (11) fresh or frozen Spinach Ricotta Cheese Ravioli (I prefer 3 x 2 inch ravioli)
⅓ cup unsalted butter, cold
1 cup (2-3 oz.) fresh sage
2 Tablespoons fresh Parmesan cheese, grated
½ teaspoon fresh lemon juice (optional)
Coarse salt
Fresh ground black pepper
Fresh Parmesan cheese, grated for serving

1. Prepare the ravioli by bringing 5 quarts of water to a boil. Salt lightly. Boil the fresh ravioli for 6-8 min.; if frozen follow the package instructions.
2. While the ravioli is boiling, melt the butter over low heat in an 8 in. saucepan. Add the fresh sage all at once. Stir as the sage wilts into the butter. Simmer for 8 to 10 min. uncovered. The butter will brown perfectly as the sage and butter simmer together. Remove from heat and remove the sage. Sprinkle in a little of the crisp sage for more sage taste, if you prefer. Stir in the Parmesan cheese and lemon juice if using. Season with a tiny amount of coarse salt and fresh ground black pepper. Stir.
3. Carefully drain the pasta. Arrange on a plate. Spoon the sage sauce over top the ravioli. Sprinkle on freshly grated Parmesan cheese to taste. Serve hot.

Serve with: Spinach with Parmesan page 211 or Green Salad. Warm Bread. This can be a main dish or a side dish.

Variation: Use spaghetti in place of the ravioli.
For Spaghetti: Cook 8 oz. spaghetti and toss with the butter sauce and freshly grated Mizathera cheese. Leave out the fresh lemon juice. Season to taste. Serve.

CONVERSATION STARTER:
What is your favorite thing to do each season of the year?

This is such an easy dinner. Friends came by so I pulled out the fresh ravioli and served it alongside another Italian dish so we had enough for everyone. They want to come again just to eat it!

PASTA WITH HOT ITALIAN SAUSAGE

Serves 4
Time: 15 minutes

1 medium/large red bell pepper, sliced in ⅛ inch strips
1 teaspoon salt
8 oz. (2 cups) bowtie pasta
2 teaspoons olive oil
2½ (about ½ pound) hot Italian sausage links, casings removed
½ teaspoon fresh ground black pepper
½ cup beef broth
¼ cup pasta water
⅓ cup grated Parmesan cheese

1. Rinse the bell pepper, core and cut into strips. Set aside.
2. Bring 5 quarts of water to a boil over high heat. Add 1 teaspoon salt. Add the pasta, stir, turn down the heat and boil for 9 min.
3. While the pasta is boiling, heat olive oil in a 10-12 inch fry pan over medium/high until hot. Add the sausage and peppers together. Stir and break up sausage as it browns. When the sausage is browned, stir in the black pepper. Add the beef broth and pasta water. Simmer for 5-8 min. or until the liquid is absorbed.
4. Drain the pasta. Pour sauce over cooked pasta. Serve. Top with grated Parmesan cheese.

Serve with: Hot Italian bread. Everyday Artisan Bread page 236, French Baguettes page 242, Two Basic Salads page 258, Artichokes or Brussel Sprouts.

This easy meal is fast and can be put together in 15 minutes! Kids love it as much as adults. Double or triple the recipe. My girls made up this recipe. The bell pepper makes it!

Meatless PESTO SAUCE

Makes about 1 cup
Time: 5 minutes

Plan Ahead: Make pesto a day ahead.

20-25 small/medium size fresh basil leaves
½ cup olive oil
⅓ cup pine nuts
1 cup fresh Parmesan cheese, grated
⅓ cup Romano cheese, grated
Coarse salt
Fresh ground black pepper, to taste

Process in a food processor or blender until well mixed. Set aside.
Or refrigerate, covered, up to 3 days. Freeze for 2 months.

Serve with: You can put pesto sauce over roasted asparagus. Use in soups and sauces. Spoon over pasta or baked chicken. Use on pizza. It's great on chicken sandwiches!

For years, most of the pesto I had tried was not my favorite sauce. I experimented with different ingredients and came up with this recipe. I have grown to love it and used it in many different ways. I especially enjoy it in tomato sauce. Try it out and experiment with this recipe. You're going to love my pesto!

Meatless RAFFAELLA'S PASTA

Serves 2
Time: 45 minutes

Plan Ahead: Prepare the sauce ahead of time. Prepare the pasta ahead of time. Dinner in 5 min.

1 red bell pepper, sliced in ½ inch strips
1 yellow bell pepper, sliced in ½ inch strips
2 Tablespoons olive oil, divided
½ cup water
½ square chicken bouillon cube or 2 teaspoons instant bouillon
1 Tablespoon chicken bouillon
1½ cups white mushrooms, sliced thin
1 cup heavy cream
2 Tablespoons tomato paste (buy it in a tube)
8 oz. (2 cups) penne pasta
Coarse salt
Fresh ground black pepper
Parmesan cheese, freshly grated

1. In a medium size fry pan over medium heat, sauté the peppers in 1 Tablespoon olive oil, water and chicken bouillon cube (or instant bouillon) until light brown and soft. About 30 min. Add more water as needed, ¼ cup at a time. Do not let the peppers go dry. (You don't want to drown out the flavor of the peppers, that is why you only add a small amount of water at a time.) Cook down to about ⅛ cup water. Remove the peppers from the pan and put in a plastic bag for 10 min. to sweat. Peel off the skins. Discard.
2. Put 1 Tablespoon olive oil in a separate small fry pan. Add ¼ cup water and 1 Tablespoon chicken bouillon. Add sliced mushrooms. Cook down for about 15 min. adding in more water as needed.
3. Cook the pasta according to package directions. Set aside. Save some pasta water if needed later.
4. Put the peeled peppers in a blender. Add cream and tomato paste. Blend until smooth. Stir in the mushrooms. If too thick, add in some pasta water. May re-heat on top of stove at this point when ready to serve. Season to taste with salt and pepper.
5. Pour over warm penne pasta. Top with grated Parmesan. Serve immediately.

Serve with: Two Basic Salads page 258, Peasant White Bread page 237 or Steamed zucchini.

Variation: May add cooked Italian sausage. Use ground or rubbed sage.

I learned how to make this pasta from beautiful Raffaella. I spent the day with her cooking in her beautiful apartment in Florence, Italy. This recipe has been handed down in her family from generation to generation. I feel so privileged to have this recipe. Raffaella said one of the most inspiring things I have ever heard, "We would rather give our children another brother or sister than more things."
My heart skipped a beat right then and there...very memorable.
Thank you, Raffaella. xo

LASAGNA SOUP

Serves 6
Time: 35 minutes

Plan Ahead: Prepare the soup ahead, reheat. Pass the garnish.

2 teaspoons olive oil
1 onion, diced
4 garlic cloves, crushed
2½ mild Italian sausage links (about ¾ pound), casings removed
¾ pound ground beef
2 teaspoons oregano
½ teaspoon red pepper flakes
1 can tomato paste
2 14.5-ounce cans diced tomatoes, with juice
6 cups chicken broth
2 bay leaves
8 oz. rotini or fusilli pasta
½ cup fresh basil

Soup Garnish:
8 oz. ricotta cheese
½ cup Parmesan cheese, grated
2 cups Mozzarella, grated
Coarse salt
Fresh ground black pepper to taste

1. Heat the olive oil in a large pot. Add onion and garlic, sautéing until onion is soft. Add sausage and ground beef, breaking the meat into small pieces as you stir. Cook until brown. Pour off extra grease. Add oregano, pepper flakes, tomato paste, diced tomatoes, chicken broth and bay leaves. Stir, and bring to a boil. Turn the heat down and simmer for 20 min.
2. Add the pasta. Cook until pasta is tender, about 12 min. Add basil. Remove from heat.
3. In a small bowl mix the ricotta, Parmesan, and Mozzarella together. Season lightly with salt and pepper. Place 2 tablespoons cheese mixture on top of each bowl of soup.

Option: Serve the soup in bowls and pass the garnish so everyone can help themselves.

Serve with: French Baguettes page 242.

Variation: May use all Italian sausage or ground beef. Use Penne pasta.

Kids like to serve themselves and stir in the cheese and watch it melt into their bowl of soup. Let's get them involved early at being chefs. Let them be in on the final preparation of the meal. (This also cools the soup just enough to not burn their mouths.) Enjoy! Thanks, Echo, for this recipe. xo

ZITI WITH ARUGULA, PESTO AND SAUSAGE

Serves 6
Time: 1 hour

Plan Ahead: Prepare the Pesto Sauce page 44 a day ahead. ½ cup homemade pesto, or store bought.

- **2 teaspoons coarse salt, for boiling the pasta**
- **3 cups (11oz.) ziti or penne pasta**
- **1 Tablespoon olive oil**
- **2½ Italian mild sausage links (about ½ pound), casings removed**
- **½ yellow onion, diced**
- **4 garlic cloves, minced**
- **2 14.5 oz. cans diced tomatoes with juice, crushed**
- **Coarse salt**
- **Fresh ground black pepper**
- **6 oz. fresh Mozzarella cheese, cubed**
- **1 cup fresh Parmesan cheese, grated, divided**
- **3 cups fresh arugula or spinach**

1. Prepare the pesto first if making homemade. Set aside.
2. Bring a large pot of water to a boil. Add salt. Add ziti or penne, stir and bring to a boil. Turn down the heat to a rolling boil and cook for 11 min. Drain, saving ⅓ cup pasta water.
3. While the pasta is cooking, prepare meat sauce. In a large fry pan over medium high heat add the olive oil, sausage, onion and garlic and sauté until the sausage is cooked through, about 10 min., breaking it up into pieces.
4. Blend tomatoes and juice in a food processor or blender and add to the meat sauce. Simmer and stir for about 8 min. Stir in the pesto. Season to taste with salt and pepper.
5. Preheat oven to 375°. In a large bowl combine the pasta, pasta water, sausage-tomato mixture, cubed mozzarella, ⅓ cup Parmesan cheese, and arugula. Mix.
6. Grease a 13 x 9 inch baking dish with olive oil. Transfer meat/pasta mixture into the baking dish. Sprinkle the remaining ⅔ cup Parmesan cheese over all. Bake until sauce bubbles and cheese melts, about 30 min.

Serve with: Everyday Artisan Bread page 236 or French Baguettes page 242.

*I love this casserole.
I like all the different tastes, especially my homemade pesto.
I added arugula because it adds so much flavor.
I am an arugula lover!
This casserole is good enough that you'll want to enjoy it for lunch the next day.*

SUMMER VEGGIES, ITALIAN SAUSAGE AND PASTA

Serves 2
Time: 20 minutes

1 cup of your favorite pasta - rotini, fusilli, butterfly, penne, or angel hair
2 Tablespoons olive oil
½ yellow onion, sliced thinly
¼ each red, yellow, and/or green peppers, sliced into thin strips
2 cloves garlic, minced
2 6-inch yellow and/or green zucchini, thinly sliced
10 pods Snow Peas, strings removed
3 large heirloom tomatoes, skin on, cut into 2-inch chunks
¼ lb. Italian bulk sausage, broken into small chunks
6 large stalks Swiss Chard, chopped, including stems
½ cup fresh Parmesan cheese, grated
Fresh basil or fresh oregano

1. If not using previously cooked pasta, boil the pasta in 3 quarts water until tender. Drain.
2. To a large 10-12 inch fry pan over medium high heat, add oil. Heat until hot. Add onion, peppers and garlic and turn heat down to medium. Stir frequently until peppers are soft. Keep garlic from burning.
3. Add zucchini, peas, tomatoes and sausage. Stir frequently until tomatoes are soft and sausage is cooked. Add drained pasta. Stir together.
4. Add chard and stir until it is wilted. Serve immediately in large, flat bowls or plates. Sprinkle with cheese and fresh herbs.

Serve with: Bruschetta with Roasted Garlic page 52.

Variation: Use hamburger. Substitute fresh carrots, fresh green beans. Instead of large tomatoes, use small pear tomatoes, cut in half.

This recipe comes from my editor Ann,
who has taught me how to use fabulous fresh or frozen
ingredients from her own garden.
She also knows how to shop at the local farmer's markets
to get the best produce.
She serves her family fresh,
delicious meals daily even though she works fulltime!

CONVERSATION STARTER:
What do you think kids know that adults don't?

ITALIAN PICNIC AT HOME

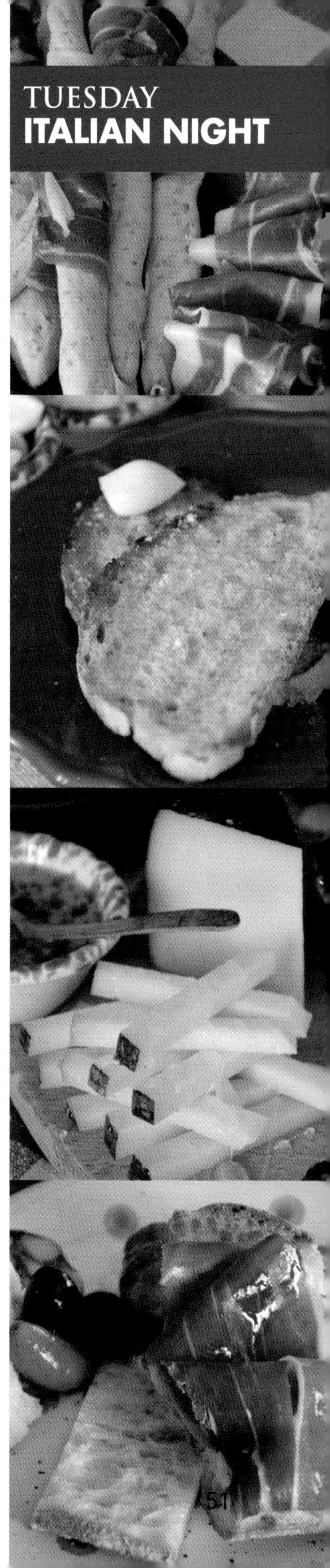

Two Choices for a Picnic at Home
Time: 5 minutes

When you want to have a fun Italian picnic at home, for lunch or dinner, buy the ingredients listed for Picnic 1 or Picnic 2.

Picnic 1:
Taleggio, Provolone, Parmesan Reggiano, or Romano Cheese
Hard Salami
Prosciutto, the sweet kind
Kalamata Olives
Hard French or Crusty Artisan Bread
Lime Slushies page 64

Picnic 2:
Table Top Grill
Italian or French Baguettes, sliced ¼ inch thick
Fresh garlic clove, peeled
Olive oil
Coarse salt
Parmesan Reggiano cheese
Honey
Italian salami
Kalamata olives

Picnic 1:
Choose one of these kinds of cheeses. The ones I have listed here are easy to find. You don't need to go to a fancy grocery store to find the other items. They are available all over also.
Put the cheese and meat on the bread or eat them separately along with the olives. It is a one-of-a-kind taste.

Picnic 2:
Place grill on the table and all other ingredients arranged on a platter. Toast bread on the table top grill. Rub garlic clove over the toasted bread. Drizzle with olive oil. Sprinkle with salt. Place a piece of cheese on the bread and drizzle with honey. This is delicious and great fun!

*Have some fun - use a table top grill. This is how I was taught to entertain in Italy. We find a scenic place to sit and eat our food. It is good to have a knife to cut the bread and cheese. Try either of these ideas at home and see how much fun your family will have enjoying these foods.
Often, we sit in front of the fireplace in the winter and serve this meal.
In the summertime,
I like to serve it outside.
Enjoy!*

Meatless BRUSCHETTA WITH ROASTED GARLIC

Serves 2
Time: 45 minutes

Plan Ahead: Roast the garlic ahead of time. See Step 1.

1 whole garlic pod, roasted
Olive oil
Coarse salt
Fresh ground black pepper
1 small red tomato, diced
1 small yellow tomato, diced
1 Tablespoon olive oil
2 Tablespoons fresh basil, chopped
Coarse salt, to taste
Fresh ground black pepper, to taste
3 oz. goat cheese
3 Tablespoons pecans, minced
Olive oil
6 slices Italian bread, ¼ inch thick

1. Peel the dry skin off the garlic pod. Slice off the top of the garlic, to expose each clove. Place in a shallow baking pan. Drizzle the top of each clove with olive oil. Lightly salt and pepper. Cover with foil and roast at 400° about 30 to 40 min. When done the clove will feel soft when squeezed.
2. In a small bowl mix together the tomatoes, 1 Tablespoon olive oil, basil, salt and pepper to taste. The tomato mixture is served at room temperature. Set aside.
3. Heat oven to 450°. Mold the goat cheese into a 3-inch round. Coat goat cheese on all sides with pecans. Place on a foil lined shallow baking pan. Drizzle cheese lightly with olive oil. Bake until warm.
4. Drizzle both sides of the bread slices generously with olive oil, coarse salt, and fresh ground black pepper. Place on a separate baking sheet and place in a 450° oven. Bake, flipping once, until both sides are toasted light-brown.
5. To serve - use a platter and place the garlic on one side. Put the tomato mixture into a small cup and place by the garlic. Place the cheese next to the bread. Serve while the garlic, cheese and bread are warm.
6. Each person creates his/her own bruschetta by spreading the warm garlic on the bread. Then the warm cheese. Top with the tomato basil mixture. Enjoy!

Variation: If you don't care for goat cheese, try using ricotta cheese. If you want to make this meal an event, use a table top grill and grill the bread over hot coals right on the table.

We tasted a bruschetta like this years ago that we never forgot.
This is our girls' favorite!
It makes a really fun meal for two people.
Use as an appetizer anytime.
For other traditional bruschetta recipes that are just as delicious, see my first book. xo

ROMANO CHICKEN WITH BEURRE BLANC

Serves 4
Time: 1 hour

Plan Ahead: Make sauce an hour ahead and re-heat. (I re-heat my leftover sauce the next day as well and it is delicious!)

2 large boneless/skinless chicken breasts, frozen
½ cup Romano cheese, grated
½ cup mayonnaise
1 roll Ritz crackers, crushed (Ritz crackers come 4 rolls per box)

Beurre Blanc:
1 Tablespoon shallot, minced finely
⅓ cup white cooking wine or white wine
⅓ cup white wine vinegar
Coarse salt, pinch
⅛ teaspoon fresh ground black pepper
½ cup cold butter (1stick), cut into 1 Tablespoon portions
⅛ teaspoon dried tarragon

1. Pre-heat the oven to 375°.
2. Line a small baking sheet with foil. Place the frozen chicken on the foil. Bake 30 min. uncovered.
3. While the chicken is baking, mix the grated cheese and mayonnaise together in a small bowl. Set aside.
4. Put the crackers in a quart size plastic bag and crush with your hands. After the chicken has cooked 30 min., take out of the oven and cut the chicken breasts in half. You will now have 4 pieces of chicken. Spoon the cheese/mayonnaise mixture generously on top of the four pieces of chicken. Sprinkle the crackers generously over top the cheese mixture- some will fall to the side.
5. Put the chicken back into the oven and continue baking for another 30 min. Prepare the Beurre Blanc while the chicken is cooking the last 30 min. Serve the chicken with the warm Beurre Blanc on the side as a dip.

Beurre Blanc:

1. In a 8½ inch sauce pan combine shallot, cooking wine and vinegar. Stir. Bring to a boil and sprinkle with salt and pepper. Turn the heat down to simmer, stir occasionally and cook until reduced to about 2 Tablespoons, about 8 to 10 min.
2. Take off the heat for a couple of minutes. Put back on the heat and add the cold butter, 1 Tablespoon at a time, stirring until almost melted, then add in the next Tablespoon until all the butter is incorporated. Stir in the tarragon. Serve warm.

Serve with: Mashed potatoes or Linguini with Butter and Parmesan page 227. Steamed carrots, broccoli, cauliflower mix.

Variation: Use Parmesan cheese in place of Romano.

This chicken is so moist and delicious you just fall in love.
The sauce is divine.
I got the idea to put the two recipes together after
I baked this chicken the very first time.
When I served this chicken to my family with this sauce,
they went crazy !!

Meatless
GNOCCHI WITH SIMPLE SAUCE

Serves 4-6, about 40 Gnocchi
Time: 45 minutes

***Plan Ahead:** Make the gnocchi ahead of time, freeze or warm up in microwave. Make sauce ahead of time. Re-heat. Purchase fresh gnocchi, eliminate one step.*

Gnocchi:

1 pound Yukon Gold potatoes (2 medium size potatoes), do not peel
Water for boiling potatoes

1 large egg, well beaten
1 Tablespoon unsalted butter, melted
1 teaspoon coarse salt
½ cup all purpose flour, plus extra for dusting
3 quarts water, plus 1 Tablespoon coarse salt

Simple Sauce:

1 28 oz. can Italian branded tomatoes, very important. (Look for the yellow and red label, San Marzano in your grocery stores.)
1 teaspoon coarse salt
½ teaspoon fresh ground black pepper
1 teaspoon dried oregano
2½ Tablespoons olive oil
Fresh Parmesan cheese, grated for garnish

1. Leave the potatoes whole. Do not peel. (Keeping the peels on keeps water out of the potatoes, very important.) Scrub them lightly. Place them in a medium saucepan and cover with water by about 3 inches. Boil until soft and tender but not breaking apart. About 30 - 40 min. Drain potatoes. Let cool to warm.
2. While the potatoes are boiling start the sauce. Drain ¾ of the juice off the tomatoes. Discard juice. Place tomatoes in a medium size fry pan. Add salt, pepper and oregano. Stir occasionally and simmer uncovered for 20 min. (The rough texture on the tomatoes is most desirable). Stir in the olive oil. Cover and set sauce aside.
3. Peel the warm potatoes with a paring knife. Mash them with a potato ricer, potato masher or use your electric mixer. Stir the egg, butter and salt into the mashed potatoes. Add the flour a little at a time, and work into a smooth manageable dough. The mixture should hold its shape and be pliable but not sticky.
4. Dust your counter top with flour. Divide the dough in half. Roll each half into about a 1-inch thick rope, no more than 1-inch, and about 2 ft. long. Dust the counter top with a little more flour as you go if needed. (If it is easier for you, divide the dough into thirds, and roll shorter ropes, about 1 inch round and 1 ft. long – 10 gnocchi per rope.)
5. Using your dough scraper cut 20, 1-inch gnocchi per rope. Take a table fork and quickly but softly run it over the edge of each little gnocchi. This makes a nice little mark and will create a space for sauce to stick to it. Cut all the gnocchi before poaching.
6. Start 3 quarts of water boiling in a pot. Add 1 Tablespoon coarse salt. When the water is ready and boiling, poach the gnocchi in 4 batches (about 10 to each batch) by dropping them into the boiling water. Leave enough room for them to move without touching until they rise to the surface and roll over. This will take only about 2 min. They cook quickly.
7. When the gnocchi rise to the surface, carefully remove them with a slotted spoon to drain. Warm the sauce and serve immediately. Pass the Parmesan.

Serve with: Green salad. Great Garlic Bread page 237.

When I make gnocchi with this sauce everyone squeals. It's so delicious. Ernest taught me how to make gnocchi the correct way in NYC on one of my Food Nanny Shows. He closed down his bakery one entire afternoon just to let us film our show and to teach me how to make gnocchi. We all love you, Ernest!

Meatless CACIO E PEPE – A QUICK MAC & CHEESE

Serves 2
Time: 10 minutes

1½ teaspoons coarse salt
6-8 oz. spaghetti, fresh or dried
2½ Tablespoons unsalted butter, divided
1 teaspoon fresh ground black pepper
¾ cup pasta water
½ cup Parmesan or Grana Padano Parmesan cheese, finely grated
½ cup Romano cheese, finely grated
½ lemon, zest only (optional)

1. Bring 3-4 quarts of water to a boil in a large pot. Stir in the salt. Add spaghetti. Cook until tender, about 2 min. for fresh; 10 min. or so for dried until tender. Remove pasta with tongs into a bowl. Set aside. Reserve pasta water.
2. In a large shallow frying pan over low heat, melt 1½ tablespoons butter and stir together with black pepper, about a minute. Add pasta water; turn the heat down to simmer. Add cooked pasta and remaining butter. Add Parmesan cheese, stirring and tossing with tongs until the cheese is melted.
3. Turn the heat off and add Romano cheese and lemon zest if using, turning with tongs. Stir in more pasta water if the sauce is too dry. Serve immediately.

Serve with: This is a starter dish in Italy. Here, in the States, it's dinner. You can serve this dish along side fish, chicken or beef. Provide plenty of green veggies such as: artichokes, brussel sprouts or broccoli. Peasant White Bread page 237.

Variations: Use fresh pasta if available. Linguini is another popular option.

This is a quick, simple but delicious meal for lunch or dinner.
It's good for just one person or for a family.
I make it for lunch for my grandkids often.
It reminds me of making Spaghetti Carbonara,
only with fewer ingredients. Enjoy!

AUTHENTIC RAGU

Serves 4 - makes about 3 cups
Time: 1 hour

½ cup flat leaf parsley (Italian)
1½ sticks celery, leaves included, cut into 2 inch pieces
1 small yellow onion, cut into chunks
1 1-inch piece of carrot, peeled
1 clove garlic, peeled
2 Tablespoons olive oil
½ lb. ground beef
½ lb. ground pork
½ cup white wine, or cooking wine
½ teaspoon fresh ground or dried nutmeg
Coarse salt
Fresh ground black pepper
1 15oz. can tomato sauce
1 cup water
1 cup beef broth
1 lb. Penne, Fusilli or Rigatoni cooked
Fresh Parmesan cheese, grated

1. Put the first 5 ingredients into a food processor or blender. Turn on the machine for about 8 sec. You want the mixture to be well minced, but not watery. Set aside.
2. In a medium size saucepan heat the olive oil over medium heat. Add minced vegetables. Stir a couple of times until the liquid is gone and the flavors all come together, about 5 min. Add ground meat. Cook and stir until browned.
3. Add the wine. Let it evaporate. Add the nutmeg, salt and pepper to taste. Add tomato sauce, water and beef broth. Stir until combined, then turn the heat down to simmer. Simmer uncovered for 20 min. Then, partially cover the pan and simmer for 30 more min.
4. Serve over Penne, Fusilli, Rigatoni, rice or Polenta. Pass the fresh Parmesan cheese.

Serve with: Green salad. Artisan Beer Bread page 247.

I will treasure the time spent with you, Vittorio, and your family. I watched Marzia prepare this homemade ragu right in her own farm house kitchen in Tuscany. I never felt more at home in a kitchen. Marzia is my age and we had so much in common. Feeding large families on a weekly basis often is what we do: in a kitchen with one oven! She had rabbit meat on the counter waiting to be cooked as well, that blew my mind!! Marzia, I love you! I will treasure our day together with you and your family forever! xo.

CONVERSATION STARTER:

Have you ever been really scared of something? Why?

ITALIAN PEASANT SOUP

Serves 6
Time: 20 minutes

- 1 pound boneless/skinless chicken breasts cut into 1-inch pieces
- 1 pound mild Italian sausage links, casings removed, cut into 1-inch pieces or use ground sausage
- 1 Tablespoon olive oil
- 1 medium yellow onion, chopped
- 4-6 garlic cloves, minced
- 2 15-oz. cans cannellini beans, rinsed and drained. May substitute great northern beans
- 1 14.5 oz. can diced tomatoes with juice
- 4¼ cups chicken broth
- 1 teaspoon dried basil
- 1 teaspoon dried oregano
- 6 cups fresh spinach, kale or Swiss chard leaves, chopped
- ½ cup fresh Parmesan cheese, grated

1. Wipe off the chicken with a wet paper towel. Cut into pieces, cut away any extra fat or gristle. Set aside.
2. In a large pot over medium heat cook sausage with 1 Tablespoon olive oil until browned and no longer pink. Drain any extra grease. Add onions and garlic. Sauté until the onions are soft. Add chicken pieces and sauté and stir until no longer pink. Add beans, tomatoes, broth, basil and oregano; stir to mix. Cook uncovered, for 10 min. Add the spinach, kale or chard and heat just until wilted. Serve with Parmesan cheese sprinkled on top.

Serve with: Food Nanny Parmesan Bread Sticks page 246. French Baguettes page 242.

Julie, we love your soup! Everyone I have ever made this soup for has really enjoyed it. Even the kids will eat spinach cooked this way in the soup. I love spinach, kale and chard as options. They are so good for you and taste really great too. Kale is a vegetable that many were raised on during the great depression. It was a vegetable that many home cooks used, especially on the East Coast. Now we are using it like it is something that has just been discovered! It is so funny how that works with food and lots of other things too.

AMERICAN LASAGNA

Serves 12
Time: 1 hour 45 minutes

Plan Ahead: Make the sauce a day ahead. Have Lasagna on the table in 45 minutes!

3 14.5 oz. cans diced tomatoes, un-drained (Italian tomatoes if possible)
2 Tablespoons olive oil
⅓ cup white or yellow onion, chopped
3 garlic cloves, minced
1 pound 3 oz. package mild Italian Sausage links, casings removed
1 6 oz. can tomato paste
3 Tablespoons brown sugar
1½ teaspoons oregano, dried
½ teaspoon basil, dried
½ teaspoon thyme, dried
1 teaspoon coarse salt
1 bay leaf
2 cups hot water
1 pound lasagna noodles, cooked
1 15 oz. carton Whole Ricotta cheese
½ cup fresh Parmesan cheese, grated
2 eggs
¼ teaspoon fresh ground black pepper
4 cups (1 pound) Mozzarella cheese, grated
3 Tablespoons butter

Sauce:

1. Put the tomatoes in a blender and pulse 4 or 5 sec. to crush. Set aside.
2. Heat the olive oil in a large pot or skillet over medium heat. Add the onion and garlic and sauté and stir until the onion is soft. Increase the heat to medium high and add the sausage. Continue to cook, stirring until the sausage is browned. Stir in the tomato paste with a wooden spoon. Cook until the mixture starts sticking to the pan, about 5 min.
3. Add the crushed tomatoes, brown sugar, oregano, basil, thyme, salt and bay leaf. Mix well. Stir in the water. Bring to a boil, decrease the heat, and simmer uncovered for an hour. (May simmer up to 2 hours, adding in more water periodically if the sauce gets too thick.)

Remove the noodles from the package and cook according to package directions. Drain. Lay out the cooked pasta in a single layer on a 15-inch sheet of aluminum foil to cool. (The foil will be re-used to cover the baking dish.)

4. Preheat the oven to 350°. Grease a 9 x 13-inch baking dish.
5. Mix the ricotta, parmesan, eggs and pepper in a medium size bowl. Assemble the lasagna.
6. Spread ⅓ of the meat sauce in the prepared baking dish. Arrange 5 noodles lengthwise over the sauce, over lapping the edges. Spread ⅓ of the cheese mixture and sprinkle 1⅓ cups of the mozzarella cheese over the pasta.
7. Repeat the layers two more times, ending with the mozzarella. Dot the butter around the edges. Cover with the foil and bake 35 to 40 min. or until bubbly. Let stand 5 min. before serving.

Serve with: Two Basic Salads page 258, Food Nanny Parmesan Bread Sticks page 246 or French Baguettes page 242.

Variations: Use hot Italian Sausage for more spice. Use this sauce over spaghetti.

This is my basic spaghetti sauce.
Use this to make American Spaghetti.
This is wonderful sauce your entire family will love!
Every time we make this lasagna friends ask for the recipe.

Meatless

MASSIMILIANO'S QUICK AND EASY PASTA

Serves 4
Time: 15 minutes

Plan Ahead: Have everything on hand and dinner is ready in 15 minutes! Now that's fun!

¼ cup olive oil
¾ cup yellow onion, diced
1 clove fresh garlic, minced (optional)
1 14.5 oz. can diced tomatoes with juice, crushed
5 cups water
1 pound pasta of choice - bowtie, penne or ziti
½ cup fresh basil, torn
1 Tablespoon unsalted butter
Coarse salt
Fresh ground black pepper
Fresh Parmesan cheese grated, for serving

Heat the olive oil in a large pot over medium heat. Add onion and sauté until soft. Add garlic. Sauté 30 sec. Add crushed tomatoes, water and pasta. Stir and bring to a boil. Turn the heat down and cook over low heat until the pasta is cooked, about 12 min. Stir in fresh basil and butter. Salt and pepper to taste. Serve. Pass the grated Parmesan cheese.

Serve with: Two Basic Salads page 258 or Great Garlic Bread page 237.

Massimiliano is the CEO of the oldest functioning Renaissance Theatre in the world, near Venice, Italy, where he lives.
The theater was built at the end of the 16th Century.
He is also a renowned pianist and composer.
He practiced 18 hours a day at one time in his life.
We worked together on the Food Nanny Show.
It took me 2 weeks to pronounce his name!
His rule of thumb is one pound pasta per four people.
He showed me this Go-To pasta that he makes all the time.
It reminds me of my mother's tomato Go-To pasta, only this one has more flavor. xo

CONVERSATION STARTER:

When you are a parent, how will you discipline your children?

CHICKEN PARMESAN

Serves 4
Time: 30 minutes or less

Plan Ahead: Prepare the chicken ahead of time and save a few minutes.

- ½ pound spaghetti, cooked
- 2 teaspoons salt
- 4 small boneless/skinless chicken breasts, flattened
- 1 egg, beaten
- 1 cup homemade bread crumbs using 2 pieces of white sandwich bread
- ½ teaspoon Italian seasoning
- 2 Tablespoons unsalted butter
- 1¾ cups homemade marinara or store bought spaghetti sauce, without meat
- ½ cup pasta water, or more
- ½ cup Mozzarella cheese, grated
- 1 Tablespoon fresh Parmesan cheese, grated

1. Boil 5 quarts of water in a large pot. Add 2 teaspoons salt and spaghetti. Cook about 10 min. or until tender. Drain. Set aside. Save ½ cup pasta water plus extra if needed.
2. Wipe off the chicken with a wet paper towel. Using the palm of your hand, flatten the chicken to even thickness or use a mallet and put chicken between 2 pieces of plastic to flatten to about ½ inch thick.
3. Beat the egg in a shallow dish. In a food processor or blender process the bread until crumbs. Place in a shallow dish and stir in the Italian seasoning. Dip chicken into egg, then in crumbs to coat.
4. In a large fry pan over medium heat, melt the butter. Brown the chicken on both sides. Add the spaghetti sauce and ½ cup pasta water. Reduce the heat to low; cover and simmer for 10 min. Sprinkle both cheeses on top. Cover and simmer again for 5 min. or until the cheese melts. If sauce is too thick, add more pasta water. Serve over drained hot spaghetti.

Serve with: Mixed vegetables or fresh green salad.

My daughter Emaly and I figured out a way to make Chicken Parmesan really fast and yummy! This is quick, easy and delicious. Dinner is on the table in less than 30 minutes! Now that's a deal!

CONVERSATION STARTER:

How many times did you tell someone you loved them today?

Meatless BOWTIE PASTA WITH BROCCOLI

Serves 4
Time: 15 minutes

1 lb. pasta Bowtie or Orecchiette
1 broccoli head, fresh or frozen, chopped
¼ cup pasta water
¼ cup olive oil
1 garlic clove, pressed
¾ cup fresh Parmesan cheese, grated
Coarse salt
Fresh ground black pepper, to taste

1. In a large pot, bring 5 quarts of water to a boil. Add the broccoli, bring to a boil and add pasta. Cook until pasta is al dente.
2. Drain pasta and broccoli, saving ¼ cup pasta water. In a bowl stir together pasta, broccoli, pasta water, olive oil, garlic and Parmesan cheese. Salt and pepper to taste.

Serve with: French Baguettes page 242 or Bruschetta page 52.

Variation: Cube (bite size) 2 cups French baguettes. Toss with olive oil and fresh Parmesan cheese. Salt and pepper to taste. Place on baking sheet and bake at 400° 10 min. or until light brown. Mix in with the cooked pasta and broccoli mixture.

*This meal is fast, easy and really healthy.
If you have 15 minutes, you've got dinner on the table.
This is a whole lot better than fast food any night!*

Meatless LIME SLUSHIES

Serves 6
Time: 10 minutes

3 fresh limes, juiced
4 Tablespoons sweetened condensed milk
¾ cup sugar
1 cup water
3 cups ice
Garnish with a slice of lime or a sprig of fresh mint

In a blender mix the juice, milk, sugar and water until well blended. Blend in the ice on medium speed. Serve in small cups or glasses as desired.

Serve with: Great with any Italian dish! Great for dessert or on a summer day.

*These slushies are fabulous. So fresh, so tasty.
They remind me of the Amalfi Coast in Italy.
It is the most beautiful place I have ever been.
Think of Positano and drink these really fun slushies.
Elizabeth gave us the idea. Katie, my daughter and her husband, Colin perfected the recipe.*

FETTUCCINE ALFREDO WITH GRILLED CHICKEN

Serves 4-6
Time: 30 minutes

Plan Ahead: Grill the chicken ahead of time and keep warm. Dinner ready in 15 minutes.

2 small boneless/skinless chicken breasts, grilled
Coarse salt
Fresh ground black pepper

Alfredo Sauce:
½ cup (1 stick) butter
1 3oz. package cream cheese
1 pint heavy cream
1 teaspoon garlic powder
½ cup fresh Parmesan cheese, grated
Coarse salt
Fresh ground black pepper

1 pound uncooked fresh or regular Spinach Fettuccine

1. Wipe off the chicken with a wet paper towel. Season well with salt and pepper. Turn the grill to medium/high heat. Fold a paper towel, sprinkle with olive oil and using your tongs go over the grill to season it so the chicken won't stick to it. Grill the chicken over medium heat, about 10 to 15 min. per side, depending on the size of the breast. Cut into chunks.
2. While the chicken is grilling make the Alfredo sauce. Boil the pasta according to package directions, just before you are ready to serve. Drain.

Alfredo Sauce:

3. Melt the butter and cream cheese in a medium saucepan over low heat. Stir in the cream and garlic powder. Increase the heat and bring to a boil. Decrease the heat and simmer 10 to 15 min., stirring often.
   Stir the Parmesan cheese into the sauce and season with salt and pepper to taste. If the sauce needs additional thickening (for example if you're serving it as a dipping sauce without pasta), you may sprinkle in flour, 1 teaspoon at a time. Keep warm.
4. Toss the sauce with the cooked pasta and grilled chicken in a large bowl and serve immediately. Season with more salt and pepper to taste.

Serve with: Green salad, vegetables such as: peas, carrots or broccoli. Bread Sticks page 246.

Variations: We make the Alfredo Sauce just to dip our bread sticks into all the time. Put this sauce on pizza with grilled chicken.

Kristen down the street called me one day to tell me she makes this meal at least once a week. She said, "Liz, I just love your Alfredo sauce, and it makes the best Chicken Alfredo ever!!" We all love using fresh fettuccini noodles when we can get them. They make this meal special.

Fish, Meatless or Breakfast for Dinner

When I go to help families create a menu plan, most often they don't want to include fish. I get them started by trying white fish such as Tilapia.
Almost everyone agrees that Tilapia does not taste fishy, and they like it!
Graduating to Salmon will be next. I have some great sauces in this chapter that will help you really enjoy eating fish even more! But, if you are absolutely against trying fish, then plan meals on this night that do not include meat.
In each chapter I have included recipes that are meatless so a couple of nights a week you can plan meals eating meat-free. I believe My Meal Plan has kept my family and me healthy. With fresh fish in our diets and a meatless dinner a couple of times a week, we have a healthy lifestyle that anyone would want to champion.
Servings of meat every night, especially red meat, are not good.
When planning the menu, you may want to try this: use Wednesday to eat some fish, or choose a meal with no meat. You will feel better and you will be on your way to a healthier lifestyle. We all know that fresh vegetables, fresh fruits and whole grains are what keep us healthy. When we do eat meat it is important to have more veggies on our plates than meat.
The longer I live, the more I see the importance of eating fish in your diet once, or twice a week, and eating no meat at all a couple of times of week.
This is why I include Breakfast in this chapter. Most breakfast foods do not require meat in the recipes and they are inexpensive meals to plan.

The Food Nanny. xo

WEDNESDAY
FMB NIGHT

Meatless

MACADAMIA NUT-CRUSTED FISH

Serves 4
Time: 15 minutes

Plan Ahead: Roast the beets. Reheat when serving.

½ pound fresh cod or any white fish
½ cup macadamia nuts, chopped
5 Tablespoons Parmesan cheese, freshly grated
6 Tablespoons panko breadcrumbs
1 teaspoon fresh parsley, minced (optional)
2 egg whites
2 Tablespoons water
1½ Tablespoons butter
1 teaspoon olive oil
Lemon wedges

1. Cut the fish into desired serving amounts. Set aside, but keep cold.
2. In a pie pan, mix the chopped nuts, Parmesan cheese, panko and parsley. Set aside.
3. Whisk the egg whites with the water in a small bowl. Set aside.
4. In a fry pan, over low to medium heat, melt the butter with the olive oil.
5. Place fish into the egg wash. Roll the fish into the nut mixture. Pat the nut mixture lightly with your fingers so it will stick to the fish. Place in hot oil and sauté until golden brown about 4 min. per side.
6. Serve immediately with a lemon wedge on the side.

Serve with: Brown Rice with Almonds page 217, Roasted Beets page 229, Jasmine Rice page 218, broccoli or green beans.

Variations: May blend the nuts to powder; add 2 Tablespoons sweetened coconut to the nut mix; or add capers and lemon juice to the butter and olive oil.

When we eat at Duke's on Waikiki I order a fish that tastes a lot like this recipe that I developed. Go there and have Chicken Quesadillas or the Salad Bar and Fish or Ribs. Dukes is the place to eat! The best ever!! xo

OREGON SEAFOOD SOUP

Serves 4-6
Time: 30 minutes

Plan ahead: Prepare the soup – all except adding the seafood. This can be made and refrigerated a day or two ahead. Prepare and add the seafood to the re-heated sauce when you are ready to have your meal. Dinner is on the table in less than 5 minutes!

6 cloves garlic, minced
1 medium yellow onion, chopped fine
2 green onions, chopped fine, include some green
2 cups finely chopped kale, Swiss chard or spinach as you like. (I prefer kale.)
1 teaspoon Herbs de Provence
½ teaspoon coarse salt
2 to 3 pinches red pepper flakes
¼ teaspoon fresh black pepper
½ bottle (2 cups) dry white wine; or re-place the wine with clam juice
¼ cup Marsala wine
1 14.5 oz. can diced tomatoes with liquid
2 cups sausage, sliced pre-cooked. Kielbasa, Andouille or Linguica are best. If raw, cook first.
16-20 fresh prawns (shrimp) – can be frozen, shelled. (I leave the tail on.)
20-30 hard shell clams. Manilla clams or steamer clams work well, about 5-6 per person.
8-12 sea scallops, can be frozen. Cut in half, or quarter if they are large. If using small bay scallops, use 28-32.

Polenta Rounds Homemade page 83, ¼ inch thick. Or buy ready-made and cut to ¼ inch. Asiago cheese, grated.

In a stock pot or large saucepan, place:

1. Minced garlic, onion, green onion, kale, Herbs de Provence, coarse salt, red pepper flakes and fresh ground black pepper. Add the wine or clam juice, Marsala wine and bring all of this to a boil.
2. Turn down to simmer and add tomatoes and sausage. Simmer until the kale and onion softens. Soup can be prepared to this point and put in the refrigerator until ready to have your meal. Do not add seafood until ready to serve the dish.

Clean and prepare seafood:

1. Bring the stock in the pot back to a boil and add seafood. Cook only until clams open. Discard ones that do not open. Be careful not to over-cook as shrimp toughens if overcooked. Remove from heat and serve over Polenta rounds with Asiago cheese.

Prepare Polenta page 83:

Or buy polenta prepared and cut into ¼ inch rounds. Spray a baking sheet with baking oil and roast in a 350° oven with a good sprinkling of grated Asiago cheese until melted. Place in the bottom of the bowl and pour the seafood soup on top.

Variations: French Baguettes may be substituted for polenta.

Every time I go to Portland, Paul makes me this soup. I look forward to it every visit. I love the polenta that gives it the final touch. It is delicious, fat free, low calorie and comes together in less than 30 minutes. If you enjoy all these flavors you are going to love this wonderful seafood soup... xo

CLAM CHOWDER

Serves 6
Time: 30 minutes

2 6½ oz. cans clams, minced
1 cup celery, finely chopped
1 cup yellow onion, finely chopped
2 cups potatoes, diced
¾ cup butter
¾ cup flour
½ teaspoon salt
⅛ teaspoon pepper
1½ teaspoon sugar
1 quart Half & Half

1. Drain the clams and save the juice. Place the clams, celery, onion and potatoes in a medium size saucepan on top of the stove. Add the clam juice and enough water to cover the vegetables. Bring to a boil; turn down the heat and simmer until the potatoes are tender. Set aside.
2. In another sauce pan over medium heat melt the butter. Add the flour, salt, pepper and sugar and stir until bubbly. Whisk in the Half & Half. Stir with a wooden spoon. Cook until thickened.
3. Add in the clams and vegetables. Heat through and serve.

Serve with: Oyster Crackers. German Brown Bread page 233. Green salad.

I have been making this clam chowder for 25 years. I knew the nicest person, Kaydawn, who gave me the recipe that many years ago.

Meatless

SPICY REMOULADE SAUCE FOR FISH

Serves 4
Time: 5 minutes

⅓ cup yogurt
2 Tablespoons mayonnaise
2 teaspoons parsley, chopped
2 teaspoons shallot, minced
1 clove garlic, crushed
2 teaspoons honey Dijon mustard; or Dijon and a few drops of honey
½ teaspoon fresh tarragon or
1 teaspoon dried tarragon
¼ teaspoon cayenne pepper
Dash of fresh ground black pepper

Plan ahead: Prepare sauce ahead of time. Re-heat when ready to serve. Remoulade is French for a mayonnaise based sauce with mustard. Use this sauce on any kind of fish.

Place all the ingredients into a small saucepan on top of the stove. Heat until warmed through. Spoon warm sauce over prepared fish.

Easy great sauce for any kind of fish - ready in minutes. You will really love this one.

STEAMER CLAMS IN WHITE WINE SAUCE

Serves 4
Time: 30 minutes

2 teaspoons dried red peppers, crushed
Olive oil
1 leek, minced
4 cloves fresh garlic, minced
1 celery stalk, chopped fine, leaves and all
½ teaspoon fennel, optional
2 cups white wine
2 pounds steamer clams, rinsed
¼ cup cream
2 Tablespoons butter
3 Tablespoons Italian parsley, minced
Crusty Sourdough Bread
Lemon Wedges
Tabasco

CONVERSATION STARTER:

Are you afraid of doing anything?

1. In a large pot sauté crushed red peppers in 1 Tablespoon olive oil. Toast them up. It just takes a few seconds.
2. Add 1 Tablespoon more olive oil to the pan then add minced leeks, garlic, celery and fennel. Sauté until the leeks and celery are soft. Add white wine and cook over low heat. Let the flavors blend about 3 min.
3. Add the rinsed clams. Cover the pot with a lid. Cook until the clams open - about 5 min. As soon as they open turn the heat off. The key here is to not over-cook them.
4. If some clams do not open - throw them away. Take the remaining clams out with tongs and place in a bowl. Stir the cream and butter into the wine sauce in the pan. Serve in bowls making sure you get plenty of sauce in the bottom of each bowl. Top with parsley.

Serve with: Warm Crusty Sourdough or Crispy Bread. Lemon wedges and Tabasco along side. To make crispy bread: Broil the bread until toasted. Take one skinned garlic clove and run it across the bread. Drizzle on olive oil.

Variations: Can use this same recipe with mussels.

The first time I ever ordered my own clams was when we were visiting Sue and Lonnie. I was so hungry! I will never forget how much wonderful bread I ate by sopping up the delicious sauce. Sue is a great cook and she taught me how to make this dish in her kitchen. You can see the ocean from there and it makes cooking so much fun.

SALMON WITH SOY SAUCE AND FRESH GINGER

Serves 4
Time: 20 minutes

Plan Ahead: Prepare your sides the day ahead.

4 salmon steaks, 4 oz. each
1 green onion, minced
2 Tablespoons soy sauce
1 Tablespoon honey
1 teaspoon fresh ginger, grated
1 teaspoon sesame seeds, toasted

1. In a small bowl whisk green onion, soy sauce, honey and ginger until honey is dissolved.
2. Place salmon in a plastic bag. Add 2 Tablespoons of the sauce just to marinate for a few minutes in the refrigerator while the broiler preheats. Reserve the remaining marinade for sauce.
3. Line a small baking pan with foil and spray with a light coat of cooking oil. Take the salmon out of the marinade and place onto the foil. Throw away the marinade in the baggie used to marinate the salmon.
4. Broil the salmon about 5 inches from the broiler until cooked through, 8 to 10 min. Drizzle with the reserved sauce and garnish with toasted sesame seeds.

Serve with: Linguine with Butter & Parmesan Cheese page 227, wasabi mashed potatoes - make your mashed potatoes as you would and add some prepared wasabi to taste. I buy it in the tube and always have it on hand. Make a salad with arugula, red and yellow heirloom tomatoes. Olive oil with balsamic vinegar dressing. Serve a small plate of raw veggies with it.

Variations: Double the sauce.

*Jen, thanks for sharing this recipe with me.
This fish is delicious and easy. xo*

STEAMED SALMON FILLETS WRAPPED IN FRESH CHARD

Serves 2
Time: 10 minutes

2 6 oz. salmon fillets, fresh or thawed
2 Swiss Chard leaves, at least 12 – 18" long, with 4-6" stem
Coarse Salt
Fresh Ground Black Pepper

1. Season salmon with coarse salt and fresh ground black pepper.
2. Wrap each fillet in a single 12-18 inch chard leaf. Lay fillet 3 inches from the top of the leaf. Fold the top of the leaf down over the salmon - if you press down the leaf it will stay creased.
3. Fold the 2 sides of the leaf over top. Fold up the remaining bottom of the leaf so the fillet is completely wrapped in the leaf. Crack the stem and fold it down. Turn the "package" over with the stem on the bottom. Do the same with the other fillet.
4. Place the fillets in a microwavable dish. Cover the dish with plastic wrap.
5. Microwave 3 to 4 min. on high or the automatic "Fish" setting.
6. After cooking, the plastic film will be shrunk tightly over the dish. Remove film. Serve the salmon in the chard "package" – a delicious salmon and vegetable entrée.

Serve with: Steamed red potatoes or Jasmine & Quinoa page 218.

Variations: Can place lettuce on top of the salmon but discard after cooking.

Tip: I know that working Moms and busy Moms (so that would include all of us) are always looking for short cuts when it comes to preparing meals. If we have a meal plan we can see what is coming up for the next night. That way we can prepare ahead of time. We can get kids to chop veggies or prepare a sauce.
The tip here is - plan ahead. Don't waste time trying to figure out what's for dinner, have that already in the plan. Use your time wisely and make it easier on yourself the next night by preparing part of the dinner tonight.

Ann gave me this recipe.
She works full time and is always coming up with great ways to save time and still be able to eat the foods she loves.

BROILED OR GRILLED SALMON WITH RED PEPPER OR DILL SAUCE

Serves 4
Time: 20 minutes

Plan Ahead: Prepare either or both of the sauces.

Salmon Marinade:
4 6 oz. salmon fillets
Juice of ½ lemon
2 teaspoons Dijon mustard

Blackened Red Pepper Sauce:
1 blackened red bell pepper, skinned
1 cup sour cream
1 cup plain yogurt
½ teaspoon tarragon
Coarse salt
Ground black pepper

Dill Sauce:
1 cup mayonnaise
2 Tablespoons dill pickle relish
2 Tablespoons yellow onion, finely chopped
1 Tablespoon parsley, chopped (fresh or dried)
1 Tablespoon fresh lemon juice
1½ teaspoons garlic salt

Salmon Marinade:

1. In a small bowl stir together the lemon juice and Dijon mustard.
2. Place the salmon in a re-sealable plastic bag. Pour the marinade over the salmon. Squish the bag around so the marinade covers the salmon. Store in refrigerator while you prepare either sauce.

Blackened Red Pepper Sauce:

1. Turn the broiler on. Place the pepper on a baking sheet about 8 inches under the broiler and let it blacken. Check and turn often.
   Put the blackened pepper in a plastic bag for 10 min. to sweat. Remove the skin.
2. Quarter the pepper and place in a food processor or blender. Mix with remaining ingredients until smooth. Season to taste with coarse salt and fresh ground black pepper. Serve the sauce at room temperature over the top of broiled or grilled salmon.

Dill Sauce:

Stir ingredients together. Place in a container with a lid. Chill.
Serve with Broiled or Grilled Salmon Fillets.

To Broil Salmon:

1. Sprinkle the marinated fish lightly with coarse salt and fresh ground black pepper. Drizzle a little olive oil on both sides. Place on a baking sheet lined with foil. Broil 2 to 3 inches from the element for 2 minutes.
2. Lightly spread some soft butter on top of the salmon. Continue to broil until the fish springs back when you touch it - about another 5 minutes. Serve immediately with Blackened Red Pepper Sauce or Dill Sauce.

To Grill Salmon:

1. Follow the directions above, only grill on top of the BBQ at medium heat until you see the salmon start to turn white on the bottom. Spread with butter and continue grilling until the salmon springs back when touched. I like to place salmon on a double layer of foil for grilling.

Serve with: Spinach Salad page 265, or Couscous Salad page 269.

I am always looking for great sauces to put on my salmon. Salmon is one of those fish that you can broil, pan fry or BBQ very nicely. Thank you Jenny and Nancy.

LINGUINE WITH LEMON SHRIMP

Serves 4
Time: 25 minutes

1 lb. large shrimp, about 15, peeled and deveined. Save the tails and shells.
Juice of 2 lemons
½ cup olive oil
5 garlic cloves, crushed
Red pepper flakes, crushed, to taste
Shrimp shells and tails
1 medium yellow onion, chopped
½ lb. linguine pasta
½ Tablespoon coarse salt
¼ teaspoon olive oil
½ cup pasta water, saved
¼ cup Italian parsley, chopped
Parmesan cheese

I cooked this meal in my first season of the Food Nanny with the Parkin Family. What a great family they were. I so enjoyed being with all of them. Every single person fell in love with this dish. I love it too.

1. **Marinate the shrimp:** Place the peeled shrimp in a large bowl with lemon zest and lemon juice. Add olive oil, garlic cloves and red pepper flakes to taste. Stir. Let sit while the stock and linguini cook.
2. **Stock:** In a small saucepan place the shrimp shells and tails. Add chopped onion and enough water to just cover the shells, tails and onion. Bring to a boil then turn down the heat and simmer for 6 min. Strain and reserve stock. Set aside.
3. Cook the linguine per package directions adding ½ Tablespoon coarse salt and olive oil, about 10 min. Drain, reserving ½ cup pasta water. Set aside.
4. Put 2 Tablespoons olive oil in a large fry pan over medium heat. The pan is ready to cook the shrimp when a small piece of bread browns quickly.
5. Take the shrimp out of the marinade with tongs and shake to get most of the marinade off – but save the marinade. Place the shrimp immediately into the fry pan. Fry quickly, turning with the tongs. When the shrimp turns pink and you cannot see through it anymore the shrimp is done. This will take 1 to 2 min. depending on your heat. Remove the cooked shrimp to a bowl.
6. Pour the remaining marinade into the hot fry pan. Add the pasta water and drained shrimp stock.
7. Add the linguine, cooked shrimp, chopped Italian parsley and stir with tongs to mix.
8. Put the shrimp and linguine in a bowl and serve. Pass fresh grated Parmesan cheese.

Serve with: Great Garlic bread page 237, steamed broccoli or asparagus page 215.

Meatless
MINESTRONE LOVERS SOUP

Serves 6
Time: 1¼ hours

4 Tablespoons olive oil
1 cup yellow onion, chopped
1 cup celery, chopped
½ cup carrots, chopped
3 cloves garlic, minced
1 14.5 oz. can, diced tomatoes with basil, garlic and oregano
1 8 oz. can tomato sauce
¾ cup cabbage, shredded
⅓ cup zucchini, chopped (zucchini optional)
8 cups chicken broth
1 Tablespoon tomato paste
1 15 oz. can cannelloni beans
2 Tablespoons dried parsley
1 teaspoon salt
¾ cup elbow macaroni
½ cup fresh grated Parmesan cheese

1. Heat the oil in a large pot over medium heat. Add chopped onion, celery, carrots and garlic. Sauté until the onions are soft.
2. Add tomatoes, tomato sauce, cabbage, zucchini, chicken broth, tomato paste, cannelloni beans, parsley and salt. Stir. Let this come to a boil. Cover and reduce heat slightly to allow soup to simmer for 40 min. or until vegetables are just tender.
3. Add pasta and simmer for 11 min. longer until the pasta is al dente but not too soft.
4. Serve with freshly grated Parmesan cheese on top.

Serve with: Everyday Artisan Bread page 236 or Artisan Beer Bread on page 247.

Variations: Pressure cook your soup in 10 min. Then stir in the already cooked pasta. Or, crock pot: cook on low for 8 hours adding in the macaroni in the beginning.

*I love Minestrone Soup especially when it is chilly outside.
It is so satisfying and so healthy for you!
Thank you, Sharee, our dear friend for over 30 years.*

Meatless
RED LENTIL COCONUT SOUP

Serves 4-6
Time: 30 minutes

1½ Tablespoons olive oil
1 medium yellow onion, chopped
3 cloves garlic, minced
2 medium carrots, peeled and chopped
1 inch slice ginger (optional)
1¾ cups red lentils
4 cups water
1 14 oz. can coconut milk
1 teaspoon salt
2½ Tablespoons lemon or lime juice
Cilantro for garnish

1. In a medium size saucepan heat the olive oil over medium heat and sauté the onion, garlic, carrots and ginger (if using) until the onions are soft.
2. Add the lentils, water, coconut milk and salt. Stir. Bring to a boil, reduce heat, cover and simmer for 30 min. or until the lentils are soft.
3. Remove from heat. Remove the slice of ginger. Stir in lime or lemon juice. Garnish with cilantro.

Serve with: Nann Bread page 239. Arugula salad.

This is a nice recipe made with a healthy food source – lentils. They are king when it comes to nutrition. Give the red ones a try. They are a bit sweeter and nuttier than others. Lentils are a key source of protein for vegetarian and vegan diets. Thanks, Jenny, for this yummy soup recipe.

TILAPIA AND ASPARAGUS "GIFT" WRAPS

WEDNESDAY
FMB NIGHT

Serves 4
Time: 25 minutes

Plan Ahead: Prepare rice quinoa or couscous 1 day ahead.

4 tilapia fillets 4 -6 oz. each
4 cups arugula or baby spinach, rinsed
Coarse salt
Fresh ground black pepper
2 Tablespoons olive oil
2 teaspoons butter
1 teaspoon dried tarragon
6 thin asparagus pieces, cut into 2 inch pieces
1 shallot, sliced
1 lemon, thinly sliced

1. Season tilapia with coarse salt and fresh ground black pepper.
2. Stretch out foil across a 9x13 inch baking dish. Now double that amount or use parchment paper. Foil will take 5 to 10 min. longer to cook.
3. Lay the foil/parchment paper out on the counter and spread one half of the foil/parchment with a little olive oil. Lay down the arugula or spinach. Place the fish on top of the greens.
4. Melt the butter and mix with the olive oil drizzle over top the fish. Sprinkle on the tarragon.
5. Scatter the asparagus and shallots across the fish. Sprinkle with more olive oil, a little coarse salt and fresh ground black pepper. Lay the lemon slices evenly over top the fish.
6. Fold the foil over the fish and tuck in the sides (like wrapping a present). The steam will not escape. Lay the fish package in the 9x13 inch pan.
7. Bake at 425° for 15 min. per inch of fish.

Serve with: Quinoa Rice page 218. Sliced tomatoes and Roasted Beets page 229.

Variations: Make individual packets and serve them individually. This makes a nice presentation.

I love making this fish. It is healthy, fast and tastes really great! When you feel like something light and healthy this is a great choice. Keep parchment paper on hand to save time on cleaning baking sheets also. xo

Meatless POLENTA WITH MUSHROOM SAUCE

Serves 4
Time: 35 minutes

Plan Ahead: Make polenta the night before or in the morning. Have everything else chopped and ready to go when you prepare the sauce.

Polenta:

4 cups water
1 cup polenta corn meal
¼ cup fresh grated Parmesan cheese
2 Tablespoons butter
Dash of coarse salt
1 Tablespoons olive oil

Mushroom Sauce:

2 cloves fresh garlic, minced
1 Tablespoon celery with leaves, chopped fine
1 Tablespoon leek, minced (optional)
½ shallot, minced
6 white mushrooms, sliced
¼ cup white wine, or apple juice
½ teaspoon beef bouillon cube for flavor
¼ cup freshly grated Parmesan cheese
1 cup + 2 Tablespoons heavy cream
Coarse salt
Fresh ground black pepper

1. In a medium size saucepan bring 4 cups water to a boil and put in 1 cup polenta corn meal. Stir. Turn the heat down to low and continue cooking and stirring for about 4 to 5 min. until thick. Add Parmesan cheese, butter and a dash of salt. Stir well.
2. Lightly brush olive oil on the bottom of a Jelly Roll pan 17 x 11. Pour the hot polenta out onto baking sheet and even it out with a spoon. Let it sit on the counter until the steam goes away. When the steam is gone place the polenta in the refrigerator for 15 min. or until it is firm.
3. Use a 2½ inch biscuit cutter to cut polenta into shapes. (I use a round biscuit cutter). Freeze any leftovers in a plastic bag.
4. In a large frying pan or a grill pan, fry 4 pieces of polenta at a time in 1½ Tablespoons olive oil. Sauté on both sides until warmed through. Continue frying adding more olive oil as needed. Set aside on a plate. Cover and keep warm. ***While the polenta is sautéing make the mushroom sauce:***
5. In a pan over medium heat, using a little olive oil to sauté garlic, celery, leek, shallot (optional) and mushrooms until the leeks are soft. Add white wine or apple juice, bouillon, Parmesan and heavy cream. Simmer slowly until thickened. Sprinkle with coarse salt & fresh ground black pepper.
6. Arrange two polenta pieces on each plate. Pour on the mushroom sauce. Serve immediately.

Serve with: French Baguettes page 242 or Sourdough Bread, Arugula salad, Roasted Beets page 229.

The first time my sister Sue served this to me I nearly died – it was one of the most delicious dishes I had ever eaten. I am so happy to share it with you.

Meatless BROCCOLI AND SWISS/CHEDDAR FRITTATA

Serves 4
Time: 15 minutes

1 Tablespoon unsalted butter
⅓ yellow onion, minced
1½ cups fresh broccoli, no stem, chopped
Salt and pepper
7 eggs
3 Tablespoons grated Swiss cheese
3 Tablespoons grated cheddar cheese
3 thin slices fresh tomato

1. Preheat the broiler to high.
2. In an 8-inch nonstick/oven proof skillet or cast iron pan melt the unsalted butter over low heat. Add minced onion. Sauté until soft about 4 min. Add chopped broccoli and continue to sauté for another 5 min. or until tender.
3. In a medium size bowl whisk the eggs together and season with salt and pepper. Turn the heat up to medium. Pour the eggs over the onions and broccoli. Sprinkle on the grated Swiss and cheddar cheese.
4. Cook without stirring until eggs are set on bottom and beginning to set on top - about 6 min. Lay the tomato slices on top and sprinkle with salt.
5. Transfer the skillet to the oven and broil about 5 inches from the heating element until the eggs are set on top and beginning to brown, 3 to 4 min. Remove from the broiler and cut into wedges to serve. Serve hot or at room temperature.

Serve with: Bacon or ham and toast.

Variations: You can make a frittata out of just about anything you have left over in your refrigerator. Use the same amounts that I have in my recipe only using some of these different ingredients: asparagus, cauliflower, mushrooms, Feta cheese, Mozzarella cheese, ham, Canadian bacon, bacon, pancetta, prosciutto. Use your imagination!

A frittata is like an omelet only not as difficult to make!
Try it out. It is healthy and good for you.
Another great way to serve eggs with vegetables.

CHRISTMAS MORNING CASSEROLE

Serves 6-8
Time: 1¾ hours

Plan Ahead: Prepare through step 4. Refrigerate overnight and bake in the morning.

8 slices sandwich white bread, crusts removed
1 pound hot spicy sausage
½ pound sage sausage
2 cups sharp cheddar cheese, grated
6 eggs, beaten
2 cups milk
1 teaspoon dry mustard
1 can cream of mushroom soup
½ cup milk

1. Prepare the bread and place in a buttered 9x13 inch glass baking dish. Set aside.
2. In a medium fry pan over medium heat brown the two kinds of sausage together. When cooked drain off all the fat.
3. Sprinkle the sausage over the top of the bread. Sprinkle the grated cheese over top the sausage.
4. In a medium bowl whisk the eggs, milk and dry mustard together. Pour over top of the cheese. Cover with plastic wrap and refrigerate overnight or at least 3 hours before baking.
5. Before baking whisk together the soup and milk. Pour this on top of the casserole. Bake at 300° for 1½ hours or less. Check around 1 hour and 10 min. to see if it looks set. This casserole will rise sort of like a soufflé and should be barely brown on top. When taken out of the oven it will fall after a couple of minutes - not to worry. Slice and serve.

Variations: Use mild sausage. Use Colby cheese. Use bacon, onion and diced green pepper in place of sausage. Use ham, tomato and herbs. Add one small can diced green chilies to the recipe.

Serve with Fresh Fruit Compote:
1 cup water
½ cup sugar
4 grapefruit, sectioned
3 oranges, sectioned
Red grapes, halved
1 banana, diced

Bring sugar and water to a boil. Refrigerate or freeze to cool. Pour over fruit. Add the bananas just as you are ready to serve.

Variation: Eliminate the grapefruit and add fresh cut-up pineapple and fresh sliced strawberries.

This breakfast casserole has been around for a long time. It is a great breakfast casserole and my entire family loves it. It is delicious and easy to prepare. Deb serves this casserole with the fruit compote every Christmas morning.

QUICHE LORRAINE

Serves 6
Time: 1 hour

1 single Food Nanny Pie Crust page 312 unbaked
½ pound bacon
1 small onion, minced
1 green Bell pepper, chopped
1½ cups milk
½ pound cheddar cheese, grated
3 eggs, beaten
1 teaspoon coarse salt
¼ teaspoon fresh ground black pepper
1 teaspoon Worcestershire

1. Prepare the piecrust. Place in a 9-inch pie plate. Set aside.
2. In a medium size skillet on medium heat sauté the bacon, onion and green pepper until the vegetables are soft and the bacon is cooked. Drain off the fat. Set aside.
3. In small saucepan over medium heat bring the milk almost to a boil. Turn the heat off and let the milk sit for about 2 min. Add the grated cheese. Stir and let it melt into the milk.
4. Add the beaten eggs, salt, ground black pepper and Worcestershire into the milk mixture. Stir until blended.
5. Spoon the bacon and vegetables into the bottom of the unbaked piecrust. Pour the cheese mixture over.
6. Carefully place the pie pan in the oven and bake at 350° for 40 min.

Serve with: Spinach Salad page 265 or Food Nanny Hot Crescent Rolls page 249.

Variations: Use 1 cup cubed ham in place of bacon and 1½ cups Swiss cheese in place of cheddar.

When Steve and I visited Washington DC for the first time I wanted to eat at one of those sidewalk cafés. I ordered Quiche Lorraine. Camille gave me this recipe and I have been making it ever since. xo

Meatless SCRAMBLED EGGS TWO WAYS

#1

Serves 4
Time: 5 minutes

- 2 teaspoons butter
- 1 teaspoon olive oil
- ¼ cup frozen corn
- 6 eggs
- ¼ cup sharp cheddar cheese, grated

1. Heat the butter and olive oil in an 8-inch non-stick skillet over medium heat. Put the corn from the freezer into the skillet. Crack the eggs into the skillet but do not break the yolks. Season with coarse salt and fresh ground black pepper.
2. With a rubber spatula slowly scrap the bottom of the pan and break the yolks. Add the cheese and continue to drag the spatula back and forth. This creates large curds. Let the eggs sit a few seconds then stir again. Avoid stirring too much but don't let the eggs sit too long either. Eggs are done when they are still a little glossy, wet. Remove from heat: they will continue cooking for a second. Serve immediately.

Serve with: Bacon, potatoes and toast. Reheat left over mashed potatoes; add horseradish and a little butter.

#2

Serves 1
Time: 5 minutes

- 2 eggs
- Coarse salt or Truffle salt to taste
- ½ teaspoon butter
- ¼ cup Half and Half
- ½ teaspoon olive oil
- 3 Tablespoons cheddar or white cheddar cheese, grated or your favorite herb cheese
- Fresh ground black pepper

1. Crack the eggs into a small bowl. Add the salt to taste and Half and Half. Whisk together. Set aside.
2. Heat the butter and olive oil over medium heat in an 8-inch non-stick skillet over medium heat. Add the eggs to the pan. Let it sit until the edges start to firm up. The eggs will be lighter in color and have tiny bubbles.
3. Add the cheese. Using a rubber spatula gently and slowly drag it back and forth across the pan making sure you cover the entire surface. This helps form large curds. After a few stirs, let the eggs sit for a few seconds then stir again. When the eggs are half set start to stir slowly but more frequently. Avoid stirring too much but at the same time don't let the eggs sit in one spot too long.
4. When the eggs are half done go slowly and turn down the heat if they are cooking too fast. Continue to scramble until glossy but still wet looking. Remove from heat. The eggs will continue to cook for a second after taken off the heat. Serve immediately.

Serve with: Bacon, pancakes, toast or potatoes.
Variations: Use any kind of cheese and experiment with your favorite salt.

These are a couple of my favorite ways to scramble eggs. Scrambling eggs can be a problem - most people get them over done or too dry. These are good instructions for a beginner cook.

MEXICAN RICE WITH CHORIZO SAUSAGE AND EGGS

Serves 4
Time: 35 minutes

½ small yellow onion, chopped
2 cloves garlic, minced
⅓ cup olive oil
1 cup long grain white rice
1 teaspoon salt
1 teaspoon fresh ground black pepper
2 teaspoons chili powder
½ pound Chorizo sausage, skin removed, cut into 12 pieces
2½ cups beef broth, boiling
7 eggs scrambled or 4 eggs fried.
Warm corn tortillas or toast
Salsa (optional)
Avocado slices (optional)

CONVERSATION STARTER:

What is your favorite vacation? Your dream vacation?

Preheat oven to 350°.

1. Place a 4-quart oven-safe roaster or saucepan on top of the stove over medium heat. Sauté the chopped onion and minced garlic in the hot oil until soft.
2. Add the rice and seasonings and brown lightly.
3. Add the sausage pieces and boiling beef broth. Stir.
4. Cover with a tight lid or foil and bake at 350° until the liquid is completely absorbed, about 35 min.
5. Serve immediately with scrambled or fried eggs and warm corn tortillas with your choice of salsa and avocado on the side.

Variations: Serve this rice in place of taco meat in corn or flour tortillas…It is delicious! Serve plain cooked Chorizo sausage mixed in with scrambled eggs.

This is my own variation of Mexican Rice.
The Chorizo sausage just makes it.
Chorizo sausage is more fatty, but it is delicious!!
Be sure you cook the sausage before adding it to the eggs.

FOOD NANNY EGGS BENEDICT

Serves 2
Time: 10 minutes if sauce is prepared ahead of time.

Plan Ahead: Prepare the Hollandaise Sauce the day before.

Hollandaise Sauce:

- 2 egg yolks
- 2 teaspoons fresh lemon juice
- ¼ teaspoon salt
- ⅛ teaspoon cayenne pepper
- 1 Tablespoon hot water
- ¾ cup (1½ sticks) unsalted, cold (from the refrigerator) butter

- 2 English muffins
- 4 Canadian bacon (precooked)
- 4 eggs

Coarse salt and fresh ground black pepper
Dash paprika

This super delicious, super rich dish stands alone. Homemade Hollandaise sauce is the best and I have made preparing it easy for you. Enjoy!

Prepare the sauce first:

1. In a 1 qt. saucepan stir 2 egg yolks slightly and add lemon juice stirring vigorously with a wooden spoon (No heat yet).
2. Add ¼ cup unsalted butter. Heat over very low heat stirring constantly until butter is melted.
3. Add ¼ teaspoon salt, cayenne and 1 Tablespoon hot water. Add an additional ¼ cup unsalted butter stirring vigorously until butter is melted and sauce starts to thicken.
4. Add the final ¼ cup unsalted butter and stir until melted and sauce is thick and creamy. (Be sure butter melts slowly - this gives eggs time to cook and thicken the sauce without curdling.) Serve hot or keep warm.

Prepare the English Muffins:

Broil or toast then lightly butter 4 English muffin halves. Place 2 halves on each plate.

1. In an 8-inch nonstick skillet over low-to medium heat, warm the bacon. Move to a plate. Cover to keep warm.
2. Crack 4 eggs in the same skillet on low-to medium heat being careful not to break the yolks. Add 2-3 ice cubes to the pan. Sprinkle with salt and pepper. Cover. Cook 3 min. for soft eggs or 5 min. for hard. Remove from heat.
3. Place the bacon on top of each English muffin, top with an egg and spoon on the Hollandaise sauce. Sprinkle with a dash of paprika if desired. Serve immediately.

Variations: Can double the Hollandaise sauce; use 1 slice whole wheat bread per person.

Serve with: Fresh Fruit Compote (middle of) page 85. Hash brown potatoes.

Meatless SOUR CREAM PANCAKES WITH ORANGE BUTTERMILK SYRUP

Makes 6 large or 12 small size pancakes
Time: 20 minutes

Plan Ahead: Make the syrup in advance.

1½ cups all-purpose flour
3 Tablespoons sugar
2 teaspoons baking powder
1½ teaspoons coarse salt
½ cup sour cream
1 cup milk
2 eggs
1 teaspoon vanilla
1 teaspoon orange zest (optional)
Oil for frying

Orange Buttermilk Syrup:
½ cup butter
1 cup buttermilk
2 cups sugar
1 Tablespoon light corn syrup
2 teaspoons baking soda
2 teaspoons vanilla
Juice of one large orange

1. In a medium size bowl stir the flour, sugar, baking powder and salt together.
2. In another small bowl whisk together the sour cream, milk, eggs, vanilla and orange zest if using. Pour the wet ingredients into the dry and mix just until combined.
3. Turn the griddle up to 360° and wipe it with a little canola oil. I like to brush on a little oil and then go over it with a paper towel so there is only a slight film of oil to prevent the pancakes from sticking. Bake pancakes on the hot griddle until you see the tiny bubbles form and break. Turn over and bake until golden brown. Serve immediately with Orange Buttermilk Syrup.

Prepare Orange Buttermilk Syrup:
1. In a medium sauce pan over medium heat bring the butter, buttermilk, sugar and corn syrup to a boil. Boil for 2 min. Remove from heat.
2. Stir in the baking soda and vanilla. The syrup will foam up pretty high. Whip until mixed together. Let it sit a minute while the foam goes down.
3. Add the juice of one large orange. Stir until combined. Serve warm over pancakes.

Serve with: Bacon.

Variations: Omit the Orange Zest in the pancakes and the orange juice in the syrup. Use the syrup over any pancake recipe. Add bananas to the sour cream pancakes and serve with plain buttermilk syrup.

*Pancakes are comfort food for me.
Often after filming a show late into the evening I would go out for pancakes. That was all I could think about eating, especially when I am tired. I love these pancakes.
I love this syrup on almost any pancake I make.
You will too. Homemade syrup is special.*

eatless

BANANA MACADAMIA NUT PANCAKES WITH COCONUT SYRUP

Serves 6 to 8
Time: 15 minutes

3 cups flour
½ cup sugar
1 Tablespoon baking powder
1 teaspoon baking soda
½ teaspoon salt
1 cup macadamia nuts, chopped
3¼ cups buttermilk
½ cup butter, melted
4 eggs
2 teaspoons vanilla
2 bananas, chopped
Oil for the griddle

Coconut Syrup:
1 13.5 oz. can coconut milk
1½ Tablespoons cornstarch
2 cups light corn syrup
½ cup sugar
½ cup shredded coconut

1. In a small bowl mix the flour, sugar, baking powder, baking soda, salt and nuts together. Set aside.
2. In another small bowl whisk together the buttermilk, melted butter, eggs and vanilla. Add this to the dry ingredients. Mix until combined.
3. Stir in the chopped bananas.
4. Wipe the griddle or frying pan with a little oil and fry on a hot griddle about 360°. Turn the pancake when you see the little bubbles come up and start to break. Pancakes should be golden brown.

Syrup:
In a medium size saucepan, whisk coconut milk and cornstarch together. Add other ingredients. Bring to a boil and remove from heat.
Store in the refrigerator up to 2 weeks.

Serve with: Serve with butter and coconut syrup.

These are the best pancakes ever!!
They take me right to Hawaii when we visit and
eat these for breakfast at our favorite place.
These pancakes and syrup are better than any that
I have had on the Islands.
There is nothing like Coconut Syrup...
These are yummy!!! Enjoy!
Thanks, Rachel, for the recipe. xo

Meatless

FLAPJACKS WITH OATS AND WHOLE WHEAT

Serves Small batch for 6
Time: 10 minutes

Plan Ahead:
Make the Mix ahead. Can store for up to 4 weeks.

Mix:
4 cups quick oats
2 cups all-purpose flour
2 cups whole wheat flour
1 cup brown sugar
1 cup powdered milk
1 Tablespoon baking powder
2 teaspoons cinnamon
2½ teaspoons coarse salt
½ teaspoon cream of tartar

2 eggs, beaten
⅓ cup canola oil
2 cups dry mix
1 cup water

CONVERSATION STARTER:

Who is your favorite Disney character? Any Character?

Make the Mix:
In a medium size bowl add the first 9 ingredients. Stir together with a spoon. (Store in an airtight container up to one month to have on hand.)

Make a small batch of pancakes, about 6:
1. In a small bowl whisk eggs. Add canola oil, 2 cups dry mix and water.
   Mix with a spoon until blended.
2. Cook on a lightly oiled griddle at 360°. When you start to see holes in the batter appear and then break turn the pancake over.

Serve with: Real Maple Syrup, Bacon or sausage and eggs.

These pancakes have great texture to them. You feel like you are eating healthy pancakes with substance. They are hearty and delicious. Thank you, Rachel, for sharing the recipe with me. xo

eatless

GRANDMA ELLEN'S SWEDISH PANCAKES

Makes 12 large pancakes Time: 30 minutes

1¾ cups flour

2 Tablespoons sugar

½ teaspoon salt

3 eggs

3 cups milk

1/4 cup Butter

Canola oil for frying

Process flour, sugar, salt, eggs, milk and butter in a food processor until thoroughly mixed. Let stand 5 min. to thicken slightly.

My editor, Ann, shared her Grandma's recipe with me. She made these frequently and word went out through the extended family. All the family could show up at Grandma's over several hours and she would make pancakes until everyone had enough!
It was a very special thing to have her say, "I think I'll make Swedish pancakes tomorrow. Why don't you come over?"

1. Heat a 10-12 inch frying pan on high and add 1 Tablespoon oil. (Add a little oil before frying each pancake.) The pan should remain very hot but not smoking. Add ⅓ to ½ cup of batter to pan and immediately swirl batter around to cover bottom of pan completely.
2. When bubbles show through the pancake take a very large pancake turner and lift the edges to get under the pancake enough to release it and turn it over. It will not break apart.
3. After it is flipped leave it for 15-20 seconds and remove it from pan, laying it flat across a plate.
4. Roll each pancake up (like a crepe) and leave them on the plate until you have enough cooked to serve everyone. You can also cover the plate with foil and place it in a warm oven.

Serving and adding toppings
Traditionally each person takes 2 pancakes and unrolls them on their plate. Put 2 or 3 spoons of topping in each one and roll it back up. The roll is sliced and eaten.

Traditional toppings include:

a. Lingonberry Preserves.
   Warm before you serve.
b. Whole cranberry sauce made from fresh cranberries cooked with sugar until the berries pop. Serve warm.
c. Fresh lemon slices are passed and the pancake is sprinkled with sugar and then some lemon juice is squeezed on the sugar.

Serve with: Served with breakfast sausages and cocoa; or bacon or sliced ham.

Meatless

BLUEBERRY LEMON SCONES

Serves 8 scones
Time: 20 minutes

2¼ cups all-purpose flour
½ cup butter
1 Tablespoon sugar
¼ teaspoon salt
1 Tablespoon baking powder
1 egg, beaten
¾ cup Half and Half
½ teaspoon lemon zest (optional)
1 cup fresh blueberries
¼ cup brown sugar

Glaze:
1 cup powdered sugar
3 teaspoons water
½ teaspoon lemon juice (optional)

1. In a small bowl (using 2 forks or a pastry blender) or in a food processor, pulse until the flour, butter, sugar, salt and baking powder together looks lumpy like feta cheese.
2. Mix the egg, Half and Half and lemon zest (if using) together. Gently fold into the dry ingredients.
3. Bring the dough together with your hands and turn out onto lightly floured surface. Fold it over a couple of times. Press the dough out into a rectangle. Cut the dough in half lengthwise. Cut 4 pieces the same size, from each piece.
4. Sprinkle on the blueberries then sprinkle the brown sugar over top the blueberries.
5. Lay scones on a baking sheet lined with parchment paper.
6. Bake at 350° for 10 min. or until light brown around the edges. Pour the glaze over the warm scones. Serve warm.

Serve: These are great for breakfast or dessert.

Variations: Leave out the lemon if you prefer. Use raspberries, blackberries, currents or elderberries.

I love English scones!
Thanks, Annie and Lisa.

Meatless BLUEBERRY PANCAKES

Serves 4
Time: 10 minutes

2 cups fresh or frozen blueberries, thawed if frozen
2 Tablespoons sugar

Carefully rinse off the blueberries if fresh. Dry on paper towels. Place in a small bowl. Sprinkle with 2 Tablespoons sugar. Stir gently. Let sit while you prepare the pancakes.

Pancakes:
1¼ cups all-purpose flour
¼ cup whole wheat flour
3 Tablespoons sugar
1¼ teaspoons baking powder
½ teaspoon baking soda
¼ teaspoon salt
2 cups buttermilk
¼ cup milk
1 egg
3 Tablespoons butter, melted
1 Tablespoon melted butter
1 Tablespoon canola oil

1. In a medium size bowl mix together the flours, sugar, baking powder, baking soda and salt. Set aside.
2. In a small bowl whisk the buttermilk, milk, egg and 3 Tablespoons melted butter. Add this to the dry ingredients and whisk until it comes together. The batter will still be lumpy. Gently fold in the prepared blueberries.
3. In a small bowl mix 1 Tablespoon melted butter and 1 Tablespoon canola oil. Brush lightly onto a hot griddle (about 360°) or frying pan, or use a paper towel dipped into the butter mixture and wipe the griddle with it.
4. Using a ¼ cup measure for the batter, pour onto a hot griddle. Cook until you see a few bubbles form and then pop. Flip over and cook until golden brown.

Serve: With hot Maple Syrup; bacon or sausage.

Variations: Omit the whole wheat flour and use All-Purpose flour.

I love Blueberry Pancakes...
Can't get enough of 'um!!
Blueberries are so good for you too!

Meatless GRANOLA

Makes 3 cups
Time: 1 hour

- 1½ cups old-fashioned rolled oats
- ½ cup raw almonds, chopped
- ¼ cup cashews, chopped
- ⅓ cup shredded sweetened coconut
- 3 Tablespoons brown sugar
- 2 Tablespoons real maple syrup
- 1 Tablespoon light corn syrup
- 2 Tablespoons canola oil
- ¼ cup raisins
- ¼ cup chocolate chips (optional)

1. Preheat oven to 250°.
2. In a medium size bowl combine all the ingredients EXCEPT RAISINS AND CHOCOLATE CHIPS. Pour onto an 17½ x 11 inch baking sheet. Spread out evenly over the pan. Bake for 35 to 50 min. depending on how crunchy you want it.
3. Remove from oven and transfer into a medium size bowl. Stir in the raisins and chocolate chips if using.

Store in an airtight container for up to 2 months.

Serve with: Yogurt or milk of choice.

Additions or substitutions:
Dried cranberries, pecans, sunflower seeds, chopped dates. You can double this recipe.

I love my granola!
The best ever! It's easy and delicious.
Substitute other ingredients
that your family loves. xo

CONVERSATION STARTER:
Whose place do you like to visit the most?

Mexican Night

As I have traveled around the U.S., I can find Mexican specialty stores all across the country. We can buy fresh tortillas, tamales, Mexican cheese and desserts almost everywhere! We have more kinds of fresh chilies available to us now, like Serrano, Anaheim and Jalapeno. We can find "Chipotle Peppers in Adobo Sauce," which I use in "Chicken Chipotle with Brown Rice," an authentic Mexican dish. Onions, tomatoes, green bell peppers, tomatillos, avocados, sour cream, cheese, black beans, pinto beans, rice, tortillas and chicken flavor bouillon are a few of the key ingredients to making great Mexican food.

I love the new flavors of pork that would be considered "American" style Mexican food. You will want to try my "Sweet Pork Verde" in this chapter, which you can make into tacos, burritos, or a salad. I have quick and delicious salsas for you to try. I teach you how to make beans from scratch. I even have the best recipe in the world for making homemade chicken taquitos. I love great taquitos!

Eating Mexican food once a week does not mean eating "Tacos" every time! However, Chicken Tacos have been an all-time favorite forever in our home! Some of our children say that "Mexican" is their favorite night.

Between my two cookbooks I have given you about 40 fabulous, healthy, choices that the entire family will enjoy every week.

I hope you will be excited about implementing a Mexican Night into your meal plan.

The Food Nanny. xo

THURSDAY
MEXICAN NIGHT

Meatless

Meatless PIÑA COLADAS

Serves 4
Time: 10 minutes

Plan Ahead: Double the recipe and freeze until ready to serve.

- 2 cups ice
- ½ of a 15 oz. can cream of coconut, located near the Margarita mix in your super market
- 1 6 oz. can pineapple juice
- ½ cup Half and Half
- 4 oz. crushed pineapple

Place ingredients in a blender and blend until smooth. Pour into glasses and serve immediately.

Variations: Can be frozen.

These Piña Coladas have become a tradition at Claudia's home. She has all the ingredients on hand at all times. Just a little bit in a Dixie size cup is enough. Just a taste. Serve these for dessert, for a snack when your kids come home from school or when you just need something cold to drink. Enjoy!!

CONVERSATION STARTER:

Who is the craziest in our family?

BEEF ENCHILADA SUPPER

Serves 4
Time: 30 minutes

1 pound ground beef
¼ cup onions, chopped
1 8 oz. can tomato sauce
¼ cup water
1 Tablespoon dried parsley, chopped
1½ Tablespoon ancho chili powder
½ teaspoon coarse salt or Mexican salt
⅛ teaspoon ground black pepper
1 10 oz. can mild red Enchilada Sauce
2 Tablespoons coconut oil
8 corn tortillas, taco size
1½ cups Mexican cheese, shredded
1½ cups sliced black olives

1. Pre-heat oven to 350°.
2. In a medium size fry pan over medium heat break up meat and fry with onions until cooked through and onions are soft. Drain off any extra grease.
3. Add tomato sauce, water, parsley, ancho chili powder, coarse salt and ground black pepper. Reduce heat, simmer uncovered 10 min.
4. Warm enchilada sauce in a small pan over low heat. Spread ¼ cup sauce in 9x13 inch baking dish.
5. Heat oil in a small fry pan and warm each tortilla in oil, about 5 seconds, until soft. Dip each tortilla, both sides, in the warm sauce and place in 9 x 13 baking dish.
6. Spread ⅓ cup meat mixture down center of each tortilla. Roll up tortilla around filling to form enchilada and place seam side down in baking dish. Do this with each one placing them closely, side by side in the baking dish.
7. Cover with remaining warm sauce, sprinkle on the shredded cheese and sliced black olives. Bake at 350° for 15 min. Serve immediately.

Serve with: Butter lettuce and Romaine with thin slices of red onion, avocado and tomato. Pass your favorite dressing or olive oil and balsamic vinegar mixture.

Variations: Use regular chili powder in place of ancho chili powder. If you prefer more sauce, add another can of enchilada sauce.

Serve this meal to your neighbors and friends. These are delicious and remind me of how much Everyone loves enchiladas. xo

Meatless PINTO BEANS

Makes about 7½ cups cooked beans
Time: 6 to 8 hours soaking;
2 to 4 hours cooking.

Plan Ahead: Use a pressure cooker or crock-pot.

1 lb. bag pinto beans. Discard broken or dirty beans or rocks. Rinse well.
10 cups water
¼ medium onion, whole
2 garlic cloves peeled, whole

1. Measure 1 lb. dried, washed beans into a large pot on top of the stove. Pour 10 cups water over the beans. Bring the beans and water to a boil. Boil for 3 min. Remove from heat and place a lid on the beans and soak over night or at least 6 to 8 hours. (The soaking takes most of the gas out of the beans).
2. The next day pour water off the beans, rinse and put them back into a clean pot and add enough water to cover by 2 inches.
3. Add onion and garlic cloves. Cover with a lid, keeping the lid ajar so steam can escape. Bring beans to a boil on top of the stove over medium high heat.
4. Decrease the heat to simmer and cook the beans, depending on where you live, anywhere from 2 to 4 hours. In high altitude it could take 4 hours. Make sure to keep the beans covered with water at all times. Beans are done when you can mash them with a fork or crush them between 2 fingers.
5. Season the beans generously with coarse salt and fresh ground black pepper to taste. Serve. Makes about 7½ cups cooked beans.

Serve with: Just about anything you can think of! Or serve them plain with homemade bread and butter.

Variations: Do the same thing with black beans. 1 cup dried beans equals 3 cups cooked beans. You don't need to cook an entire pound. This is your basic recipe. You may add ham or a little bacon or even a can of tomato sauce. Make refried beans out of these.

I cooked this exact recipe on my Food Nanny TV show with Pam and her children. I will always remember Pam and those beautiful children. They were wonderful and very, very kind. My Mom made these beans often.
Just basic food. Satisfying and delicious, especially with homemade bread and butter.

MEXICAN CHICKEN AND RICE

Aaroz con Pollo
Serves 4
Time: About 40 minutes

8 chicken thighs
1½ Tablespoons olive oil
1½ Tablespoons unsalted butter
½ cup onion, chopped
3 cloves garlic, minced
1 cup long grain white rice
2 large fresh tomatoes, chopped
2¼ cups chicken broth
½ teaspoon chili powder
1 teaspoon coarse salt
Fresh ground black pepper
1½ cups frozen peas

1. Remove the skin from the chicken thighs, if desired. Wipe off the chicken with a wet paper towel. In a medium size pan over medium high heat, add olive oil and unsalted butter. Place the chicken in the pan and fry, about 7 min. per side. Remove chicken to a plate.
2. To the drippings, add the onion, garlic and rice. Stir and fry until light brown.
   Add chopped tomatoes, chicken broth, chili powder, salt and fresh ground pepper to taste.
3. Turn up the heat and bring to a boil. Return the chicken to the pan; lower the heat, cover and simmer about 30 min. or until the rice is tender. Mix in the peas just before serving.

Serve with: Chips and salsa; additional vegetables; warm homemade flour tortillas; fruit.

Variations: Use chicken breasts on the bone. Use a whole cut-up fryer. Mix and match as you please.

Chicken and rice is a comfort meal for me. You can buy chicken thighs very inexpensively. Thighs have more fat so use the breast if you need to. This meal is so inexpensive, yet so delicious.

CONVERSATION STARTER:

What is your oldest memory?

PORK VERDE WITH LIME DRESSING

Serves 6
Time: 6 hours

Plan Ahead: Cook pork the day before.

Can be made into Tacos, Burritos or a Salad.

Lime Ranch Dressing:
1 packet Hidden Valley Ranch Buttermilk Dressing
1 cup buttermilk
1 cup mayonnaise
2 tomatillos, peeled and cut into pieces
½ bunch cilantro, leaves only - cleaned and chopped
2 cloves garlic, minced
Zest and juice of one lime
1 jalapeno pepper, chopped Use the seeds if you like extra heat. Go easy according to your taste.

Sweet Pork:
1½ pounds boneless pork roast
Garlic salt, to taste
1 12 oz. can of regular (not diet) Coca Cola
8 oz. salsa – or Everyday Salsa page 227
1 cup brown sugar

Lime Ranch Dressing:
1. Empty the buttermilk packet into a food processor or blender. Add the buttermilk, mayonnaise, tomatillos, cilantro, garlic, zest and juice of one lime and the jalapeno. Mix until well blended.
2. Keep refrigerated until ready to use. Serve at room temperature.

Sweet Pork:
1. Place the roast in a crock-pot and sprinkle generously with garlic salt. Pour in enough water just to cover the roast. Cook on high for 3½ hours.
2. Drain all the water off the roast and divide the roast into 4 sections.
3. Use an immersion blender or regular blender to mix coke, salsa and brown sugar together until smooth. Pour over the roast and continue to cook on high for another 1½ hours.
4. Shred pork with a fork.
5. Pour the Lime Ranch Dressing over the pork and enjoy with rice and beans; or make Tacos, Burritos or a Sweet Pork Salad.

Sweet Pork Salad:
1. Place a 6 to 8 inch flour tortilla sprinkled with Mexican blend cheese on a cookie sheet. Broil about 6 inches away from the broiler element until the cheese melts.
2. Place the flour tortilla in a one-serving size pasta bowl.
3. Top with shredded pork.
4. Food Nanny Lime Rice or Mexican Rice (Book #1).
5. Black Beans.
6. Romaine lettuce, chopped.
7. Fresh Roma tomatoes, chopped.
8. Avocado, chopped.
9. Corn tortilla strips, available in any store.
10. Lime Ranch Dressing over all. Serve immediately.

Variations: You may serve this pork with Food Nanny Lime Rice and black or pinto beans on the side. The pork is also terrific in tacos, burritos. Always serve the Lime Ranch Dressing on the side.

*I love all the flavors and can't get enough of the pork or this dressing. Love it in the salad!
Try it in tacos and burritos too. There are so many great new Mexican flavors out there. This is one of our favorites! xo*

CHICKEN CHIPOTLE WITH BROWN RICE

Serves 4
Time: 50 minutes

Plan Ahead: Cook the rice. Prepare the bacon.

1 cup long grain brown rice cooked or ready-to-serve brown rice
¾ pound bacon, cooked and torn into pieces
4 small boneless/skinless chicken breasts
Fresh ground black pepper
Chicken flavor bouillon
2 Tablespoons olive oil
2 cups sour cream
¼ cup milk
1 7 oz. can Chipotles in Adobo Sauce
Fresh corn tortillas, homemade or store bought

Prepare the rice:

1. In a medium size saucepan add 2½ cups water, 1 cup uncooked brown rice and 1 teaspoon salt. (Salt is optional). Stir. Bring to a boil. Turn the heat down to low and cover with a lid. Simmer 45 to 50 min. or until the water is absorbed.
2. Start frying the bacon.

Prepare the chicken:

3. With a wet paper towel wipe off the chicken breasts. Pound the chicken between 2 gallon-size plastic bags with a meat mallet. (We are tenderizing the chicken and also flattening to about ¼ inch so it is easier to cook.)
4. Lay the chicken breasts out on a baking sheet when flattened. Sprinkle generously with fresh ground black pepper on both sides. Spread about 1 teaspoon chicken flavor bouillon on each side of the breast.
5. In a large frying pan over medium heat add the olive oil. Sauté the chicken for about 3 min. per side. Remove from heat.

Prepare the sauce:

6. Place the sour cream, cooked bacon pieces, 1 to 2 chipotles from the can and ¼ cup milk in a food processor or blender and blend well.
7. Pour the sauce over the cooked chicken and return to medium heat and bring to a boil. Stir the sauce into the chicken juices. Cover and let simmer until the chicken is fully cooked and sauce is like gravy. Pour over the rice.

Serve with: Plenty of veggies. Steamed broccoli or cauliflower; green beans. Fresh corn tortillas are a must. Go to your nearest Mexican market and buy fresh corn tortillas like I do.

Variations: Use white rice. May use chicken tenders.

*I got this recipe from a good friend.
I have made it my own and we all enjoy this delicious Mexican Chicken.*

TAMALE CASSEROLE

Serves 4
Time: 45 minutes

Plan ahead: Prepare meat mixture ahead of time.

1¼ cups beef broth
½ pound lean ground beef
½ onion, chopped
3 cloves garlic, minced
½ green bell pepper, chopped (optional)
1 8 oz. can tomato sauce
1 medium fresh tomato, diced
1 cup whole kernel corn, (frozen or canned), drained
¼ cup chopped black olives
2 teaspoon chili powder
1 teaspoon ground cumin
1 teaspoon salt
½ teaspoon ground black pepper
1½ teaspoon sugar
1 cup cheddar cheese (shredded)
sour cream for garnish

Tamale Corn Meal Topping:

1 cup instant corn masa mix for tamales
1¼ cups + 1 Tablespoon chicken broth
¼ teaspoon baking powder
½ teaspoon salt
5 Tablespoons butter melted

1. Pre-heat oven to 350°.
2. In a medium size pan over medium heat, brown the ground beef. Add the onions, garlic and green pepper if using, stir and cook until soft.
3. Add the tomato sauce, fresh tomato, corn, black olives, chili powder, cumin, and salt. Add 1 1/4 cups beef broth. Stir. Turn the heat down to low and simmer about 5 - 10 min. Add in the cheese and stir until melted.
4. Pour into a buttered 8x8 in. baking dish.

Prepare the topping

5. Stir together the instant corn masa, chicken broth, baking powder, salt, and melted butter.
6. Spread evenly on top of casserole. Bake uncovered at 350 about 30 minutes.
7. Pass the sour cream

Serve with: Chips and salsa or Guacamole. Fruit Salsas and Chips page 129, Homemade Flour Tortillas page 121.

Variations: May double the recipe.

The topping makes this casserole for me! This meal is easy and is a nice change from regular Mexican food. This one is yummy!! Double the recipe and serve it to company with my Piña Coladas.

Meatless MELT IN YOUR MOUTH BURRITOS

Serves 4
Time: 20 minutes

Plan Ahead: make and freeze to use on a busy day.

1 16 oz. can refried beans
⅓ to ½ cup water
1 cup cheddar cheese, shredded
2 eggs
2 Tablespoons milk
⅛ teaspoon salt
½ cup vegetable oil
4 flour tortillas, 8 inch round
4 pieces aluminum foil 8 x 12 inches
Salsa
Sour Cream

These burritos will melt in your mouth. They are soft and delicious! Kids love these! A great way to serve breakfast in the morning to company or for a busy family. Eat them on the way to school or work. Take them with you in a thermos or insulated carrier. xo

1. Pre-heat oven to 375°.
2. Spoon the refried beans into a medium size saucepan on top of the stove. Pour the water into the pan with the beans. Bring the beans to a low boil over medium high heat stirring until the water is mixed and the beans are easy to stir and easy to spread. Remove from heat. Cover to keep warm.
3. Shred 1 cup cheese. Set aside. In a pie dish beat eggs, milk and salt with a fork. Set aside.
4. Pour oil in a medium size frying pan and turn the heat up to medium high.
5. Quickly warm one tortilla at a time in the microwave for 10 seconds. With your fingers, dip the warm tortilla in the egg mixture, turn and do the other side. Place the tortilla into the hot oil and fry each side until the egg mixture is cooked or until barely brown. Place on paper towel for a few seconds to soak up excess oil.
6. Move the cooked tortilla to a small plate and measure out ¼ cup warm beans and spread down the middle of the tortilla. Measure out ¼ cup of the shredded cheese and sprinkle down the middle on top of the beans. Fold in and tuck the ends, then roll to form a burrito.
7. Wrap each burrito in its own piece of foil. Place onto a baking sheet. Do this 3 more times until the burritos are wrapped and placed on the baking sheet. Place in a pre-heated oven at 375° on the middle rack and bake for 10 min.
8. Remove from the oven. Serve each person their own foil wrapped burrito on a plate. Help little ones to unwrap the hot foil. Pass salsa and sour cream (optional).

Breakfast Burrito: Follow the same directions as for Bean and Cheese Burrito except fill fried flour tortillas with ¼ cup scrambled eggs, warm. Sprinkle on 3 Tablespoons shredded cheddar cheese, a slice of warm bacon and 3 Tablespoons warm hash brown potatoes. Roll up the same as above and wrap in foil as directed. Bake 10 min. in the oven. These are so delicious!

Serve with: Chips and Salsa. Use one of my fresh Fruit Salsas. Sliced Avocados.

Variations: It is endless what you can do with these burritos. Try using vegetarian refried beans. Double or triple the recipe and freeze them. To freeze: Let the burritos cool, then wrap each one tightly in plastic wrap, then in foil. When ready to use, thaw. Unwrap the plastic and wrap again in the same foil. Place in oven at 250° until warmed through.

QUICK AND EASY HONEY LIME CHICKEN ENCHILADAS

Serves: 4
Time: 1 hour

Plan Ahead: Marinate chicken ahead of time. Then, these easy enchiladas will take you just minutes to get into the oven.

⅔ cup honey
½ cup fresh lime juice
2 Tablespoons chili powder
1 teaspoon garlic powder
1 pound cooked (purchased) Rotisserie Chicken*, shredded, equivalent of 2 medium chicken breasts
2 10 oz. cans green enchilada sauce
1 lb. Monterey Jack cheese, shredded
8 flour tortillas (taco size)
½ cup heavy cream
Sour Cream

1. Pre-heat oven to 350°.
2. In a medium size bowl, mix the marinade sauce: honey, lime juice, chili powder and garlic powder. Save half this marinade sauce for later. Set it aside.
3. Toss half the marinade with the cooked chicken. Cover with plastic wrap and place in the refrigerator for at least 30 min. and up to 2 hours.
4. Spray a 9x13 inch-baking dish with cooking oil. Pour a thin layer of enchilada sauce on bottom to coat.
5. Set aside 1¼ cups of the shredded cheese for topping. Lay the flour tortillas out on the counter or a baking sheet. Divide the chicken and shredded cheese evenly over the tortillas.
6. Roll up each enchilada and place in the baking dish side by side. Mix the remaining marinade with the rest of the green enchilada sauce and cream. Pour over the enchiladas and sprinkle with remaining cheese. Bake for 30 min. Serve immediately. Pass the sour cream.

Serve with: Chips and Salsa. Food Nanny Lime Rice and black beans.

Variations: *Prepare your own chicken by cooking 1 lb. of chicken breasts in the oven. Clean them off with a wet paper towel, place on baking sheet and sprinkle with olive oil, coarse salt and fresh ground black pepper. Bake at 350° for 35 min. Cool. Shred.

This is a great recipe for chicken enchiladas. I was doing a presentation in Raleigh-Durham and Jenny had a dinner party for me and her friends. She served these delicious enchiladas - what a memorable meal that was!

Meatless

SALSA WITH CORN, BLACK-EYED PEAS, TOMATOES AND AVOCADO

Serves 6
Time: 10 minutes

- 1 11 oz. can Shoe Peg white corn
- 1 15 oz. can black-eyed peas or black beans
- 3 Roma tomatoes, diced
- 1¼ cups salsa (Everyday Salsa page 127 or store bought)
- ¼ cup fresh cilantro, diced
- ½ fresh lime, juiced
- Coarse salt
- Fresh ground black pepper
- 3 avocados, diced

1. Mix everything up in a medium size bowl except the avocadoes. Season to taste with coarse salt and fresh ground black pepper. Cover with plastic wrap and refrigerate.
2. Just before serving add the diced avocadoes.

Serve with: Tortilla chips of choice.

*Kristin and Caiser bring this to every family gathering.
We love seeing them
and their growing family.
And, we love their salsa!!
So will you!!*

CONVERSATION STARTER:

Describe the birth of each of your children.

Meatless MEXICAN LAYERED DIP

Serves 12-16
Time: 20 minutes

1 large can refried beans
2 4 oz. cans green chilies, diced
4 medium to large tomatoes, diced. Save 2 diced tomatoes for topping
Green onions, diced, to taste (optional)
1 2.25 oz. can sliced olives, divided
1½ to 2 pints sour cream
1 cup cheddar cheese, shredded
1 cup mozzarella cheese, shredded
1 small green pepper, diced (optional)
Chives (optional)

1 Avocado Guacamole:
1 avocado
3 dashes Tabasco
½ teaspoon garlic salt
½ fresh lime, juiced

Preheat oven to 350°.
Layer in order given in a 9x13 inch-baking dish. Bake until heated through and cheese is barely melted. Top with guacamole, more diced tomatoes, more olives, green pepper (optional) and chives (optional).

***1 Avocado Guacamole:**
Mash avocado with a fork. Place in a small bowl. Stir in Tabasco, garlic, salt and lime juice. Mix well.

Serve with: Serve as an appetizer or make a meal out of this layered dip.

Variations: You can choose not to heat up the dip: serve it at room temperature.

Judy and I have been making this layered dip for over 30 years! It's still a family favorite!

Meatless
HOMEMADE FLOUR TORTILLAS

Makes 8 tortillas
Total time: About 1 hour

1¾ cups all purpose flour
½ teaspoon salt
¼ teaspoon baking powder
¼ cup vegetable shortening, may use canola oil
½ cup very hot water

1. In a medium size mixing bowl add the flour, salt and baking powder. Stir with a whisk to combine the dry ingredients.
2. Add the shortening (or oil) and work into the flour with a fork or a pastry cutter until the crumbs are the size of peas. (This is like making piecrust). Add hot water and stir with a fork to combine.
3. Pour this mixture out on a lightly floured board or your counter and knead with your hands for 4 min. to form smooth dough. Place the dough back in the bowl and cover with a towel or plastic wrap and let rest 15 min.
4. Divide the dough into 8 equal balls and roll between the palms of your hands until the ball is as smooth as possible.
5. Cut 2 pieces of plastic from a grocery bag slightly larger than 7 inches. (Plastic wrap will not work.) Place the dough in-between them and roll out each ball of dough with a rolling pin to form a thin circle about 7 inches across. Save plastic for future use.
   Or, simply place the tortilla in a tortilla press. (At most kitchen stores.) Set the dough in-between the 2 pieces of plastic and press down with a tortilla press.
6. Preheat a dry griddle over medium high heat or 350° on the griddle (cast iron or pancake) preferably non-stick. Place the tortilla in the hot pan or on the griddle and cook for 1 min. or until small air bubbles appear. Flip over and cook for 1-2 min.
7. During the 3rd min. the tortilla will usually puff up and then deflate. Small browned spots will form on the surface. Remove to a plate and cool. Once finished, the tortillas are ready to eat. They can be frozen for future use.

Serve with: You can serve these homemade tortillas with tacos, burritos, taquitos, enchiladas or on the side with most any Mexican dish.

Variations: Serve them with cinnamon and sugar. Make cheese crisps by placing a tortilla on a baking sheet and put under the broiler. Heat one side, turn over and sprinkle with shredded cheese, let melt and serve.

When you live out in the country like I do, sometimes it is nice to know that you can make your own tortillas. Food Nanny Corn Tortillas are in my first book. Here is a great recipe to make your own flour tortillas. I love Mexican Night!!

CHICKEN TAQUITOS

Makes 16 Taquitos
Time: 30 minutes

2 boneless/skinless chicken breasts
½ stick celery, cut in half
¼ yellow onion, whole
2 cloves garlic, whole
2 chicken bouillon cubes or 2 teaspoons chicken bouillon powder
1 Tablespoon olive oil
1 teaspoon butter
½ yellow onion, minced
½ green pepper, minced
2 medium fresh tomatoes, diced
2 fresh garlic, minced
⅓ cup chicken broth
Coarse salt
Fresh ground black pepper
16 small corn tortillas
Vegetable oil for frying
Everyday Salsa page 127
Sour cream

Caso Fresco Cheese
(It is a crumbly white cheese and can be bought in most grocery stores or any Mexican market.)

I learned how to make these Taquitos from Lucy, a great cook from Mexico. I have never tasted better Mexican Food.! She "had no recipes". These quick Taquitos are my favorite.

1. Place the chicken breasts in a medium size saucepan. Make sure the chicken is covered with an inch of water. Add the celery stick, onion, whole garlic cloves and chicken bouillon.
2. Bring to a boil; turn the heat down to low, making sure the water is at a steady, low boil. Boil for 10 min. Turn off the heat, cover and let sit and steam for 10 min.
3. Take the chicken out, shred with 2 forks or pull it apart with your hands. Set aside. Save the broth.
4. In another fry pan, add olive oil and butter. Add the onion, green pepper, tomatoes and garlic. Sauté until the onion and green pepper are soft.
5. Add the shredded chicken and ⅓ cup chicken broth. Season with salt and pepper. Sauté until most of the broth has evaporated.
6. Warm 8 tortillas (stacked) at a time in the microwave for 30 seconds then put them in a plastic bag for 5 min.
7. Lay the tortillas, one at a time, on a baking sheet. Put 1½ Tablespoons chicken mixture on each tortilla. Roll up as tight as you can. Insert a toothpick if you can't get the tortilla to stay closed.
8. Heat a 10-inch skillet over medium heat on top of the stove. Add canola oil about ¼ the way up the pan. Fry the Taquitos, a few at a time, in the oil turning them as they begin to brown.
9. When cooked and crisp, lay the Taquitos on paper towels to drain off the excess oil.
10. Serve warm, sprinkled with *Caso Fresco cheese, salsa and sour cream.

Serve with: Food Nanny Lime Rice, Food Nanny Mexican Rice.

Variations: Serve with guacamole. May use any left over meat such as pork or steak.

Meatless

CRANBERRY AVOCADO SALSA

Makes 3½ cups
Time: 20 minutes

Plan Ahead: Can make a day ahead. Add the avocado and cilantro when ready to serve.

- 1 yellow bell pepper, blackened
- 1 12 oz. bag (3 cups) fresh cranberries
- ½ cup sugar
- ¼ cup orange juice
- 1 small jalapeno seeded and minced (optional)
- 1 Tablespoon grated orange peel
- 2 ripe avocados halved, pitted, peeled and diced
- ⅓ cup cilantro, chopped fine

1. Char or blacken the yellow bell pepper over a gas flame on top of the stove or under a broiler until blackened on all sides. Enclose in a paper or plastic bag for 10 min. Peel, seed and chop pepper. Set aside.
2. Combine cranberries, sugar and orange juice in processor. Pulse to coarsely chop berries. Transfer to medium bowl and combine with chopped pepper, jalapeno and orange peel. Can be prepared 1 day in advance. Cover and refrigerate. Stir avocados and cilantro into salsa when ready to serve.
3. Season to taste with salt and pepper.

Serve with: Tortilla Chips. Serve it with burritos, tacos or enchiladas.

*I love anything with cranberries in it.
When Nicole shared this recipe with me years ago
I was dying over it. I still am. It's delicious!!*

Meatless

ONE AVOCADO GUACAMOLE

Serves 2
Time: 5 minutes

Plan Ahead: Have ripe avocados on hand.

- 1 avocado, peeled, pitted and mashed
- 3 dashes hot sauce
- ½ teaspoon garlic salt
- ½ fresh lime, juiced
- Fresh ground black pepper

Mash avocado with a fork on a plate. Place in a small bowl. Stir in hot sauce, garlic salt and lime juice. Mix well. Adjust seasoning as desired. Add pepper to taste. Serve immediately.

Variations: You can do this exact recipe with one, two or 10 avocados.

Serve with: Goes with almost everything!

This is a really good, fast and easy recipe for guacamole.

Meatless
EVERYDAY SALSA

Serves 6
Time: 5 minutes

1 10 oz. can diced tomatoes with green chilies
1 14.5 oz. can diced tomatoes
½ cup fresh cilantro leaves
½ yellow onion, cut in half
2 medium garlic cloves
½ teaspoon cumin
1 teaspoon cider vinegar

Mix everything in a blender or food processor. Pulse it if you like it chunkier.

Serve with: Tortilla Chips of choice.

Variations: Of course you can add jalapeno or serrano chilies to this recipe if you like it with a lot more heat!

Jamie and Adam made this recipe for us years ago and it has become our go to salsa when we need salsa in less than 5 minutes.
I keep a few cans of diced tomatoes and green chilies, on my shelf just for this salsa.

CONVERSATION STARTER:
How old were your parents when they got married?

eatless

FRUIT SALSA WITH CINNAMON STRIPS

Serves 8
Time: 15 minutes

4 cups fresh fruit of choice, finely diced. Pineapple, blackberries, raspberries, strawberries, mango, cantaloupe
1 Tablespoon honey
1½ teaspoons fresh lemon juice
⅛ teaspoon cinnamon

6 8-inch flour tortillas
Homemade or store bought
Unsalted butter
2 teaspoons cinnamon
2 Tablespoons brown sugar

Salsa:

1. In a medium size bowl place the mixed diced fruit.
2. In a small bowl mix the honey, fresh lemon juice and cinnamon together. Pour over the fruit.

Tortilla Cinnamon Strips:

1. Pre-heat the oven to 400°
2. Butter both sides of the flour tortillas. Mix cinnamon and sugar together. Sprinkle over both sides of the flour tortillas.
3. Place on a baking sheet and bake at 400° for 10 min. or a little longer to crisp. Flip over and bake another couple of minutes.
4. Let cool slightly. Cut into 2 inch strips then cut in half. Serve warm with Fruit Salsa.

Variations: Use your favorite fresh fruit in season. Experiment. Use Cinnamon Drops in place of cinnamon/brown sugar mixture. Use white sugar in place of brown sugar.

Lisa is always bringing us something new to try. She brought this salsa to a summer BBQ a few years ago. We all went crazy over the cinnamon in the salsa and strips. You will too!! It is refreshing and fun to eat. Cinnamon has always been a favorite spice of the Mexican culture.

Pizza Night

Everyone is tired from a hard week at work.
We want to be together with family or friends and enjoy the laughter and
be grateful we are together again! It's what keeps families close.
It's what bonds families together.
Making pizza on Friday night has long been a tradition in our family.
Our married children with their own families all make great pizzas.
We experiment with different kinds.
It is fun to meet at local pizza places occasionally - which causes
a total ruckus when we all show up with the 24 grandkids!!!
Thanks to Rick and Nancy, our Friday night pizzas have become a fun tradition.
Make your Friday nights the most memorable night
of the week because of your Pizza Tradition.

The Food Nanny. xo

FRIDAY PIZZA NIGHT

Meatless

Meatless
TUSCAN SUN PIZZA DOUGH

Makes: 3 pizzas (10-12 inch)
Time: 1 hour

¼ cup warm water 105-115°
1 teaspoon sugar
2¼ teaspoons active dry yeast
1 Tablespoon olive oil
3-4 cups bread flour or all purpose white flour (You can use any kind of flour with this recipe - white spelt, whole wheat, kamut, gluten free, whatever you prefer)
½ teaspoon coarse salt
1¼ cups warm water or 1¼ cups (12 oz.) warm beer

Michelle has a farmhouse right in the heart of the Tuscan region of Italy. She shared this recipe with me. It is my most favorite dough ever, because it is so authentic to Italy. I love thin crust. Michelle thinks the beer makes all the difference...!!!!! The Basic Pizza Dough page 137 is also wonderful.

1. Combine ¼ cup warm water, sugar and yeast in a small bowl. Mix with a spoon. Let sit until foamy 4 to 5 min. Add olive oil.
2. In a large bowl add the flour and salt. Make a well. Stir in the yeast mixture and the warm water or warm beer. Use your hands if you want to. When you can't stir anymore and the dough is thick, yet sticky, bring it together with your hands and put out on a lightly floured counter or a breadboard and knead with your hands for 5 to 7 min., adding more flour if it is still sticky, until the dough is very smooth. Shape into a ball.
3. Oil a large bowl with a little olive oil. Place dough in bowl smooth side down, then turn the dough over and cover with a wet dish towel or oiled plastic wrap. Let rise until double in bulk. (About 1 hour).
4. When the dough has doubled, punch down and divide into 3 equal balls, or 6 balls for Tuscan thin crust. (Meanwhile turn the oven to 500°.) Roll the dough very thin into a 10 - 12 inch round or rectangle.
5. Place the dough onto a lightly oiled (or use parchment paper) pizza pan, baking sheet or Pizza Peel. If using a Pizza Peel, mix 1 Tablespoon flour and 1 Tablespoon corn meal. Sprinkle on peel. Place the dough on the peel then move it to a stone or tile. (Work quickly: moisture will start to form in the dough and will make it difficult to slide the pizza off the peel onto a stone or tiles.)
6. Prepare the pizza with toppings to your liking. Bake in a 500° oven for 6-8 min. on bottom oven rack until crisp.

Tip: To freeze dough - after you have divided the dough and made 3 equal size balls, wrap each dough ball separately in plastic, then again in foil and freeze up to 2 months. When ready to use, take out of freezer and let the dough come to room temperature and form dough into pizzas. Bake as directed.

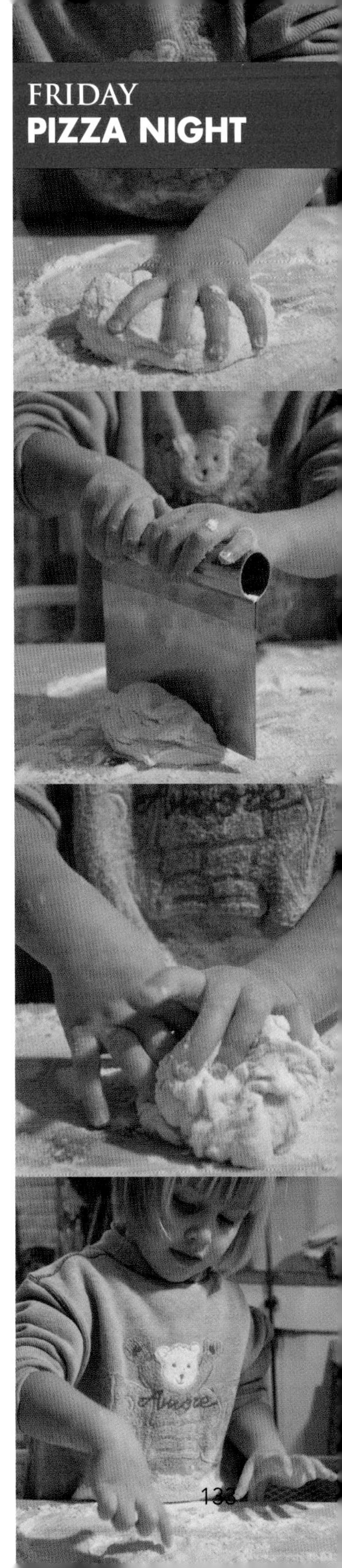

Meatless FRESH TOMATO PIZZA

Makes: One 10-12 inch pizza
Time: 15 minutes, if dough is prepared ahead.

One pizza dough ball, Tuscan Sun recipe page 133 (Can freeze ahead of time and thaw to use.)

1 large tomato, skin on, thinly sliced (I use a mandolin, takes 2 seconds)
Olive oil
¼ pound fresh Buffalo Mozzarella, sliced thin
¼ pound fresh Mozzarella, sliced thin
Oregano fresh or dried
Coarse salt
Fresh ground black pepper

Prepare dough, or have thawed dough ready to go.
Pre-heat oven to 500°.

1. Prepare dough per the directions for Tuscan Sun Pizza dough. Roll out your dough one ball at a time. Place the dough on an oiled pizza pan or baking sheet. Or, on a pizza peel with a little flour and cornmeal to move pizza to a stone or tile.

Prepare in order given:

2. Slice tomato and space evenly about the dough. Brush the entire dough and tomatoes with olive oil.
3. Lay on ⅓ cup fresh Buffalo Mozzarella cheese evenly dispersed around the dough. Lay on ⅓ cup fresh Mozzarella cheese evenly dispersed around the dough.
4. Sprinkle lightly with oregano. Drizzle on more olive oil. Salt and pepper to taste.
5. Bake in a 500° oven for 6-8 min. on bottom oven rack until crisp.

Serve with: Another flavor of one of my gourmet pizzas. Athens Greek Salad page 257 or Two Basic Salads page 258.

Variation: You can use any kind of flour in your dough to make it as healthy as possible. Use all Fresh Mozzarella in place of Buffalo Mozzarella. The key is to use all the ingredients evenly and sparingly. This makes for a delicious Tuscan Pizza!

Tip: To re-heat Pizza - place pizza slices in a pan on top of the stove over low heat. Cover with a lid so the pizza slices will steam warm and crispy. Takes 5 min. This is fabulous! It works and you will never throw away another pizza slice again. Store leftover pizza slices in a gallon size plastic bag in the refrigerator so the pizza does not smell up the rest of the refrigerator. Freeze left over pizza slices then thaw and re-heat as directed.

I made up this recipe because it uses some of my most favorite ingredients. It is so simple, yet gourmet because of the way it is put together. My Signature Pizza in my last book was the Arugula Pizza. This pizza is just about as easy as the Arugula and is fresh tasting.

Meatless

EASY PIZZA SAUCE FOR KIDS TO MAKE

About 1 cup sauce; enough for one 16-inch pizza
Time: 5 minutes

1 8 oz. can tomato sauce
½ teaspoon dried basil or oregano
¼ teaspoon garlic salt
⅛ teaspoon ground black pepper
Pinch of sugar (optional)

Mix the tomato sauce, basil, garlic salt and pepper in a small bowl. Spread on dough.

This is the sauce I started out with 30 years ago. I made it up. My kids loved it then and my boys still prefer it. David now makes this sauce at home with his own kids.

Meatless

BASIC PIZZA SAUCE

Makes enough for three 10-12 inch pizzas
Time: 5 minutes

2 14.5 oz. cans diced (Italian) tomatoes with juice
2 teaspoons dried oregano
3 Tablespoons olive oil
½ teaspoon coarse salt
¼ teaspoon fresh ground black pepper, or to taste

Put the tomatoes in a food processor, or use an immersion blender, or regular blender and pulse to crush tomatoes. Pour them into a bowl and mix in the oregano, oil, salt and pepper. Spread on dough.

Tip: *To re-heat Pizza* - Place pizza slices in a pan on top of the stove over low heat. Cover with a lid so the pizza slices will steam warm and crispy. Takes 5 min. This is fabulous! It works and you will never throw away another pizza slice again. Store leftover pizza slices in a gallon size plastic bag in the refrigerator so the pizza does not smell up the refrigerator. Freeze left over pizza slices, then thaw and re-heat as directed.

This is your basic pizza sauce which is always made with fresh or dried oregano.
It can also be made with 8 fresh tomatoes: substituting 4 fresh tomatoes per can, instead of canned. xo

thefoodnanny

Meatless
BASIC PIZZA DOUGH

Makes one 16-inch medium crust pizza or two 12-inch thin-crust pizzas or four 8-inch thin-crust pizzas
Time: 15 minutes

- 1 tablespoon active dry yeast
- 1 cup warm water 105 – 115°
- 2 Tablespoons olive oil
- 1 Tablespoon honey
- ¼ teaspoon salt
- 3 to 4 cups all-purpose flour or half all-purpose flour and half whole wheat (see Note)

1. Mix the yeast and water in a small bowl, cover and let stand until foamy 5 min.
2. Mix the oil, honey, salt and yeast mixture in a large mixing bowl. If using a food processor add 1 cup of flour at a time, up to 3 cups, mixing well after each addition. You may have to stir in the third cup of flour by hand, depending on your machine. Or mix in all 3 cups of flour by hand with a wooden spoon. If the dough seems too wet, mix in more flour, ¼ cup at a time, until the dough is soft. Turn the dough onto a floured surface and knead in more flour, ¼ cup at a time, until the dough is moderately stiff and somewhat firm to the touch, about 3 min. Cover. Rest 5 min.
3. Lightly grease pizza pan(s) or a cookie sheet(s) with oil or use parchment paper. If you are making two or more thin-crust pizzas, divide the dough. With a rolling pin, roll out the dough on a floured surface. Gently stretch the dough to fill the pan(s) or place on a peel with flour and cornmeal then slide onto stone or tiles.
4. Let the dough rise (it will not rise very much) while you make sauce and continue with the pizza recipe of your choice.
5. Bake a 16-inch medium crust pizza at 450-500° for 10 to 15 min. Bake thin crust pizzas at 450-500° for 7 to 10 min.

I like this pizza crust best with half all-purpose flour and half whole wheat. I keep my whole wheat flour in a canister right beside my all-purpose, so I can add whole wheat flour to almost any bread dough or pancake or waffle batter. This is the basic pizza dough that I raised my family on. I have shared the recipe with everyone I know. xo

CONVERSATION STARTER:
What is your favorite activity? Sporting event?

Meatless MEDITERRANEAN PIZZA

Makes: One 10 to 12 inch Pizza
Time: 15 minutes

Plan Ahead: Pizza dough.

1 pizza dough ball, from the Tuscan Sun Pizza dough recipe page 133
Olive oil
½ fresh tomato, sliced thin
Coarse salt
Fresh ground black pepper
1 2.5oz. can sliced black olives (use half, freeze the rest)
Red onion, sliced very thin (7 or 8 slices)
1 cup fresh baby spinach,
1 6oz. jar artichoke hearts (use half the jar)
⅓ cup Feta cheese, crumbled

1. Roll out the pizza dough very thin. Place the dough on an oiled pizza pan or baking sheet. Or, on a pizza peel with a little flour and cornmeal to move pizza to a stone or tile.
2. Brush the dough with olive oil. Lay on the sliced tomatoes. Sprinkle with coarse salt and fresh ground black pepper.
3. Sprinkle the olives and red onion around. Evenly disperse the spinach. Place the artichoke hearts evenly. Sprinkle on the Feta Cheese.
4. Bake in a 500° oven for 6-8 min. on bottom oven rack until crisp.

Serve with: Serve with salted green olives in garlic olive oil, on the side.

Variations: Use arugula in place of spinach.

*I love the Mediterranean!
This pizza reminds me of Greece.
I can taste the fresh vegetables and
feta cheese now!*

CONVERSATION STARTER:
*What one thing is
the most prized by you?*

FABULOUS THAI CHICKEN PIZZA

Makes: Two 10-12 inch Pizzas
Time: 20 minutes

Plan Ahead: Prepare dough ahead. Prepare sauce ahead. Prepare chicken ahead.

Peanut Sauce:

¼ cup balsamic vinegar
2½ Tablespoons granulated sugar
2 Tablespoons brown sugar
2 Tablespoons soy sauce
½ teaspoon crushed red pepper
⅛ teaspoon coarse salt
1 fresh garlic clove, crushed
2 Tablespoons chunky peanut butter

2 pizza dough balls, to make two 10 to 12 inches pizzas; Tuscan Sun Pizza dough recipe page 133.

2 Tablespoons olive oil
2 fresh garlic cloves, crushed
1 cup chicken breast, cooked and torn into pieces or shredded
6 thin slices fresh Buffalo Mozzarella cheese
½ cup shredded Mozzarella cheese
1½ Tablespoons shredded carrot
Sliced red onion to taste (optional)
¼ cup cilantro leaves
½ cup whole peanuts

1. Pre-heat oven to 500°.
2. Prepare the dough for your pizza. Or use 2 frozen dough balls, thawed.

Prepare the Peanut Sauce:

3. In a small sauce pan over medium heat bring the vinegar, sugar, brown sugar, soy sauce, red pepper, salt and garlic to a boil stirring frequently.
4. Remove from heat. Whisk in the peanut butter. Set aside. Sauce must be slightly warm to spread on pizza.

Prepare the pizza dough:

5. Roll out your dough one ball at a time. Place the dough on an oiled pizza pan or baking sheet. Or, on a pizza peel with a little flour and cornmeal to move pizza to a stone or tile.
6. Mix 2 Tablespoons olive oil in a small bowl with garlic. Brush mixture over the entire pizza dough.
7. Spread on half the Peanut Sauce. Spread the chicken pieces around. Disperse the cheeses evenly. Sprinkle carrots and onion, if using. Bake in a 500° oven for 6-8 min. on bottom oven rack until crisp. Remove from oven and sprinkle on the cilantro and peanuts.

Tip: After traveling to Italy many times, I soon learned that they made their pizza much differently from the way we make ours. We go heavy on the cheese, meat and other toppings. In Italy I learned they disperse their ingredients very sparsely compared to what we do. Most importantly they add even amounts of cheese, meat, veggies etc...This makes for a beautiful "pie" as well as a more enjoyable and delicious pizza. You don't feel "stuffed" after dinner. Perfection!!

This sauce is so fabulous you will want to drink it! If you are a Peanut Sauce fan like me you are going to go crazy for this Pizza! Enjoy! xo

Meatless
ROASTED CHERRY TOMATO PIZZA

Makes: 1 pizza (10-12 inch)
Time: 20 minutes

Plan Ahead: Make Pizza dough ahead. Pre-heat oven to 500°.

1 pizza dough ball, Tucson Sun recipe page 133
½ to ¾ pounds cherry tomatoes
1½ Tablespoons olive oil
Coarse salt
Fresh ground black pepper
Olive oil
⅓ cup fresh Parmesan cheese, grated
⅓ cup fresh Mozzarella cheese, diced
Fresh basil or fresh oregano

1. Place the tomatoes on a large baking sheet. Brush all over with olive oil. Generously sprinkle with the coarse salt and fresh ground black pepper. Shake the pan so that the tomatoes roll around so they are covered on all sides with the olive oil, salt and pepper. Place in the oven at 400° and roast for 10-12 min.
2. Roll out the pizza dough very thin. Place the dough on an oiled pizza pan or baking sheet. Or, on a pizza peel with a little flour and cornmeal to move pizza to a stone or tile. Brush olive oil over the entire pizza.
3. Sprinkle on the Parmesan cheese. Scatter the cherry tomatoes, juice and all on the dough. Place the diced mozzarella cheese evenly around.
4. Bake in a 500° oven for 6-8 min. on bottom oven rack until crisp. Garnish with basil or oregano if desired.

This is delicious! The first time I ever ate roasted tomatoes, we were in Rome. Roasting the tomatoes is key here. If you are not a tomato lover you will be now. Tomato is a fruit, did you know that? Think of this pizza being roasted fruit! It 's that good! Enjoy.

eatless

ARUGULA PIZZA & CHERRY TOMATOES

Makes: One 10-12 inch pizza
Time: 15 minutes

Plan Ahead: : Make Tuscan Sun Dough and freeze 2 of the 3 dough balls for future use.

1 pizza dough ball – Tuscan Sun Pizza dough page 133
⅔ cup fresh Mozzarella cheese
2 cups fresh arugula
½ cup fresh cherry or grape tomatoes, cut in half
Olive oil, for drizzling
Coarse salt and fresh ground black pepper

CONVERSATION STARTER:

What do your friends like best about you?

1. Preheat the oven to 500°.
2. Roll out the dough. Place the dough on an oiled pizza pan or baking sheet. Or, on a pizza peel with a little flour and cornmeal to move pizza to a stone or tile. Brush olive oil over the entire pizza.
3. Slice the fresh mozzarella cheese and place it on the crust or top with shredded regular mozzarella.
4. Bake in a 500° oven for 6-8 min. on bottom oven rack until crisp.
5. Remove from the oven and immediately pile the arugula pieces onto the hot melted cheese and top with tomatoes. Drizzle a little olive oil on top. Season lightly with coarse salt and fresh ground pepper.

I am including this pizza here because it was my biggest pizza hit in my first book. Well, so was my BBQ Chicken Pizza...anyway....enjoy!! xo

FRIDAY
PIZZA NIGHT

TRADITIONAL TUSCAN PIZZAS!

Time: 15 minutes

Plan ahead: Take out of freezer
Use 1 frozen pizza dough ball, thawed, Tuscan Sun Pizza Dough page 133.

Pizza with Potatoes
Roll out the dough very thin. Place the dough on an oiled pizza pan or baking sheet. Or, on a pizza peel with a little flour and cornmeal to move pizza to a stone or tile. Brush dough all over with olive oil. Slice raw or leftover baked potatoes very thin with a mandolin or with a sharp knife. Can also use steamed or boiled potatoes. Place the sliced potatoes on top of the dough but not overlapping. Sprinkle with coarse salt and fresh ground black pepper and drizzle on more olive oil. Bake in a 500° oven for 6-8 min. on bottom oven rack until crisp.

Pizza with Ham
Roll out the dough very thin. Place the dough on an oiled pizza pan or baking sheet. Or, on a pizza peel with a little flour and cornmeal to move pizza to a stone or tile. Brush dough all over with olive oil. Spread Easy Pizza Sauce page 135, over the dough. Sprinkle with mozzarella cheese. Slice about ⅓ cup leftover ham (any kind) or prosciutto, very thin with your mandolin or a sharp knife. Place the ham evenly around the dough. Sprinkle on a little olive oil. Bake in a 500° oven for 6-8 min. on bottom oven rack until crisp.

Pizza with Mushrooms
Roll out the dough very thin. Place the dough on an oiled pizza pan or baking sheet. Or, on a pizza peel with a little flour and cornmeal to move pizza to a stone or tile. Brush dough all over with olive oil. Dot dough evenly with fresh mozzarella cheese. Evenly disperse fresh sliced white mushrooms. Sprinkle with coarse salt and fresh ground black pepper and a little more olive oil. Bake in a 500° oven for 6-8 min. on bottom oven rack until crisp.

Pizza with Red Onions - A Tuscan Tradition
Roll out the dough very thin. Place the dough on an oiled pizza pan or baking sheet. Or, on a pizza peel with a little flour and cornmeal to move pizza to a stone or tile. Brush dough all over with olive oil. Slice 1 large red onion as thin as possible on the mandolin or with a sharp knife. Mix with 3 Tablespoons olive oil and coarse salt to taste. Pile the onions around the dough leaving an edge of about 1 inch. Bake at 350° for 30 min.

You can make a pizza out of almost anything!
Here are four more reasons why I love Pizza so much:
1. It can be SO fast and easy. 2. It is delicious. 3. It is inexpensive.
4. You get to serve it and eat it with the people you love most.
Another favorite with the kids in Tuscany is with Hot Dogs on top! Imagine!!!!
See what YOU can come up with. xo

LITTLE ITALY PIZZA

Makes: 1 pizza (10-12 inch)
Time: 15 minutes

Plan Ahead: Prepare the Pizza dough.

½ large red bell pepper, blackened
1 pizza dough ball, Tuscan Sun Pizza Dough recipe, page 133
Olive oil
1¼ cups baby spinach, fresh
½ cup white mushrooms, sliced
Coarse salt
Fresh ground black pepper
½ cup Italian sausage, cooked (optional)
½ cup Provolone cheese, sliced or shredded

I so enjoy pizza with fresh veggies, fresh ingredients make for clean eating. A little bit of sausage for flavor. I love it !!!

1. Turn the oven to broil.
2. Place the pepper on a baking sheet and place it under the broiler, about 6 inches from the element. Turn it as it gets blackened. When the skin is blackened remove from oven. (The entire pepper does not need to be black.) Place in a plastic bag for 10 min. Let sweat. Peel off the skin. Cut into long thin strips.
3. Roll out the dough. Place the dough on an oiled pizza pan or baking sheet. Or, on a pizza peel with a little flour and cornmeal to move pizza to a stone or tile. Brush olive oil over the entire pizza. Place spinach in one layer. Lay the mushrooms on top of the spinach evenly dispersed. Disperse roasted red peppers evenly.
4. Sprinkle lightly with coarse salt and fresh ground black pepper. Drizzle on a little more olive oil very lightly. Add the sausage, if using. Sprinkle on the Provolone cheese dispersed evenly.
5. Bake in a 500° oven for 6-8 min. on bottom oven rack until crisp.

Tip: *To re-heat Pizza* - Place Pizza slices in a pan on top of the stove over low heat. Cover with a lid so the pizza slices will steam warm and crispy. Takes 5 min. This is fabulous! It works and you will never throw away another pizza slice again. Store leftover pizza slices in a gallon size plastic baggie in the refrigerator so the pizza does not smell up the refrigerator. Freeze left over pizza slices, then thaw and re-heat as directed.

Meatless

FRESH RICOTTA CHEESE PIZZA

Makes: One 10-12 pizza
Time: 10 minutes

Plan Ahead: Make pizza dough.

1 pizza dough ball, Tuscan Sun Pizza Dough recipe, page 133
3 fresh garlic cloves, crushed
2 Tablespoons olive oil
½ cup whole Ricotta cheese
1 fresh tomato, skin on, sliced thin (I use my mandolin)
Olive oil
Coarse salt
Fresh ground black pepper

1. Pre-heat the oven to 500°.
2. Roll out the dough. Place the dough on an oiled pizza pan or baking sheet. Or, on a pizza peel with a little flour and cornmeal to move pizza to a stone or tile. In a small bowl combine the garlic with the olive oil. Stir. Brush oil mixture over the entire pizza dough.
3. Spread the Ricotta cheese evenly on top. Slice the tomato and lay over top the Ricotta cheese. Sprinkle with a little olive oil, coarse salt and fresh ground black pepper.
4. Bake in a 500° oven for 6-8 min. on bottom oven rack until crisp. Sprinkle on a little more olive oil and serve immediately.

Variations: Remember you can vary the flour in the pizza dough recipe. You can also choose to use whole Ricotta or part-skim, your choice.

Often on Pizza Night my husband, Steve, and I are in the mood for a light pizza. Nothing too filling.
We try and only eat meat a couple of nights a week. Vegetables, fruits and grains keep us healthy. That is what I love about my Gourmet Pizzas - which is what I call them. They are light and delicious and we feel like we are eating under the Tucson Sun!
Enjoy!

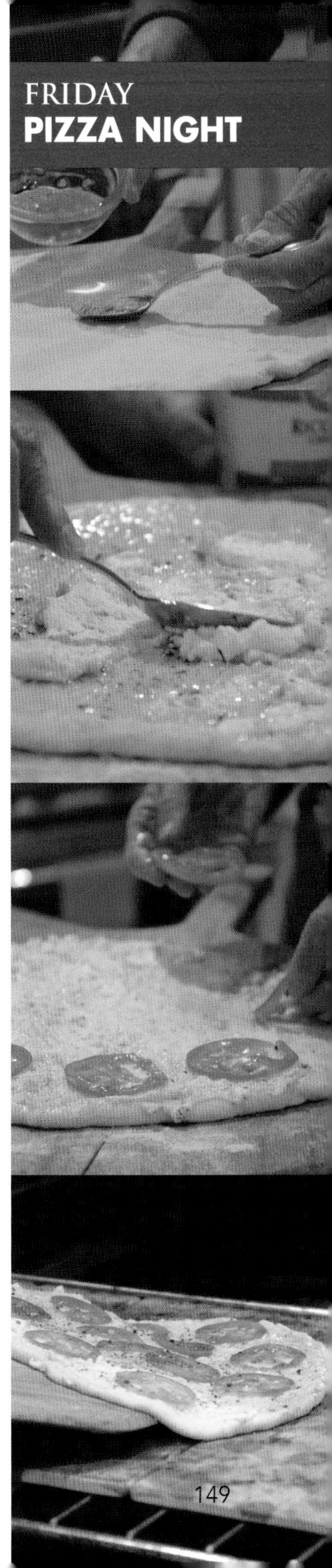

Fresh Strawberry Pizza
Makes: 1 pizza Time: 20 minutes

1. 1 pizza dough ball from the Tucson Sun Pizza Dough recipe page 133.
2. Roll out the pizza dough very thin on a lightly floured surface. Place the dough on an oiled pizza pan or baking sheet. Or, on a pizza peel with a little flour and cornmeal to move pizza to a stone or tile. Brush with olive oil all over the entire pizza.
3. Slice 1 cup strawberries, thin. (I use my mandolin). Do not overlap the strawberries nor let them touch: one layer dispersed evenly around the dough. Sprinkle very lightly with sugar if desired.
4. Bake in a 500° oven for 6-8 min. on bottom oven rack until crisp. Remove, dust generously with powdered sugar. Slice and serve warm or at room temperature.

Pizza Nutella
Makes: 1 pizza Time: 20 minutes

1. Prepare 1 pizza dough ball from the Tucson Sun Pizza Dough recipe page 133.
2. Roll out the dough very thin. Place the dough on an oiled pizza pan or baking sheet. Or, on a pizza peel with a little flour and cornmeal to move pizza to a stone or tile. Brush with olive oil all over the entire pizza. Bake in a 500° oven for 6-8 min. on bottom oven rack until crisp. Remove from the oven and spread on about ½ cup Nutella while still hot.
3. Slice and serve hot. Great warm and at room temperature too. Serve as dessert for Pizza Night.

Pizza Dough with Baked Apples, Sugar and Cinnamon
Makes: 1 pizza Time: 20 minutes

1. Prepare 1 pizza dough ball from the Tucson Sun Pizza Dough recipe page 133.
2. Roll the dough very thin. Place the dough on an oiled pizza pan or baking sheet. Or, on a pizza peel with a little flour and cornmeal to move pizza to a stone or tile. Brush with olive oil all over the entire pizza. Slice ½ apple, any kind, as thin as possible. (I use my mandolin). Lay the apple slices on top of the dough in one layer, evenly dispersed.
3. Sprinkle generously with cinnamon and a light dusting of granulated sugar.
4. Drizzle lightly with olive oil. Bake in a 500° oven for 6-8 min. on bottom oven rack until crisp. Remove, dust lightly with powdered sugar.
5. Slice and serve warm or at room temperature. Serve as dessert for Pizza Night.

*All of these desserts are delicious.
Michelle makes these easy delicious Dessert Pizzas
in her farmhouse often for her children and their friends in Tuscany.
You are going to love these Pizza Night desserts!! xo*

Meatless SCARLETT'S PIZZA NIGHT DESSERT

Makes: 30 Scarlets
Time: 15 minutes

1 pizza dough ball – Tuscan Sun Pizza Dough recipe page 133
5 Tablespoons white granulated sugar
1 teaspoon vanilla extract
¼ cup unsweetened cocoa powder
3 Tablespoons Nutella
2 teaspoons olive oil
¼ cup pizza dough
Canola oil for frying.

1. Prepare the vanilla sugar: In a pie plate mix the sugar and vanilla with a spoon. Cover with plastic. It will dry out quickly if not covered. Set aside.
2. Place the cocoa in a sifter or small sieve and set over a small bowl. Set aside.
3. Mix the Nutella and olive oil together in a small bowl and set aside.
4. Pinch off enough dough to measure ¼ cup. On a lightly floured surface roll the dough into a rope 1 inch thick. Take a sharp knife and cut 1-inch lengths. You will have ten 1-inch length pieces. Roll each piece into a skinny rope and tie in a knot. Set on the counter to rise a little bit as you roll and tie each Scarlett.
5. Heat oil (1 inch deep) over medium heat until the oil is hot enough to fry the dough quickly. Test the oil with a piece of extra dough before frying. When the oil is ready place the Scarlett's in the frying pan and fry, turning each one with tongs, over and over until light brown. Quickly remove to a paper towel.
6. As soon as you can touch them, roll all 10 of them in the vanilla sugar mixture. Place them on a plate and sift the cocoa lightly over top. Drizzle a little bit of Nutella on top the cocoa.
7. Place on a clean plate and serve warm. These are great at room temperature too! Serve as dessert for Pizza Night.

These are delicious!!!
I learned how to make the Scarletts in Rome.
This is my version! I named them Scarletts after our precious little granddaughter who only lived 90 minutes.

CONVERSATION STARTER:
What would the world be like if everyone were the same?

Grill Night

I am so excited about my new Grill recipes!!
I have been working a long time to perfect them. Try my BBQ Cheese Crusted Steak. I first ate it in Italy and perfected it at home. Grilled Thin Steak with Béarnaise Sauce is something we order every time we visit France. They serve it with fresh green beans. Some American Favorites are my Jalapeno Pepperoncini Salt Crusted Tri-Tip. It's wonderful! You will love my Sliders, Flank steak, Jalapeno Burger and Southwestern Lime Chicken. You will love these fabulous recipes!!!
If you cannot make a great steak to save your life, try my Fillet Mignon. It comes out perfectly every time. My Brisket recipe from Texas cannot be beat.
All it takes is a little planning ahead on your part.
That is the key to my entire meal plan: planning ahead. Go through the book and choose the meals you are going to cook for two weeks. Make a grocery list and go shopping. Keep the meal plan posted somewhere so family members can see what is coming up for dinner. Everyone will look forward to being home for dinner with their family. There is nothing like a family BBQ in the summertime.
We do it all summer long. Around 6:30 p.m. especially on Saturday, we start to smell the BBQ warming up with something yummy to eat.
We serve these recipes over and over and always get rave reviews from family and friends. All these recipes can be cooked under the broiler in the oven as well.
Try some Saturday Grill Night specials all year long.

The Food Nanny. xo

SATURDAY GRILL NIGHT

Meatless

BBQ APRICOT CHICKEN THIGHS

Serves 4 to 6
Time: 35 minutes

Plan Ahead: May grill a few hours or 1 day ahead and reheat in saucepan over low heat with a lid on.

6 Chicken thighs, remove skin if desired
Coarse salt
Fresh ground black pepper
2 Tablespoons fresh ginger, grated
¾ cup apricot preserves
⅓ cup plus one Tablespoon soy sauce
2 Tablespoons water
¼ teaspoon red pepper flakes

1. With a wet paper towel wipe off the chicken thighs. Sprinkle lightly with coarse salt and fresh ground black pepper.
2. In a food processor or blender place the fresh ginger, apricot preserves, soy sauce, water and red pepper flakes. Puree. Save out ½ cup sauce. Pour the rest into a bowl.
3. Preheat the grill to medium heat. Oil the grill by folding up a paper towel and drizzle it with olive oil and running it over the grate with your tongs.
4. Place the chicken thighs on the hot grill. Let them grill for 5 min. Turn. Grill for 5 more min. Turn. Turn every 5 min. for 15 min. Then brush the thighs heavily with the sauce turning after 5 min., brush with sauce again. Finish grilling the last 5 min. adding on no sauce.
   Serve with extra sauce at room temperature.

Serve with: I love this chicken best when served with my Bangkok Stir Fry page 25, when not using chicken in the stir fry. You can serve with Jasmine Rice page 218 or my Lemon Potatoes page 161.

Variations: Use peach preserves. You can broil by putting the meat about 7 to 10 inches under the broiler element on a baking sheet. Follow the same instructions as for the Grill. If the meat is thicker lower the rack to the middle position.

This chicken is moist and delicious. Another great option, really quick and inexpensive too!!!

JALAPENO PEPPERONCINI SALT CRUSTED TRI-TIP

Serves 6
Time: 40 minutes

Plan Ahead: Marinate the meat 24 hours in advance.

1 3lb. Tri-Tip beef steak
1 16 oz. jar jalapenos with juice
1 16 oz. jar pepperoncini with juice
3 Tablespoons coarse salt

1. Marinate the meat in the jalapenos and pepperoncini (including the juice from the bottles) in a gallon re-sealable bag. Let it sit for 24 hours. Flip the meat half way through so the juices and peppers cover both sides of it equally. This will help to brown the meat.
2. When you are ready to grill, take a cookie sheet and sprinkle coarse salt on the bottom. Get a good salt crust on one side of the piece of meat. Turn the grill to high. Take a paper towel folded into fourths and pour on some olive oil, then using your tongs run it over the grill to oil.
3. Place the salt crusted side down on the grill and sear the meat on the outside. Once it is seared, turn the heat to low turning the meat every 10 min. Grill until the meat is medium rare. This will take 30 min.
4. Take the meat off the grill and place on a cutting board with grooves to hold the juices, or place on a platter. Cover with foil. Let the meat rest 10 min. The meat will continue to cook and give the juices time to settle down into the meat.
5. Slice the meat in thin pieces and serve immediately. Keep it covered in foil as much as possible while slicing.

Serve with: Grilled Red and Green Bell Peppers page 159 or Sautéed Spinach with Parmesan page 211. Corn on the cob. Baked Potatoes. Grilled Garlic Parmesan Bread page 173.

Jenn and Brad had been begging me to try their new recipe for months. The first time I served this recipe to my family everyone agreed it was a keeper! This is seriously wonderful flavor! You are going to love this.

CONVERSATION STARTER:
What is one thing, for sure, that you want to do?

Meatless

GRILLED RED AND GREEN BELL PEPPERS

Serves 4
Time: 10 minutes

Plan Ahead: Marinate the peppers overnight, or up to 2 days.

1 red bell pepper
1 green bell pepper
¼ cup olive oil
2 teaspoons balsamic vinegar

1. Rinse off the peppers. Cut into fourths. Place in a re-sealable plastic bag and add the olive oil and vinegar. Squish around and place in refrigerator until ready to grill.
2. When ready to grill take them out of the marinade, throw the marinade away and grill the peppers over high heat, turning often for about 10 min. The peppers will be lightly charred and moist.

Serve with: Anything you are grilling!!

*These are one of my favorite grilled vegetables.
I love to serve these peppers with everything!
They are full of Vitamin C!! You will love them too.*

EASY GRILLED TERIYAKI CHICKEN

Serves 6
Time: 10 minutes

Plan ahead: Marinate 12 hours, but no less than 4.

1½ to 2 pounds (10 to 15) chicken tenders
2 cups lemon lime soda
1 cup Teriyaki Sauce
1 Tablespoon olive oil

1. Place the chicken tenders in a re-sealable plastic bag, add soda, teriyaki sauce and olive oil. Squish the tenders around in the sauce. Seal the bag and place in the refrigerator up to 12 hours, but not less than 4 hours.
2. When you are ready to BBQ, preheat the grill to high. Use a paper towel folded into quarters and sprinkle with olive oil. Use your tongs to go over top the grill to oil it. Oil the grill well or the chicken will stick to it.
3. Throw away the marinade and grill the chicken over high heat 5 min. on each side.

Serve with: Store-bought Mango Chutney. Jasmine Rice page 218. Use chicken broth instead of water to cook your rice. Fresh green beans.

Variations: If you don't have chicken tenders on hand, make them out of boneless/skinless chicken breasts. Cut each breast into 3 or 4 tenders. You can broil by putting the meat about 7 to 10 inches under the broiler element on a baking sheet. Pretty much follow the same instructions as for the Grill. If the meat is thicker lower the rack to the middle position.

*You won't believe how easy and moist this chicken is!
It makes a really delicious meal served
with Mango Chutney. xo*

Meatless

GRILLED LEMONY RED POTATOES

Serves 4
Time: 20 minutes

Plan Ahead: Boil the potatoes earlier in the day.

- **4 medium size red potatoes with skins on, boiled until soft**
- **2 Tablespoons olive oil**
- **1 garlic clove, minced**
- **¼ teaspoon lemon zest**
- **⅛ teaspoon dried parsley flakes**
- **Coarse salt**
- **Fresh ground black pepper**

1. Wash potatoes. Place the potatoes, whole, into a medium size saucepan. Cover with water; bring to a boil; turn the heat down to a slow boil and continue cooking until the potatoes are soft, about 15 min. Drain the water off the potatoes and place on a plate.
2. Preheat the BBQ Grill to high.
3. Mix the olive oil, garlic, lemon zest, parsley salt and pepper to taste in a small bowl.
4. Cut the potatoes in half and dip each cut end into the olive oil/lemon mixture. Save the extra mixture.
5. Place the potatoes cut side down over high heat onto the grill. When you see black grill marks the potatoes are done, about 5 min. Pour remaining olive oil mixture over top the potatoes to serve.

Serve with: Almost anything you are grilling!

These potatoes of mine are as easy as it gets and have a great lemony flavor. You will be grilling these little gems all the time!!

CONVERSATION STARTER:

What is one thing that you would change about your school?

SOUTHWESTERN LIME CHICKEN

Serves 4-6
Time: 20 minutes

Plan Ahead: Marinate overnight.

4 ¾ - 1 inch thick boneless/skinless chicken breasts
¼ cup olive oil
6 Tablespoons soy sauce
½ cup fresh lime juice
2 Tablespoons brown sugar
2 Tablespoons dried oregano
1 Tablespoon dried rosemary
1 Tablespoon fresh garlic, minced
1½ teaspoons chili powder
½ teaspoon cayenne pepper
4 slices Monterey Jack or Pepper Jack Cheese

1. With a wet paper towel clean off the chicken breasts. Set aside.
2. In a small bowl mix together the olive oil, soy sauce, lime juice, brown sugar, oregano, rosemary, garlic, chili powder and cayenne pepper. Place the chicken in a re-sealable plastic bag. Pour the marinade over the chicken and toss and turn the bag to make sure the chicken is thoroughly coated. Place the bag in the refrigerator overnight or up to 12 hours. Turn occasionally.
3. Preheat the grill to medium high. Take a paper towel and fold it into fourths. Sprinkle with olive oil. Using your tongs, run the paper towel over top the grill to oil it.
4. Remove chicken breasts from marinade. Grill 6 min. on one side. Turn over. Close grill cover and grill 6 more min. on the other side. Turn. Grill 2 more min. per side. Cut into the chicken to see how it looks. If almost done, place a slice of cheese on top of each piece of chicken. Cover. Grill until the cheese melts about 3 more min.

Serve with: Food Nanny Lime Rice; Black Beans; Corn on the cob; Everyday Salsa page 127, Chopped Romaine lettuce, Lime Ranch Dressing page 112 and warm flour tortillas.

Variations: Use fresh herbs in place of dried. If you are using thin breasts you will only need about 10 min. cooking time, then place the cheese on top to melt.

You can broil by putting the meat about 7 to 10 inches under the broiler element on a baking sheet. Pretty much follow the same instructions as for the Grill. If the meat is thicker lower the rack to the middle position.

This chicken is very earthy tasting.
Rich, delicious and moist.
Marinating chicken makes all the difference especially when grilling!!

WEST VIRGINIA HOT DOGS, CHILI SAUCE & COLESLAW

Serves 4
Time: 2 hours

Plan Ahead: Make the Chili Sauce and Coleslaw 1 day ahead of time.

4 Hot Dogs
4 Hot Dog Buns
Mustard
¼ cup white onion, chopped (onion optional)

Chili Sauce:
1 pound ground beef
1 medium onion, minced
1 6 oz. can tomato paste
3 tomato paste cans of water
1 cup ketchup
1 teaspoon apple cider vinegar
1 teaspoon salt
1½ teaspoons chili powder

Coleslaw:
1 cup green cabbage, shredded
2 Tablespoons carrot, peeled and grated
¼ cup mayonnaise or more to taste
Coarse salt
Fresh ground pepper

Prepare Chili Sauce:
DO NOT BROWN MEAT. Combine all ingredients in saucepan, adding water 1 can at a time and stirring after each addition. Cook over low heat at least 1½ hours stirring occasionally.

Prepare Coleslaw:
Shred the cabbage and carrot as fine as you can get them and place in a small bowl. (I use my mandolin or food processor.) Add mayonnaise and stir. Add more or less mayonnaise to your liking. Add salt and pepper to taste. Cover with plastic wrap and keep in refrigerator until ready to use.

Prepare Hot Dogs:
Grill the hot dogs. Place in a bun. Spread with mustard. Spoon on the chili sauce and top with the coleslaw. Sprinkle on the onions. Serve.

Serve with: Potato chips, pickles of choice and olives.

Tip: Freeze leftover chili sauce for next time.

I was with the Kaleidoscope Food Nanny team doing a show in Solvang, California when Jan, who was from West Virginia, made us her famous West Virginia hot dogs. We all fell in love with Jan and her hot dogs. My favorite hot dogs ever!

GRILLED JALAPENO BURGERS

Serves 4
Time: 20 minutes

Plan Ahead: Make Homemade Hamburger Buns page 253 or Food Nanny French Baguettes or store bought Potato Buns.

1 pound ground beef, 80/15, ground chuck or Skirt steak.*
Coarse Salt
Fresh ground black pepper
1 teaspoon olive oil
1 teaspoon unsalted butter
3 jalapenos, sliced lengthwise
1 yellow onion, sliced thin
4 slices bacon, cooked
4 hamburger buns
Jalapeno cream cheese, room temperature

**Whether you get the meat from a butcher, grind it yourself, or finely chop it in a food processor - to get deliciously juicy results you need to use meat with some fat in it such as ground chuck or skirt steak. Do not over handle the meat. You don't want to make a dense hamburger.*
You want to delicately form a patty that looks like it might not stay together. You can broil by putting the meat about 7 to 10 inches under the broiler element on a baking sheet. Follow the same instructions as for the Grill. If the meat is thicker lower the rack to the middle position.

1. Form the hamburger patties 1 inch thick and about ½ inch bigger than the bun you are using. Don't over-handle the meat. (Remember, packing the meat together too tight will not allow the meat juices to flow.) Salt and pepper the hamburger on both sides and set aside.
2. In an 8-inch skillet melt butter and add olive oil. Add jalapenos and onions and sauté over low heat until soft about 10 min. Set aside.
3. Lightly butter the buns on both sides. Oil the BBQ grate. Fold a paper towel into a pad, add oil, and use long handled tongs to rub it over the grate.
4. Turn the heat up to high and BBQ the burgers for 5 to 6 min. on each side or until the internal temperature reaches 160°. While cooking, do not press on the burger with a spatula. Just flip it. Let rest for a minute before placing on the grilled bun.
5. Place the buns on top of the grill until just toasted. Spread the bottom bun generously with jalapeno cream cheese. Place the burger on top; add the bacon and grilled jalapenos and onions, distributed equally over 4 burgers.

Serve with: Baked Beans with Bacon and Pineapple page 226 or Potato Chips; Fresh Raw Veggies.

Variations: Mushroom Swiss - do the same thing only melt a piece of Swiss cheese on top of the burger just before it is finished cooking. Sauté sliced white mushrooms, onions and pineapple tidbits together until soft. Distribute evenly over top the burgers. Spread on the mayonnaise and top with a tomato slice and lettuce.

The Jalapeno Burger is my new favorite!

MARINATED FLANK STEAK

Serves 4
Time: 25 minutes

Plan Ahead: Marinate the Steak 8 hours ahead.

¾ cup canola or olive oil
½ cup soy sauce
3½ Tablespoons honey
2 Tablespoons red wine vinegar
1 Tablespoon garlic powder
½ teaspoon black pepper
¼ teaspoon onion flakes
1¾ pounds flank steak, whole

CONVERSATION STARTER:
What foreign language would you like to learn?

1. In a small bowl mix the canola oil, soy sauce, honey, vinegar, garlic powder, black pepper and onion flakes. Place the flank steak in a re-sealable plastic bag. Pour the marinade over. Place in the refrigerator at least 8 hours or up to 24 hours.
2. When ready to grill, pour the marinade off the meat into a small saucepan. (If you want to serve extra sauce with the meat place the marinade in a small pan and bring to a boil. Turn the heat down and simmer for 5 min.) Sprinkle the meat with coarse salt and fresh ground black pepper on both sides. This will help to form a savory crust on the steak.
3. Fold a paper towel into fourths. Sprinkle with olive oil and using your tongs go over the grill to oil it.
4. Score the meat four times down the middle by making 4 slits in the meat about ⅛ inch deep. Place the meat on the grill. Grill 6 min. per side.
5. Place the meat on a cutting board. Cover with aluminum foil to hold the heat in and to keep steak from drying out. Let rest about 10 min. Cut very thin slices across the grain and at a slight diagonal so the slices are wide.

Serve with: Creamy Horseradish Sauce page 170, Grilled Red and Green Peppers page 159, Grilled Creamy Potatoes page 175, Grilled Lemony Potatoes page 161 or Corn on the cob; broccoli and cauliflower; sautéed mushrooms; green salad.

Variations: Cut the meat into serving size strips and marinate. Grill for the same amount of time.

You can broil by putting the meat about 7 to 10 inches under the broiler element on a baking sheet. Pretty much follow the same instructions as for the Grill. If the meat is thicker lower the rack to the middle position.

This is a great taste for an inexpensive cut of meat. You always cook an inexpensive cut of meat on high heat when grilling. I find that it works much better. It is quick and delicious! Remember when cutting meat, whatever way the grain is going, cut the opposite way for a more tender piece of meat!

SLIDERS

Makes 12 sliders
Time: 20 minutes

Plan Ahead: Bake the hamburger buns ahead of time.
Cook bacon ahead of time.

1 pound hamburger, 80/15 mix, to make 12 slider-size 2-inch round hamburger patties
Coarse salt
Fresh ground black pepper
3 slices bacon
2 Tablespoons real maple syrup
1½ Tablespoons brown sugar
¼ cup mayonnaise
1 heaping Tablespoon chili sauce
4 teaspoons sweet BBQ sauce
1 teaspoon Worcestershire sauce
1 teaspoon sweet pickle juice
12 Slider Buns, 2½ inches round. (Hamburger bun recipe Half/Wheat, Half /White page 253)
½ cup Colby or Jack Cheese, grated
¼ cup arugula (optional)

1. Form the sliders into 2 inch patties. Season both sides generously with coarse salt and fresh ground black pepper.
2. Preheat the oven to 425°. Place the bacon on a small baking sheet and bake for 10 min. Drizzle the bacon with maple syrup and sprinkle with brown sugar. Bake 10 min. more. Remove the bacon to paper towels to soak up the extra grease.
3. Make the sauce: In a small bowl put the mayonnaise, chili sauce, sweet BBQ sauce, Worcestershire and sweet pickle juice. Mix. Set aside.
4. When the bacon is cool, stack them and cut into 4 equal pieces. You will have 12 small pieces of bacon. Set aside.
5. Turn the oven to broil. Place patties on a broiler pan or in a black iron skillet. Broil the sliders on the middle oven rack for 5 min., turn and place a piece of bacon on top, a teaspoon of grated cheese on top of the bacon. Broil until cooked through about another 4 min. Remove.
6. Cut the slider buns almost all the way through. Lay out on a baking sheet. Quickly run the buns under the broiler and toast until light brown.
7. Put a dab of sauce on the bottom bun and then a hamburger patty. Top with a piece of arugula and serve immediately.

Serve with: Potato Chips; Warm Orzo Salad with Chicken page 259, Spinach Salad page 265.

Variations: Grill the Sliders instead of broiling. Instead of making your own buns use my French Baguette page 242. Cut 2-inch rounds, 1 inch thick. Use Blue Cheese dressing on page 264 in place of the hamburger sauce or just sprinkle on dry blue cheese. Add chopped sautéed mushrooms and Gruyere cheese. Sauté some mushrooms, add a little Gruyere cheese to the mushrooms until it melts and spoon a little on each Slider.

Add Grilled Onions to the Slider: Melt 1 Tablespoon unsalted butter in a large skillet over medium heat. Add very thin slices of 1 red onion or 1 yellow onion. Cook slowly 15 to 20 min. stirring occasionally until the onions are caramelized. Sprinkle with coarse salt and fresh ground black pepper to taste.

Mini Sliders for a party: Cut the hamburger bun dough 1½ inches round. Make the hamburger 1 inch round.

One of my favorite things to eat on Grill Night is a Slider. Especially when you serve them hot just out of the broiler or off the grill. These are yummy !!! Enjoy.

GRILLED BALSAMIC HONEY GLAZED SALMON

Serves 4
Time: 10 minutes

4 Salmon fillets, about 4 oz. each
Coarse salt
Fresh ground black pepper
⅓ cup balsamic vinegar*
¼ cup honey

****One of my favorite Balsamic Vinegars is "Cherry Wood Aged Balsamic". You can find it at a quality food store. But use whatever you have. Any kind will work.***

1. Heat the grill to medium high.
2. Layer two large sheets of aluminum foil and fold in the edges to make "sides". Place the salmon fillets on the foil sheets. Season lightly with coarse salt and fresh ground black pepper. (Season both sides if the fillets have no skin on them.)
3. In a small bowl mix the vinegar and honey together. Save about ⅓ of the sauce in another bowl to serve along side the grilled salmon.
4. Place the salmon fillets on the grill, cover, and cook 4 min. Brush with balsamic/honey mixture. Cover, grill 1 min. Turn salmon over and brush with more sauce. Cover, grill another minute. Continue to baste the salmon until the fish flakes easily when tested with a fork, 4 to 6 min. per ½ inch thickness. Serve with reserved sauce.

Serve with: Creamy Grilled Potatoes page 175, Bruschetta page 52, Fresh Green Beans page 213.

I love balsamic vinegar and I love honey! When I put the two together it was magic. This is one of my favorite ways to grill salmon. Nothing gets easier than this. xo

FARMHOUSE GRILLED PORTERHOUSE WITH ARUGULA

Serves 4
Time: 40 minutes

3 to 4 Porterhouse Steak, 1 inch thick. One steak per person, room temperature
Coarse salt
Fresh ground black pepper
½ cup olive oil
5 cloves garlic, crushed
2 teaspoons dried thyme or 2 sprigs, fresh
1 teaspoon dried rosemary or 1 sprig, fresh
4 cups baby arugula, rinsed
2 cups red grape tomatoes, rinsed
2 cups yellow grape tomatoes, rinsed
Balsamic vinegar

1. Place steaks on a baking sheet and sprinkle both sides with coarse salt and fresh ground black pepper. Let sit at room temperature while you prepare the tomatoes and preheat the BBQ to high.
2. Heat olive oil and garlic in a medium size fry pan over low heat, about 6 min. or until the garlic begins to color and you can smell the aroma. Add thyme and rosemary. Cook 1 min. Add tomatoes. Cover and cook 5 min. Turn off the heat.
3. On 4 dinner plates, place one cup arugula each.
4. Oil the BBQ grill by pouring some olive oil on a folded paper towel and using your tongs to run paper towel over the grate. Place the steaks on the grill over high heat for 3 min. per side. Remove from heat and place on a platter. Cover with foil and let rest 10 min.
5. Pour the juices from the steaks into the tomato mixture and warm it up.
6. Place the steaks on top of the plated arugula and pour the warm olive oil/tomato mixture evenly over the steaks. Sprinkle each plate with a little coarse salt and fresh ground black pepper. Drizzle with balsamic vinegar and serve immediately.

Serve with: Lemony Red Potatoes page 161, Beer Bread page 247, Spinach with Parmesan page 211, Butternut Squash Rolls page 243.

Variations: You can broil by putting the meat about 7 to 10 inches under the broiler element on a baking sheet. Pretty much follow the same instructions as for the Grill. If the meat is thicker lower the rack to the middle position.

I love this steak. I love that you can serve it just the way it is without any sides. This kind of eating makes me happy!

CREAMY HORSERADISH SAUCE FOR STEAKS

Serves 6
Time: 3 minutes

¼ cup heavy cream
¼ cup prepared horseradish
½ teaspoon coarse salt
¼ teaspoon fresh ground black pepper

Whip the cream in a small bowl until thickened. Fold in the horseradish, salt and pepper. Keep cool in the refrigerator until ready to serve, up to an hour.

Serve with: Grilled or broiled steaks. Prime Rib, Fillet Mignon.

I love good horseradish. This is a great one!

FOOD NANNY FILLET MIGNON

Serves 4
Time: 10 minutes

Plan Ahead: Let seasoned steaks sit out for 30 min. at room temperature.

4 1-inch to 1½ inches thick center cut Black Angus beef tenderloin steak (Fillet Mignon) room temperature
1 Tablespoon coarse salt
2 Tablespoons crushed peppercorns
1 Tablespoon canola oil
4 Tablespoons cold butter

Sauce (optional)
4 Tablespoons cold butter
¼ cup shallot, minced
¼ cup Merlot or red wine
¼ cup beef broth
¾ cup heavy cream
1 Tablespoon parsley, fresh or dried, minced

Fillet Mignon:

1. Pat steaks dry with a paper towel. Place on a platter or baking sheet. Season each steak on both sides with coarse salt and crushed peppercorns. (Or use your pepper grinder on the largest grind.) Be sure to let seasoned steaks sit out for 30 min. at room temperature.
2. Pre-heat oven to 500°. When oven is ready continue.
3. If NOT making the sauce, preheat a cast iron pan over high heat. (I don't like the way this sauce turns out in a cast iron skillet. It seems muddy….) If you ARE making sauce, choose a non-cast iron, oven-safe pan. The pan is ready when you sprinkle with a few drops of water and it sizzles. If the pan is smoking turn down the heat. Add canola oil. Place the meat in the pan and sear 3 min. per side. Set your timer.
4. Quickly place 1 Tablespoon cold butter on top of each steak and move pan into the hot oven on the middle rack and continue cooking steaks without turning, 4 more min. for medium rare. Set your timer. Remove from oven. Place the pan on top of the stove.
5. If not making with sauce, serve immediately. If making sauce, quickly remove steaks to a platter and cover with foil to keep warm.

Sauce:

1. To the pan drippings on top of the stove add, 2 Tablespoons butter, ¼ cup minced shallot. Stir until shallots are browned about 3 to 4 min.
2. Add Merlot, or any red wine or cooking wine and beef broth. Stir, scraping up any brown bits. Boil over moderately low heat until reduced to a syrupy consistency.
3. Add heavy cream and any meat juices accumulated on the platter where the meat is resting. Boil down to half. Swirl in 2 to 3 more Tablespoons cold butter and the minced parsley.
4. Season to taste with coarse salt and fresh ground pepper.
5. Cut steaks into thin slices or serve whole and pour the sauce over meat.

Serve with: Baked Potato, Fried Potato Rounds page 219 or steamed red potatoes. Broccoli or brussel sprouts and carrots. Grilled Garlic Parmesan Bread page 173.

I found that an iron skillet is the best for frying steak and hamburgers at home. I have experienced really good luck finishing off my steaks in the oven. The steaks seem to come out perfect every time. If you have a steak 2 inches thick, you will need to allow for more time. You will have fun serving these delicious steaks anytime of the year! xo

Meatless
GRILLED GARLIC PARMESAN BREAD

Makes 12 Slices
Time: 10 minutes

12 slices (1 loaf) French or Artisan Bread, sliced ½ inch thick

½ cup (1 stick) unsalted butter, softened
½ cup Parmesan cheese, grated
½ teaspoon garlic salt
½ teaspoon dried parsley
1 teaspoon dried oregano
1 teaspoon dried basil
Coarse salt and fresh ground black pepper, to taste

Slice the bread. Blend the butter, cheese, garlic salt, parsley, oregano and basil together. Spread on both sides of the bread. Grill over medium heat for 3 min. per side until you see the grill marks or when the cheese is melted. Serve hot.

Serve with: Anything you are grilling!

Variations: Use my French Baguettes page 242. Delicious without the cheese. The garlic salt can be optional.

Kids and adults love warm garlic bread. It's great for any BBQ Dinner.

CONVERSATION STARTER:
What foreign country would you like to visit?

RIB EYE SHISH KABOB WITH GARLIC MARINADE

Serves 4
Time: 30 minutes

4 14-inch metal skewers
2 ¼-inch Boneless Rib Eye Steaks, about 1 pound, cut into 16pieces
1 green bell pepper, cut into 8 pieces
16 white button mushrooms
8 red grape tomatoes
8 yellow grape tomatoes
½ yellow onion
3 garlic cloves, chopped
3 Tablespoons olive oil
Coarse salt
Freshly ground black pepper
2 to 3 fresh or dried herbs of your choice: rosemary, oregano, marjoram or thyme

1. Season the steaks with coarse salt and fresh ground black pepper to taste. Cut each steak into eight 1 inch by 1 inch pieces per steak. Cut around any fat. Set aside.
2. Cut the green pepper into 8 equal pieces. With a wet paper towel wipe off the fresh mushrooms. Rinse the tomatoes. Cut the onion into 8 pieces.
3. In a small bowl combine the garlic, olive oil, salt and pepper with your choice of herbs, ¼ teaspoon each. Mix. This is the marinade.
4. Place the meat and veggies in a dish and pour the marinade over top and toss with your hands to coat. Take one skewer at a time and start with a piece of meat, green pepper, mushroom, red or yellow tomatoes, onion, then repeat 4 times. Start over with another skewer.
5. Preheat the BBQ grill to medium high heat. Take a paper towel and fold it into fourths. Drizzle with olive oil and run it over the grate to oil it. Place the skewers on top of the BBQ grate and grill turning often for 10-12 min. Cover the grill every time after you turn the skewers. Serve immediately.

Serve with: Grilled Potatoes with Cream page 175 or Grilled Red Potatoes page 161. Lettuce Wraps page 210. Grilled Garlic Parmesan Bread page 173. Fresh broccoli and cauliflower. Crusty Bread.

Variations: Toss meat and veggies with olive oil, coarse salt and freshly ground black pepper.

Chicken Variation: Use 1 lb. boneless/skinless chicken cut up, and marinate in a re-sealable bag with the following sauce at least 2 hours before grilling.

Sauce: ¼ cup soy sauce; 2 Tablespoons lemon juice; 2 cloves minced garlic; 1 teaspoon fresh minced ginger; ¼ teaspoon dried ginger; ⅛ teaspoon dry mustard. Reserve marinade. Use the same veggies as above only adding in green or red bell pepper and fresh pineapple chunks. While grilling brush with marinade and grill for 15-20 min. turning often. Serve over Jasmine Rice page 218.

Often times Shish Kabob is a great choice when you are not in the mood for a big steak. It is also very cost effective. You can feed 4 adults with 2 great steaks. I like to use good steak for my Shish Kabob so that every bite of meat is delicious. This is a nice way to welcome summer! xo

Meatless

CREAMY GRILLED POTATOES

Serves 4
Time: 20 minutes

4 Russet potatoes, peeled and sliced
Table Salt
Fresh ground black pepper
4 Tablespoons butter
½ cup heavy cream
Aluminum foil

1. Peel potatoes, cut in half lengthwise and place cut side down. Make 5 lengthwise cuts. Cut in half lengthwise again to make strips of potatoes.
2. Measure out two 14-inch pieces of foil. Double them up. Place the strips from 2 potatoes in the middle of the foil. Dot with 2 Tablespoons butter, salt and pepper. Pour ¼ cup heavy cream over top. Bring the long sides of the foil up and fold over 2 times to seal in the potatoes. Fold the two ends up.
3. Repeat with the same process with the other 2 potatoes.
4. Place on a grill that has been preheated to medium high. Cook for 10 min., turn and cook another 10 min. Be careful when you open the foil to check and see if the potatoes are done, the escaping steam could burn you.
5. Serve immediately right out of the foil.

Serve with: Beef, chicken, fish, grilled veggies.

They are quick and easy and a nice change that goes well with grilled meats.

CONVERSATION STARTER:
What name would you choose for yourself?

BBQ CHICKEN SALAD

Serves 4
Time: 20 minutes

4 small boneless/skinless chicken breasts, grilled and sliced
Coarse salt
Fresh ground black pepper
½ cup BBQ Sauce, plus additional for adding to the salad (your favorite kind)
6 cups Romaine lettuce, sliced or torn
1 tomato, diced
1 cup corn, (fresh or frozen), cooked
1 cup black beans, drained and rinsed
1 avocado, chopped
¼ cup cilantro, chopped
¼ cup Ranch Dressing
1 lime, cut into wedges
Tortilla strips for topping

1. With a wet paper towel wipe off the chicken. Season with salt and pepper. Turn the grill to medium high heat.
2. Oil the grate. Take a paper towel and fold it into a square. Drizzle with oil, using your tongs run it over the top of the grate. Grill the chicken 4-6 min. per side, basting the chicken with BBQ sauce as you go. Let the chicken cool a bit and slice.
3. In a medium size bowl combine the lettuce, tomato, corn, black beans, avocado, cilantro and ranch dressing. Mix. Add in the warm sliced chicken and more BBQ sauce, to your liking. Squeeze lime juice onto the salad and top with Tortilla Strips. Serve.

Serve with: Grilled Garlic Parmesan Bread page 173.

*This salad is so delicious.
It's a great option for Grill Night.
Lisa made it for us one summer day.
It was perfect. Paired with my grilled herb bread it is fabulous!*

3 DAY BRISKET

Serves 4-6
Time: 3 days

Plan Ahead: You need 3 days to make this Brisket.
Make the BBQ Sauce ahead.

1 3 lb. brisket. Have any butcher cut it that size for you

Marinade:

- **1 4-oz. bottle liquid smoke, mesquite flavor**
- **1¼ teaspoons salt**
- **1 teaspoon onion salt**
- **1 teaspoon garlic salt**

BBQ Sauce:

- **3 Tablespoons brown sugar**
- **1 cup ketchup**
- **¾ cup water**
- **2 teaspoons celery seed**
- **4 Tablespoons Worcestershire Sauce**
- **3 teaspoons dry mustard**
- **3½ teaspoons fresh ground black pepper**

1st Day: Put the brisket in a gallon size re-sealable plastic bag. Do not cut off the fat. Mix the liquid smoke with the salt. Pour over the meat. Toss and turn the bag to make sure all the meat is covered. Place the bag in a baking dish and refrigerate over night.

2nd Day: Place the meat fat side up in a small baking dish. Pour the marinade from the bag on top and sprinkle the meat on both sides with onion and garlic salt. Cover with foil. Bake for 4½ hours at 250°. While still hot drain the marinade off the brisket. Let the meat cool down. Put the meat back into the pan and refrigerate overnight.

3rd Day: Prepare the BBQ Sauce - in a medium size sauce pan add the brown sugar, ketchup, water, celery seed, Worcestershire, dry mustard and black pepper. Bring to a boil, turn down the heat and let simmer for 20 min.

When ready to serve the meat, take it directly from the refrigerator. Cut most of the fat off the top. Slice the meat very thin, cutting across the grain. Pour the BBQ sauce over the meat. Cover with foil. Bake for 30 min. at 350°. Serve.

Serve with: Corn on the cob. Baked Beans page 226. Baked Potatoes, Corn Salad page 268. Macaroni Salad page 222. Orange Muffin Rolls page 235.

I have been making this brisket for years.
You don't have to be serving an Army to enjoy great brisket!
It is easy just as long as you know when you are going to serve it. I think it is the best recipe ever, so does my family.
Texas knows how to do brisket!
I learned how to do this while living there.
This is yummy!!!

BBQ CHEESE CRUSTED STEAK

Serves 6
Time: 20 minutes

Plan Ahead: Have the butcher cut Top Sirloin ¼ inch thick. Set the meat out 30 min. in advance.

1½ lbs. Top Sirloin, 4 pieces, cut ¼ inch thick,
⅓ cup olive oil
1¼ cup panko bread crumbs
1¼ cup Romano cheese, grated
1 teaspoon dried basil
¼ teaspoon coarse salt
¼ teaspoon fresh ground black pepper

1. Let the meat come to room temperature for 30 min.
2. Measure the olive oil into a pie pan. In another pie pan, mix the bread crumbs, cheese, basil and salt and pepper together.
3. Dip each piece of meat into the olive oil, then into the bread crumb and cheese mixture. Use your fingers to pat down the mixture so it will stay on as much as possible. Place each piece on a platter.
4. Prepare the grill. Turn the heat up to high. Fold a paper towel into a square and pour olive oil onto the paper towel. Use your tongs to run the oil over the grill. Place the breaded steaks onto the hot grill and grill 5 min per side. Serve immediately.

Serve with: Linguine with Butter & Parmesan page 227. Grilled Lemon Potatoes page 161. Brown Rice page 217 and vegetables.

Variations: You can broil by putting the meat about 7 to 10 inches under the broiler element on a baking sheet. Follow the same instructions as for the Grill. If the meat is thicker lower the rack to the middle position.

*This is my version of something I ate in Italy that was so yummy!!! Everyone has their own version of it.
This steak is crunchy and delicious. The cheese just makes it.
It is quick and so easy to make for a crowd.
My family loves this meal! Enjoy!!*

Meatless GRILLED PINEAPPLE SALSA

Serves 12
Time: 30 minutes

1 fresh pineapple cut into ½ inch rounds, grilled then diced
4 yellow tomatoes, diced
4 red tomatoes, diced
1 Anaheim pepper, diced
3 Tablespoons red onion, diced
1 Tablespoon olive oil
1½ Tablespoon adobo chipotle sauce
2 teaspoons coarse salt
Fresh ground black pepper
Cilantro leaves to taste

1. With a sharp knife cut the top off a large pineapple. Cut off the bottom. With a sharp knife remove the pineapple skin from the sides.
2. Start from the top and cut ½ inch rounds all the way down the pineapple. Cut out the middle (the core) of each round. Brush the grill lightly with oil.
3. Place the pineapple on a cleaned, medium hot grill. Grill until you see the grill marks. Turn and grill the other side.
4. Lay the pineapple out on a cutting board. Dice into small pieces. Put the pineapple into a medium size bowl. Clean off the cutting board. Dice the tomatoes and peppers on the cutting board and add to the bowl.
5. Mix the olive oil, adobo chipotle sauce, salt and pepper in a different bowl. Add to the rest of the ingredients. Stir in cilantro leaves to taste.

Serve with: This Salsa is especially great on fish tacos. Spoon it over any kind of fish you are grilling, broiling, baking or pan-frying. It is a perfect accompaniment with rice. Serve with tortilla chips as well.

Angie shared this recipe with me at the "Food Feud Cook-off." She entered this salsa and got a prize for it! If you are a pineapple lover like me this will be a treat for you. I love what the grill does to the pineapple flavor.

GRILLED SALMON

Serves 4
Time: 20 minutes

4 salmon fillets, about 4 oz. each
2 Tablespoons butter, softened
Lemon pepper
Brown Sugar

1. Heat the grill to medium high.
2. Layer two large sheets of aluminum foil and fold in the edges to make "sides." Place the salmon fillets on the foil sheets. Spread a thin coating of the butter on the fillets. Sprinkle on a dusting of the lemon pepper. Make a few shallow slits in each fillet and sprinkle on the brown sugar.
3. Place the salmon fillets on the grill, cover and cook 4–6 min. per ½-inch thickness, or until the fish flakes eaily when tested with a fork.
   Serve immediately.

Serve with: Grilled Pineapple (see above), Creamy Grilled Potatoes page 175. Jasmine Rice or Jasmine Quinoa page 218.

Everyone loves this salmon!!!

THIN STEAK WITH BÉARNAISE SAUCE

Serves 4
Time: 20 minutes

Plan Ahead: Make the sauce up to 1 hour ahead. Keep warm.

The Vinegar Mixture for Béarnaise sauce:
1½ Tablespoons red wine vinegar
1½ Tablespoons white wine or cooking wine
¼ teaspoon dried tarragon
1½ teaspoons shallot, minced
⅛ teaspoon coarse salt
⅛ teaspoon fresh ground black pepper

Béarnaise Sauce:
2 egg yolks
2 teaspoons Vinegar Mixture
¼ teaspoon salt
⅛ teaspoon cayenne pepper
1 Tablespoon hot water
¾ cup (1½ sticks) unsalted cold butter, directly from the refrigerator

Steak:
4 - ¼ inch thick pieces Top Sirloin Steak, 9 inches long, 4 inches wide; about 2 lbs.
½ cup olive oil
4 medium size garlic cloves, crushed
Coarse Salt
Fresh ground black pepper

The Vinegar Mixture for Béarnaise sauce:
Boil the vinegar, wine, tarragon, salt and pepper in a small saucepan until the liquid has reduced to about 2 teaspoons. This will only take 1 or 2 min. Let cool. Set aside.

Béarnaise Sauce:
Before beginning the Béarnaise sauce have the butter ready to go, the salt and cayenne measured out and hot water ready.

1. In a 1 qt. saucepan stir 2 egg yolks slightly and add 2 teaspoons Vinegar Mixture stirring vigorously with a wooden spoon until well combined. (No heat yet)
2. Add ¼ cup unsalted butter and turn the heat to very low and heat, stirring constantly, until butter is melted.
3. Quickly add salt, cayenne and hot water. Add an additional ¼ cup butter stirring vigorously until butter is melted and sauce starts to thicken.
4. Add the final ¼ cup butter and stir until melted and sauce is thick and creamy. Be sure butter melts slowly: this gives eggs time to cook and thicken the sauce without curdling. Serve hot or keep warm.

Steak:

1. Let the steak come to room temperature.
2. Mix the olive oil and crushed garlic together. Spread 2 Tablespoons of the olive oil/garlic mixture evenly over both sides of each steak. Use up all 8 tablespoons for 4 steaks. Season generously with coarse salt and fresh ground black pepper on both sides.
3. Preheat the grill to high. Take one paper towel and fold it into fourths. Sprinkle with olive oil. Using your tongs run it over the grill to oil it.
4. Lay the steaks on top of grill and turn after 3 min. Grill 3 more min. Take off the grill and cover to keep warm. Let sit a few minutes and serve with the Béarnaise sauce.

Serve with: Grilled mushrooms, Fried Potato Rounds page 219, or baked potatoes and Grilled Red and Green Bell peppers page 159. Fresh Green Beans page 213.

When we are in France we always order this meal. Nothing is better than homemade Béarnaise sauce, which I have made so easy for you to make.

Traditionally Sunday

Often times I hear from other families that Sunday is the only day
of the week they sit down together as a family.
It has been proven that if we can do this at least 3 times during the week we will have stronger families. Dinnertime is a protection that helps to keep our families together.
Sunday is no exception. It is an important day for restoration – a day for relaxing with family and friends over good food. We need this for our mental health.
It's fun on this day to enjoy traditional recipes that have been handed down from generations past. My husband and I told stories about growing up in the "old days" over dinner. We shared our passions and our dreams. We talked of our parents, grandparents and siblings. We enjoyed the food and the company
because we had more time to devote to the dinner meal.
I made Sunday a tradition for serving homemade rolls hot out of the oven.
No matter how elegant your home or how humble your surroundings,
all that matters is that you can prepare simple hot food and share it with those you love most. Make it a Tradition in your home to never let go of your family values and forever hold on to each other - because that IS all that matters.
Try making some of my homemade rolls or bread and count how many smiling faces you see when you serve them hot - right out of the oven!

The Food Nanny. xo.

SUNDAY **TRADITIONS**

Meatless

ROSEMARY LAMB CHOPS

Serves 2
Time: 25 minutes

4 lamb chops - 1inch to 1½ inches thick

Marinade:
¼ cup extra virgin olive oil
2 cloves garlic, minced
1 Tablespoon fresh rosemary leaves, chopped
½ lemon, juiced
1 teaspoon coarse salt
½ teaspoon fresh ground black pepper

About Lamb: Lamb has long been overshadowed by its bigger beefier competition, beef! I wish more Americans would try this wonderful meat.
We have lamb being raised here in America that compares with the Australian lamb which has been king for years.
Leaner cuts of lamb are very good on cholesterol and comparable to chicken. Lamb is becoming more tender than ever and without the gamey flavor your grandmother used to cook. Give it a try - you are going to love it!

1. Rub chops all over with oil, garlic, rosemary and lemon juice. Let sit for 30 min.
2. Preheat the oven to 400°.
3. Place a medium skillet over medium high heat for a few minutes and then brown the chops in the pan. Cook for 3 min. on each side. Sprinkle with coarse salt and fresh ground black pepper.
4. Place the chops on a small baking sheet or use the same pan if ovenable, and finish in the oven about 7 to 10 min. or until desired doneness.
5. Serve with Mint Apple Jelly or Red Jalapeno Mint Jelly.

Serve with: Rice pilaf, Baked potato or Linguine page 227. Broccoli and zucchini chopped, sauted in olive oil, seasoned with coarse salt and fresh ground black pepper. French Baguettes page 242.

This is an easy lamb chop recipe with little fuss. It is so delicious! I am always looking for quick lamb recipes that make me happy and keep me healthy.

ASIAN FRIED DUMPLINGS

Serves 6
Time: 45 minutes

4 cups green cabbage, sliced very thin
½ cup yellow onion, minced
⅓ cup carrots, chopped
2 teaspoons freshly grated ginger (optional)
½ pound ground pork
⅓ cup scallions, minced
1 teaspoon teriyaki sauce
3 cloves fresh garlic, minced
Coarse salt and black pepper
¼ cup sunflower oil
2 egg whites
40 store-bought 3-inch round dumpling wrappers

Dipping Sauce:
3 Tablespoons soy sauce
1 Tablespoon rice vinegar
¼ Teaspoon sugar
Mix together. Set aside.
Garnish with chives and sesame seeds (optional)

1. Heat 1 Tablespoon sunflower oil in a large skillet or Wok over high heat. Stir fry the cabbage until soft about 3 to 4 min. Season with coarse salt. Remove to a platter.
2. Add another teaspoon of oil to the pan and sauté the onions, carrots and ginger (if using) until soft. Season lightly with coarse salt. Add to cabbage.
3. Add an additional 2 teaspoons oil and sauté the ground pork with scallions, teriyaki sauce and minced garlic until the pork is cooked through. Season with coarse salt and ground black pepper to taste. Let cool for 5 min.
4. Combine the cabbage, onions, scallions, carrots and seasoned pork in a food processor or blender and coarsely chop.
5. Working with one dumpling wrapper at a time, moisten edge with egg whites using your finger then place about 2 teaspoons filling in center. Fold in half to form a "taco." Press edges to seal well and place on a baking sheet with waxed paper or foil so they will not stick while you get the frying oil ready.
6. Heat 1 Tablespoon oil in frying pan over medium high heat. Place 6 or 8 dumplings in the oil at one time and sautè on both sides for about 1 min. Place on a platter and cover to keep warm until all the dumplings are fried. (You can fry all the dumplings to this point and steam them later before serving.)
7. To steam dumplings: In a frying pan add ¼ cup water to a small batch of 6 dumplings. Cover the pan with a lid and steam for about 2 min. May do larger batches depending on the size of your pan.
8. Arrange the fried dumplings onto a platter and scatter on the minced chives and sesame seeds, if desired.
9. Pour dipping sauce into individual ramekins for each person to dip their dumpling into or serve soy sauce in a small bowl and let each person spoon on what they desire.

Serve with: Brown rice and broccoli.

Variations: May use ground turkey or chicken instead of pork.

They are expensive to buy in a Chinese restaurant and these taste just like the restaurant ones.

ROASTED LEG OF LAMB

Serves 6 to 8
Time: 3½ hours

Plan Ahead: Pressure cook in 50 – 60 minutes.

4-5 lb. boneless leg of lamb
Olive Oil
Coarse salt
Fresh ground black pepper
4 large garlic cloves
Fresh rosemary, oregano and thyme - a few sprigs of each or 1 teaspoon of each dried
2 red onions, peeled and quartered
2 cups carrots peeled, sliced diagonally
1 red potato per person, washed, skins left on
1 bunch fresh asparagus washed, stem end removed
1½ cups chicken stock, divided

Prepare the gravy:
4 Tablespoons flour
3 Tablespoons butter
¾ cup cream and additional butter

1 jar mint apple jelly or jalapeno mint apple jelly

Preheat the oven to 425°.

1. Pat the lamb dry with paper towels. Rub meat with olive oil. Generously add salt and pepper. Crush the garlic and the spices (fresh or dry) and spread over top of lamb. Place in a roaster or 9x13 inch pan. Pour in ½ cup chicken stock.
2. Stir the prepared onions, carrots and potatoes together and drizzle with olive oil and salt and pepper. Place the veggies around the roast.
3. Arrange the asparagus in single layer on a small sheet pan, drizzle with olive oil and season with salt and pepper. Set aside until later.
4. Place the lamb and veggies, except the asparagus, in the oven and roast at 425° uncovered for 20 min. Turn the heat down to 325°, cover loosely with aluminum foil and bake for 2½ to 3 hours.
5. The last 15 min. of baking put the asparagus in the oven to roast, uncovered.
6. Remove the roast and veggies from the oven and place the roast on a cutting board to rest covered with aluminum foil. Remove the veggies to a platter – for not more than 15 min. Cover to keep veggies warm.
7. Place the roaster or metal pan on top of the stove turning up the heat to medium high. Get all the good stuff off the sides of the pan. Add 4 Tablespoons flour and 3 Tablespoons butter to the liquid. Stir for 2 min. with a whisk.
8. Add remaining chicken stock. Stir until slightly thickened. Add cream and additional butter. Bring just to boiling. Adjust for texture; too thick, add more cream or stock; too thin, and add more flour. Turn off the heat. Adjust seasoning with salt and pepper. Check the asparagus.
9. Slice the meat across the grain, nice and thin. Place the meat in the middle of a platter and arrange the veggies around it. Place the asparagus over top of the carrots, onions and potatoes to make a beautiful presentation. Drizzle on a little of the sauce over all and pour the rest of the sauce in a dish. Serve immediately with mint apple jelly or jalapeno mint apple jelly on the side.

Serve with: German Brown Bread page 233. Orange Muffin Rolls page 235. Strawberry Days Salad page 267.

I served this recipe for Easter Dinner many times. Rachelle came last year to eat with our family. It was so memorable having her here with us. It is a treat and well worth the effort. Everyone loves it even people who think they don't like lamb! Not every recipe has to be fast. Memorable meals take longer.

DELICIOUS MOIST TURKEY EVERY TIME

Preparation 10 minutes
Cook Time: Depends on size of the turkey

1 turkey, 16 lbs. or more
Coarse salt
Fresh ground black pepper
¼ cup (or more as needed) fresh or dried sage, crumbled
½ cup vegetable shortening or lard. More as needed
Cheese cloth, 2 thicknesses thick to fit over top of your turkey

1. Thaw the turkey.
2. After thawing, run it under cold water and take out everything inside from both ends including the neck end. Pat the turkey dry with paper towels inside and out. Place onto a wire rack in a roasting pan. (Wash your hands with soap and water after handling the turkey.)
3. Generously season with coarse salt and fresh ground black pepper, fresh or dried crumbled sage. Pat down the spices with your hands. (Wash your hands with soap and water.)
4. Melt the shortening in a small pan on top of the stove over low heat, or in a microwaveable bowl in microwave. Let cool for a minute. Dip the cheese cloth into the shortening and let it soak in completely. Squeeze with your hands to remove excess from the cloth. Drape the cloth over the turkey and pat down.
5. Cover and bake as directed on package. Sounds crazy, I know!

Serve with: Liz's Crescent Dinner Rolls page 251. Mashed potatoes with corn (middle of) page 199.

I have tried so many brines and ways to get a moist turkey for Thanksgiving. Nothing was ever worth the effort! It was Thanksgiving in 2 days and I was trying to decide what to try this year. Melissa, a fellow passenger, told me she uses her Grandma's recipe and said you might not like the sounds of it, but if you try it you will eat the best, most moist turkey ever! I tried it!!!! I will never go back! This is it...and it's this easy. Makes the BEST gravy too!

CONVERSATION STARTER:

Do you know which side of the plate the fork goes on? The knife? The spoon?

EASY WHITE WINE SUNDAY CHICKEN

Serves 4
Time: 20 minutes

2 chicken breasts - bone in, cut in half
2 chicken thighs
Coarse salt
Fresh ground black pepper
1 shallot, chopped
Olive oil
½ cup white wine or cooking wine
½ cup chicken broth
3 sprigs fresh thyme
3 Tablespoons cold butter

Preheat oven to 450°.

1. Wipe off the chicken with a wet paper towel. Leave the skin on. Cut the chicken breasts in half with a sharp knife. Season generously with coarse salt and fresh ground black pepper.
2. In a medium size oven-proof frying pan over medium high heat lay the chicken pieces, skin side down and fry for 4 to 5 min. on each side until golden brown. The skin will help create the fat. Do not burn the chicken; turn down the heat if you need to.
3. Place the frying pan into the 450° oven and bake for 10 min. Take out of the oven with 2 hot pads together because the handle will be very hot. Place on top of the stove. Move the hot pan to the back. Remove the chicken to a plate. Cover to keep warm. Let the pan cool down a bit.
4. Using a metal spoon, spoon out all but about 2 teaspoons of the remaining grease. You may not have much to spoon out. Leave the nice little brown bits that will make the sauce taste great.
5. Turn the heat to low and add the chopped shallot to the fat. You may need to add a little olive oil. Sauté until soft. Pour in white wine, chicken broth and fresh thyme sprigs. Stir. Reduce to about ¾ cup over medium heat.
6. Stir in the cold butter. Check your seasoning. Add extra coarse salt and fresh ground black pepper as needed. Add the chicken back into the sauce along with the juice that is left on the plate. Let the chicken simmer for 1 min. If you are concerned that the chicken is not done, check it with a meat thermometer. Breasts-160° internal temperature; thighs-175°.
7. Remove the chicken to a plate and pour the sauce over top the chicken. Serve immediately.

Serve with: Linguini with Parmesan page 227, Cauliflower, asparagus page 215 or sautéed fresh summer squash. Great with mashed or baked potato.

Variations: Use whatever chicken with bone-in that you have. The bone-in will make for a nice sauce. Try using Champagne in place of wine… really good too. Use white grape juice in place of white wine.

This is a fast recipe that makes a nice statement. I always feel really fancy when I make this simple little dish in my farmhouse kitchen. This is the way I love to eat. It is so easy especially when you are cooking for 4. It tastes so good! xo

FOOD NANNY BEEF BOURGUIGNON

Serves 6
Time: 3 hours

1½ lb. boneless Top Sirloin cut into 2 inch cubes
Coarse Salt
Fresh ground black pepper
2 Tablespoons olive oil
1 Tablespoon butter
¼ lb. thick-cut bacon, diced
3 cloves garlic, minced
2 cups red wine or Pomegranate juice
1 bay leaf
2 sprigs fresh thyme, or 1 teaspoon dried
1½ cups beef broth
1 Tablespoon tomato paste
¼ teaspoon coarse salt
¼ teaspoon fresh ground pepper
4 fresh carrots peeled, sliced ½ inch thick

To make the Roux:
⅓ cup flour
4 Tablespoons unsalted butter at room temperature
8 oz. pearl onions, frozen and skinned
1 Tablespoon butter
1 Tablespoon sugar
¼ teaspoon salt
1 cup water
½ lb. white mushrooms, quartered
1 teaspoon unsalted butter
1 teaspoon olive oil
Salt to taste
Fresh parsley
⅓ cup grated Gruyere (optional)

To Prepare the meat

1. Dry meat off with paper towels or the meat will not brown well. Sprinkle cubes of meat on both sides with coarse salt and fresh ground black pepper.
2. In a large fry pan, stew pot, or Dutch oven brown the meat one minute per side in 2 Tablespoons olive oil and 1 Tablespoon butter over high heat. Remove, place on a plate as you finish browning. Repeat until all the meat is browned. Set aside.
3. In the same pan sauté bacon until crisp. Remove with a slotted spoon. Set aside on paper towels to drain. Drain all the grease from the pan except 1 Tablespoon.
4. Add minced garlic and sauté until you can just smell it.
5. Add 2 cups red wine, cooking wine or Pomegranate juice, bay leaf and thyme. Bring to a medium boil until all the crisp bits have been scraped from the bottom and sides of pan. Boil gently for 3 min.
6. Add 1½ cups beef broth, tomato paste, salt and pepper. Cook gently for 4 to 5 min.
7. Return the beef and bacon to the pan. Add sliced carrots.
8. To make roux: mix together ⅓ cup flour and 4 Tablespoons unsalted butter (at room temperature) with a spoon. Slowly stir this roux into the meat, stirring constantly. Bring to a boil, cook for 2 min. and turn off heat.
9. Heat oven to 300°.
10. Cover pan with tight lid or foil and place in the oven for 2½ to 3 hours. Add water or more wine to thin down the sauce if desired.
11. The last 40 min. of cooking stir in the prepared pearl onions and white mushrooms.

To prepare the onions and mushrooms

- In a small saucepan, cook the onions in 1 Tablespoon butter, 1 Tablespoon sugar, ¼ teaspoon salt and 1 cup water until onions are browned and liquid is evaporated - about 5 min. Set aside.
- Wipe out the pan. Add in 1 teaspoon unsalted butter, 1 teaspoon olive oil, the quartered mushrooms with a little salt and sauté until mushroom liquid is gone and mushrooms are light brown.

To present this fabulous dish:
Remove the bay leaf and thyme if desired. May be served in the same stew pot or Dutch oven if desired. Sprinkle with tiny bits of fresh parsley and a small amount of grated Gruyere cheese.

Serve with: Food Nanny Mashed Potatoes with Corn on page 199.

I can't help but think of Julia Child because I learned so much from her. This amazing traditional French meal is one of my favorites.

Meatless YAMISTA - GREEK STUFFED PEPPERS AND TOMATOES

Serves 6
Time: 1½ hours

1 small bunch shallots (green onions), finely chopped
½ green bell pepper, chopped
½ cup of mixed fresh aromatic herbs leaves, chopped: dill, parsley, & mint
1 small peeled zucchini
1 small red onion, skin removed
5 medium size tomatoes, peeled
2 fresh garlic cloves, minced
1 cup long grain white rice, uncooked
5 medium size green bell peppers
3 cups beef or chicken stock - plus ¼ cup
½ cup Extra Virgin olive oil - plus ¼ cup
Coarse salt
White pepper to taste
2 large Russet potatoes, cut lengthwise in half, then divided into 3 slices on each side. 6 slices in all.

For the Stuffing:

1. In a medium size bowl mix the shallots, green pepper and fresh herbs. Grate the zucchini, onion and 1 tomato into the same bowl.
2. Slice the garlic cloves in half lengthwise and with the tip of your paring knife flick out the little center part which is called the "heart." Discard. Mince the garlic and add to bowl.
3. Stir in the uncooked rice, stock, olive oil, salt and pepper to taste. Set aside.
4. Wash the 4 remaining tomatoes and cut straight back on the top still leaving a small portion connected. Cut around the inside of the tomato with a paring knife. Using the point of the knife on the outside of the tomato, in the back where the top is connected, stab into the tomato making a small slit which will release the inside pulp and you will be able to gently pull it loose and lift it out. Very cool!! Ha! Clean out the rest of the tomato.

Prepare the peppers and tomatoes for stuffing:

5. Wash the green bell peppers and cut the tops off. Discard. Remove the seeds and clean out the inside with your paring knife, discard.
6. Spray a 9x13 in. baking pan with non-stick spray.
7. Fill the tomatoes lightly (do not pack down) with the stuffing mixture. Place the tomato upside down into the pan, two on each end, saving the middle for the stuffed peppers.
8. Stuff the peppers the same way and place them upside down in the pan (even though they do not have a top) laying them in the middle of the tomatoes.
9. Peel the potatoes and cut into 6 wedges. Place the potato wedges in-between the tomatoes and peppers so they are standing up.
10. Mix the ¼ cup stock and ¼ cup olive oil together and drizzle over all the vegetables.
11. Bake at 375° uncovered for one hour.

Serve with: Greek Salad page 257, French Baguettes page 242, hamburger patties, steak, lamb or fish.

Variations: Use Heirloom tomatoes any time of year to make this delicious meal. Use Greek Olive Oil. Greek Olive Oil is more green. Use brown rice.

This is a dish that will melt in your mouth.
It is a delicious, traditional meal served in Greece in the summer when vegetables are so fresh, and at their peak.
I learned this doing a Food Nanny show in Athens with some of the best chefs. Enjoy!

DANISH FRIKADELLER (DANISH MEATBALLS)

Serves 6
Time: 35 minutes

2 lbs. fine ground pork
(Note: If it isn't ground really fine, chop it with a knife - it must be fine)

- 1 Tablespoon coarse salt
- 1 Tablespoon black pepper
- 1 medium yellow onion, chopped
- 2 eggs, beaten
- ½ cup milk
- 3 Tablespoons flour or breadcrumbs
- 2 Tablespoons olive oil
- 2 Tablespoons butter

CONVERSATION STARTER:

Do you know your Mom's Birthday? Dad's Birthday?

1. In a medium size bowl mix the ground pork, salt, pepper, onion, eggs, milk and flour or bread crumbs together with your hands or a fork.
2. Heat oil and butter in a large frying pan until hot but not burning.
3. Take a heaping tablespoon of the meat mixture and form into an egg shape by cupping it in your hands. (It will be like a meatball only shaped a little differently.)
4. Fry the Frikadeller over medium heat until brown on both sides and cooked all the way through. Cook in batches until all the meat is used up.
5. Remove to a platter, cover and keep warm. Save the drippings for gravy if desired.

To prepare the gravy: Add the following to the pan drippings

- 2 cups water
- 1 Beef flavored bouillon - extra large cube; or 2 teaspoons beef bouillon granules
- 1 teaspoon Worcestershire Sauce
- 1 to 2 Tablespoons flour to thicken the gravy

Bring the water, bouillon and Worcestershire to a low boil. Whisk in the flour a little at a time. Boil for a couple of minutes and season with coarse salt and fresh ground pepper. Pour the gravy over the Frikadeller.

Serve with: Danish Cabbage page 214; steamed or boiled red potatoes; mashed potatoes; peas and carrots.

Variations:

- Use 1¼ lbs. ground pork and ¾ lb. ground beef.
- Replace 2 cups water with 2 cups evaporated milk, like many Danish cooks.
- Make a Béchamel sauce with fresh parsley and pour over the Frikadeller as well.
- Try it on my French Baguette page 242 with Dijon mustard!

My Grandmother was a Dane! Susie in Solvang, California, showed me this great dish, when I was doing "The Food Nanny Show" there. Make the Danish Sweet Red Cabbage to go with the Frikadeller too. The cabbage just complements this meal perfectly. My recipe for the cabbage is wonderful. Just ask Greg, one of my photographers!!

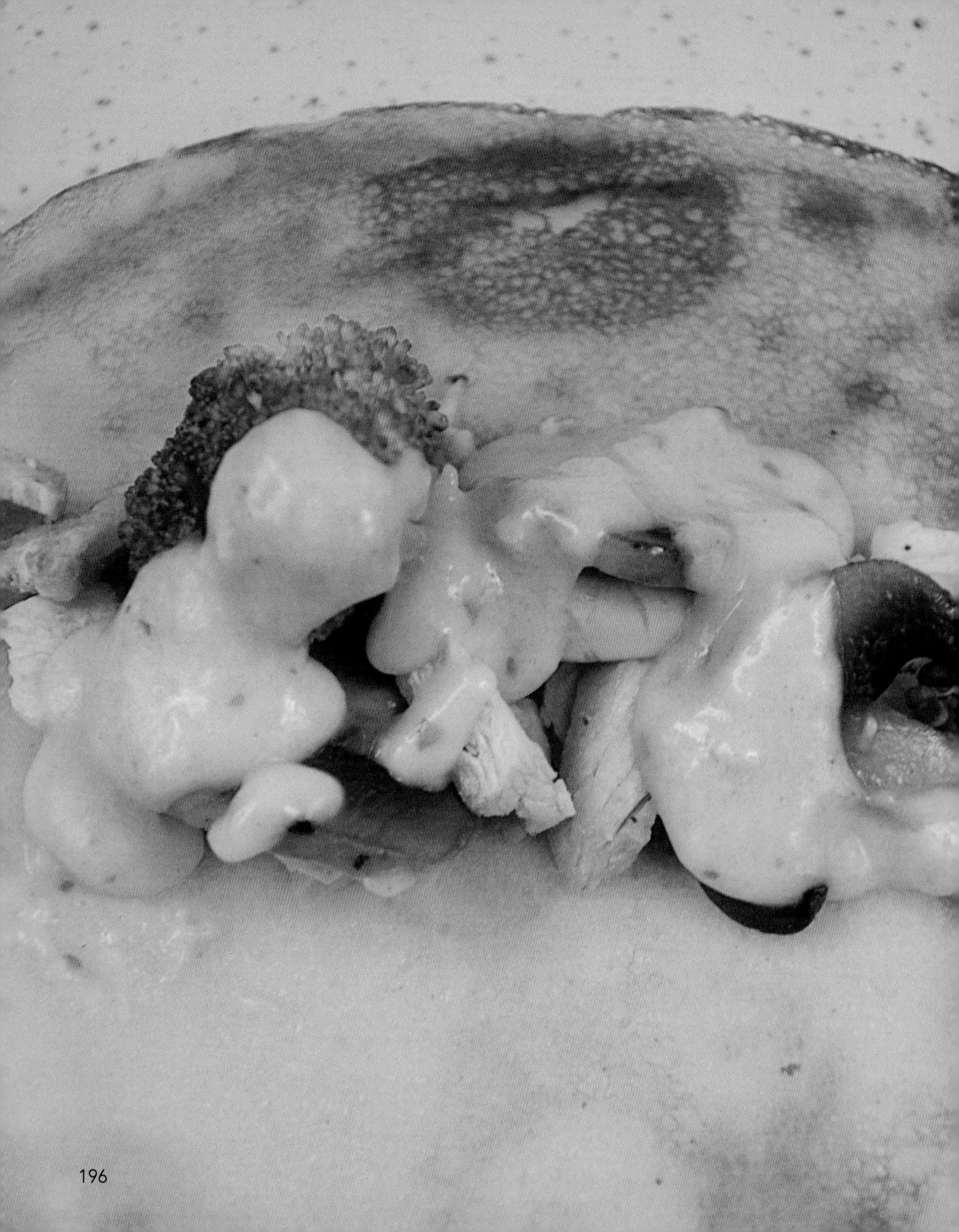

CHICKEN DIVAN CREPES WITH CHEESE SAUCE

Serves 8
Time: 40 minutes

***Plan Ahead:** Prepare the chicken, freeze for future use. Prepare crepes ahead. Reheat for use. Prepare the mushrooms and broccoli the day before. Make the sauce earlier in the day.*

Crepes:
1 cup milk
2 eggs
2 teaspoons canola oil
2 teaspoons rum or Grand Marnier (optional)
⅔ cup flour
⅛ teaspoon salt
Canola oil for frying the crepes

Chicken:
1 Tablespoon olive oil
2 small boneless/skinless chicken breasts, chopped

Sauce:
1 teaspoon butter
½ cup sliced fresh mushrooms, sautéed (mushrooms optional)
3 Tablespoons butter
2 cloves fresh garlic, crushed
½ teaspoon tarragon leaves, crushed
3 Tablespoons flour
1 cup plus 1 Tablespoon chicken broth
1 teaspoon Worcestershire sauce
½ cup Swiss cheese, grated
1¼ cups Cheddar cheese, grated and mixed together
1 cup sour cream plus 2 Tablespoons
1 10 oz. pkg. frozen broccoli spears or about 1 lb. fresh broccoli cooked

Prepare the crepes:

1. In a medium size bowl whisk together the milk, eggs, canola oil and rum or Grand Marnier if using.
2. Stir the flour and salt together. Add flour and salt to the milk and egg mixture. Whisk or blend in a blender until smooth like the consistency of cream.
3. In a large skillet over medium high heat pour in ½ teaspoon canola oil each time you prepare a crepe. (The skillet is hot enough when a small piece of bread dropped in browns.) Pour ¼ cup crepe batter into the pan and tilt the pan until batter covers the bottom.
4. When you start to see a few bubbles appear after about 1 min. flip and cook the other side until light brown. Stack on a plate until all are cooked.

Prepare the chicken:

Preheat oven to 350°.

1. With a wet paper towel wipe down the chicken. Remove fat or gristle. Chop.
2. Place the oil and chicken in a small skillet. Season with coarse salt and fresh ground black pepper to taste. Sauté over medium heat until done. About 5 min. Remove to a bowl.

Prepare the Sauce:

1. Wipe out the pan. Sauté the sliced mushrooms in 1 teaspoon butter and 1 teaspoon olive oil. Season with coarse salt and sauté until light brown. Remove to bowl. Wipe out the pan.
2. Melt 3 Tablespoons butter in same pan over LOW heat. Add crushed garlic and sauté until you smell the aroma. Stir in tarragon and flour. Cook until it starts to bubble. Add the chicken broth and Worcestershire sauce. Whisk until thickened.
3. Add half the cheese. Stir in the sour cream. Stir in the sautéed mushrooms. Season with coarse salt and fresh ground black pepper. Stir and set aside.

Assemble Chicken Divan Crepes:

1. On a baking sheet lined with parchment paper, take one crepe at a time and place some cooked chicken and one broccoli spear on each crepe.
2. Spoon 2 Tablespoons sauce over each. Roll up the crepe around the filling and place seam side down in a buttered 9x13 inch baking dish or in 2 buttered 8x8 inch pans.
3. Pour remaining sauce over all. Sprinkle with remaining cheese. Cover with foil and bake in oven for 20 to 30 min. or until heated through.

Serve with: Two Basic Salads page 258. Liz's Crescent Dinner Rolls page 249.

Variations: Normally in the U.S., cheddar means an orange colored cheese. You may use white which is the natural cheddar with no dye added.

CHEF JEAN LOUIS COQ AU VIN

Serves 4
Time: 2½ hours

Plan Ahead:
Prepare the potatoes ahead of time. Reheat.

Olive oil
1 fryer chicken, cut up; or use
2 breasts with bone-in, cut in half, and 4 thighs
1½ cups fresh pearl onions, peeled; or frozen already peeled
¼ cup flour
1 liter (or 4 cups) red wine or pomegranate juice
3 - 4 sprigs each of fresh rosemary, thyme and oregano. (Can tie altogether to make an herb bouquet or "bouquet garni," in French.)
3 cups white mushrooms cleaned, cut in half

Mashed potatoes with corn:
(Step 8 - 9 - 11)
2 medium to large Russet potatoes
⅓ cup cream
4 Tablespoons butter
¼ cup fresh or frozen corn
Coarse salt
Fresh ground pepper

1. In a large fry pan over high heat brown the chicken in olive oil on both sides until golden brown. Salt and pepper lightly.
2. Brown onions in a small sauce pan in olive oil on high heat stirring often to prevent burning them. They should be nice and brown.
3. Turn the heat down on the chicken and toss in one handful of flour (this is called "sash"), then toss in another handful of the flour….isn't it fun?!!! This will thicken the drippings.
4. Add onions and one-liter wine or pomegranate juice to the chicken and let cook 1 min.
5. Place individual sprigs of herbs or the garni, in the bottom of an oven proof pan and pour the chicken mixture and onions over top.
6. De-glaze the pan you fried the chicken in by adding in a little more juice until all the drippings and anything stuck to the pan are incorporated in the juice. Add this to the chicken in the pan.
7. Cover with foil and bake 1 hour and 15 min. at 350°.
8. Quarter the potatoes and boil them with salt and pepper in enough water to cover until done. Mash with a fork, not a potato masher.
9. Heat the cream, butter and corn in a small saucepan on top of the stove and keep warm.
10. When 20 min. are left to finish cooking the chicken add the mushrooms. Cover and finish cooking.
11. When ready to serve, stir the cream mixture into the potatoes with a fork. Mix together with a little more salt and pepper and divide among four plates.
12. Spoon over the chicken mixture and serve. Bon Appetit!!!

Serve with: Steamed Honey Glazed Carrots page 211. German Brown Bread page 233.

Variations: May use all chicken breasts with bone-in or part breasts and thighs.

Jean Louis taught me that there really are no rules when it comes to cooking! If you prefer Russet potatoes for mashing over Yukon Gold - it's your preference - own it! I wanted a centuries old peasant meal that we could all cook in our own kitchens without being intimidated, thus Coq au Vin. You and your family will feel like you are eating in the French countryside where this dish originated.

CHICKEN TARRAGON WITH CREAM

Serves 6
Time: 30 minutes

6 small boneless/skinless chicken breasts
Coarse salt
Fresh ground black pepper
¼ cup flour
3 Tablespoons butter
1 Tablespoon olive oil
2 Tablespoons yellow onion, finely chopped
½ cup white wine or cooking wine
2 Tablespoons flour
¾ cup chicken broth
2 Tablespoons fresh tarragon or 2 teaspoons dried tarragon
½ cup heavy cream

1. Wipe off the chicken breasts with a wet paper towel. Cut away any extra fat. Season with coarse salt and fresh ground black pepper on both sides.
2. Measure the flour into a pie plate and dip the chicken in the flour shaking off excess. Place on a plate.
3. In a large skillet over low to medium heat, melt the butter and add olive oil. Place the chicken in the skillet and sauté until light brown on both sides. Remove chicken to a platter. Cover.
4. Add 2 Tablespoons minced onion to the skillet. Sauté 2 min. Add the wine. Turn up the heat to high and cook until the wine is about ¾ cooked down and the brown bits are loosened from the bottom of the pan.
5. Turn the heat down to low and whisk in flour to form a thick paste. Add the fresh or dried tarragon, chicken broth and whisk until smooth.
6. Return the chicken to the skillet. Cover and cook until tender over low heat about 15 - 20 min. Remove breasts to a platter. Cover to keep warm.
7. Stir heavy cream into the sauce in the skillet. Check the seasoning. Add more coarse salt and fresh ground black pepper as needed. Pour this sauce over the warm chicken and serve immediately.

Serve with: Plate of raw veggies. Fresh green beans with butter and fresh dill. Angel Hair pasta with Lemon infused olive oil and a little butter and Parmesan cheese. Baked or Mashed potatoes with corn page 199.

Quinoa and rice mixture: 1 cup rice, ¼ cup quinoa. Add 2½ cups water or chicken broth, stir, bring to a boil and turn down the heat and cover. Cook over low heat for 25 min.

Variations: Use Half & Half in place of cream. For the chicken breasts you can use fresh or frozen. If frozen, thaw in the microwave.

CONVERSATION STARTER:

What year were your Grandparents born?

I am a nut for the herb tarragon. I love it in anything! I especially love it in a sauce. My Aunt Evelyn gave this recipe to me. There are many nights that you just need something quick but delicious. This is one of those recipes. Try it with the rice and quinoa. You will love that too!

BRILLIANT OVEN BBQ CHICKEN

Serves 6
Time: 1hour & 45 minutes
Bake at 350°

Plan Ahead: Make the sauce.

Sauce:

- ½ stick butter
- ⅓ cup yellow onion, minced
- 2 cloves fresh garlic, minced
- 2 teaspoons paprika
- 2 teaspoons chili powder
- ½ cup cider vinegar
- 1 Tablespoon Worcestershire sauce
- ½ cup brown sugar
- ¼ cup molasses
- ¼ teaspoon ground cayenne pepper
- 2 teaspoons coarse salt
- 1 teaspoon ground black pepper
- 1 6 oz. can tomato paste
- 1 cup water

Chicken:

- 1 fryer chicken cut up
- 2 Tablespoons olive oil
- 1 Tablespoons butter

Prepare the sauce first:

1. In a Dutch oven melt one half-stick butter.
2. Add the minced onion and cook until the onion is soft. Add minced garlic and sauté until you smell the aroma. Add the next 11 remaining ingredients including the water.
3. Bring the mixture to a boil stirring with a whisk until smooth. Immediately turn the heat down to simmer.
4. Simmer uncovered for 25 min.

Prepare the chicken:

1. Wipe off the chicken pieces with wet paper towels. Season generously with coarse salt and fresh ground black pepper. (Very important.)
2. Heat a large skillet or frying pan. Add olive oil and butter.
3. When the olive oil/butter begins to sizzle, place the chicken pieces in the pan and brown on both sides until golden brown.
4. Remove to a platter lined with paper towels to catch the excess oil.
5. Lightly oil (using olive oil) a 9x13 inch baking dish.
6. Place the browned chicken pieces in the baking dish. Spread on half of the BBQ sauce and cover with foil. Bake for 50 min at 350°.
7. Remove the foil and spread on the rest of the sauce. Continue baking for another 10 min. Serve immediately and use any extra sauce from the bottom of the pan.

Serve with: Orange Muffin Rolls page 235 or corn bread. Baked or mashed potatoes with corn page 199.

Variations: Use all breasts with the bone-in. Use boneless/skinless. Or use thighs and legs. Quick BBQ Chicken: Butter the casserole dish well with melted butter. Dip the chicken pieces in milk and then cover in flour. Shake off excess flour. Set in baking dish and cover with tons of home-made BBQ sauce or your favorite store bought BBQ sauce. Cover with foil. Bake for 1 hour at 350°.

I get really hungry for my great BBQ Chicken during the winter months. This has the perfect amount of "KICK" that will please the entire family. It could be my very favorite, ever!! My BBQ Chicken could become your Super Bowl Tradition!

CREAM OF ZUCCHINI SOUP

Serves 4
Time: 25 minutes

1 medium onion, chopped coarsely
2 Tablespoons butter
3¾ cups zucchini squash, peeled and cubed
3 cups chicken broth
⅛ teaspoon freshly ground black pepper
⅛ teaspoon nutmeg
⅛ teaspoon salt
Dash cayenne pepper
½ cup Half and Half
½ cup cheddar cheese, grated

1. Clean, chop and cook onion in butter until soft and transparent but not browned.
2. Wash, peel and cube zucchini into about 2 inch pieces. Combine onion, zucchini and chicken broth in large saucepan. Bring to boil, simmer 15 min. or until squash is tender. Add seasonings.
3. Using a blender or an immersion blender, puree mixture until smooth. Return to saucepan if using a blender. Add Half and Half and adjust seasoning to taste. Reheat but do not boil.
4. Serve hot, garnished with grated cheddar cheese.

Serve with: French Baguettes page 242; fresh tomatoes with olive oil and capers.

Variations: Pepper Jack Cheese or Colby Jack Cheese to garnish.

This soup is a quick, light meal.
Think of it when your garden is full of zucchinis.
Rosemary is very health conscious and
it's one of her favorites. xo

CONVERSATION STARTER:
What is your most favorite food?

CROCK POT TURKEY BREAST

Serves 4-6
Time: 8 hours on low heat

1 turkey breast, thawed
Coarse salt
Fresh ground black pepper
Season All spice mixture, or your favorite poultry seasoning
¾ cup chicken broth

Gravy:
4 cups chicken broth
⅓ cup flour
Coarse salt
Ground black pepper
Tony Chachere's Louisiana Style Seasoning

CONVERSATION STARTER:

Did your Mom and Dad have a black and white TV in their home?

1. Put thawed turkey breast in the sink. Run cold water over it to rinse it off. Place on paper towels. Pat the breast dry with paper towels. Season generously with coarse salt, ground black pepper and spice mixture.
2. Place the turkey breast in the crock pot. Pour the chicken broth in the bottom. Cover. Cook on low for 8 hours.
3. Remove turkey from the crock pot and slice breast into serving pieces.
4. Measure 1 cup of broth from the crock pot and pour over the sliced turkey. Cover with foil or a lid so the turkey will absorb the liquid until you are ready to serve it.

Prepare the Gravy:
1. Measure the broth you have left from cooking the turkey into a small saucepan. Add water to equal 4 cups.
2. Take out 1 cup of broth and pour into a small bowl. Add the flour and whisk until smooth. Turn the heat up to medium high and whisk in the broth and flour mixture. Continue to stir with a wooden spoon or whisk until thickened for gravy.
3. Adjust seasoning with coarse salt and ground black pepper. Add in some Tony Chachere's seasoning for a little spice.

Serve with: Mashed Potatoes and Gravy. Cranberry sauce. Anytime Fruit Salad page 317. Corn Salad page 268.

Variations: Can put the turkey breast into an oven bag if desired.

Marlene gave me the idea to slice the meat right after it is cooked and pour the broth over the meat so that it will soak up all the juice. This makes for the most wonderful turkey ever! It is so moist!!

Sides

When I was raising my family I usually served two vegetables with dinner.
Often, three. I wanted the meat to be the least important.
I wanted the sides to be as plentiful as the meat.
From the time our children were small,
I knew it was important to expose them to as many vegetables as I could.
I put at least one of our favorite vegetables such as corn, peas,
green beans or broccoli on the table each night in case there was someone who didn't
like what was being served. Even if it took years for someone to try a new vegetable,
at least they were exposed to them. Now, most of our kids eat all vegetables.
The vegetables and sides that I have in this chapter will be fun for your family to
get acquainted with. They will get to know cauliflower, asparagus, carrots, spinach,
beets, green beans and even quinoa - all cooked in delicious ways.
Brown Rice and Lettuce Wraps are so good too.
Choose something from this chapter often so that you can broaden
their tastes and have fun doing it.

The Food Nanny. xo

FAVORITE SIDES

Meatless

meatless

ROASTED PARMESAN CAULIFLOWER

Serves 6
Time: 40 minutes

1 head cauliflower, rinsed and cut into small pieces
½ cup heavy cream
½ cup Monterey Jack cheese, grated
½ cup fresh Parmesan cheese, grated
3 oz. cream cheese, cut into small pieces
Coarse salt
Fresh ground black pepper

1. Preheat oven to 400°. In a large bowl combine the cauliflower pieces and cream. Line a large baking sheet with aluminum foil. Spread half the cauliflower mixture in the middle of the pan.
2. In a small bowl combine the Jack, Parmesan, and cream cheese. Sprinkle half the cheese over top the cauliflower.
3. Spread the rest of the cauliflower over top the cheese. Sprinkle the remaining cheese over top the cauliflower. Season to taste with salt and pepper. Bake at 400° for 20 to 30 min. until tender and the cauliflower just starts to brown on top. Serve.

Serve with: Beef, lamb or chicken.

This dish is seriously one of the best veggies I have ever eaten. Jan, our neighbor, called one day and said, "Hey, do you want a great recipe?" Yes! Everyone I have served it to goes crazy for it. Even people who are not fond of cauliflower! I could sit down and eat the entire dish for dinner myself, it is that good! Thanks Jan! xo

LETTUCE WRAPS

Serves 8 people as a side dish
or 4 people for a main meal
Time: 15 minutes

Sauce:

2 Tablespoons sugar
¼ cup warm water
1 Tablespoons soy sauce
1 Tablespoon rice wine vinegar
1 Tablespoon ketchup
1½ teaspoons fresh lime juice
¼ teaspoon sesame oil (in the Asian section of your grocery store)
***½ teaspoon red chili paste, and more for garnish (in the Asian section of your grocery store)**

Filling:

12-16 Butter lettuce leaves (one head), rinsed and dried. Sometimes called Boston Bib. (Butter lettuce has very soft cupped leaves, perfect for lettuce wraps). Or Iceberg lettuce, rinsed and dried.
3 Tablespoons sesame oil, or olive oil
1 lb. fresh ground pork, finely ground
¼ cup shallot or onion, diced
3 cloves garlic, minced
⅓ cup canned water chestnuts, diced
2 Tablespoons brown sugar
2 Tablespoons soy sauce
2 teaspoons rice wine vinegar

Plan Ahead: Buy sesame oil, rice wine vinegar and red chili paste. You will use these ingredients over and over again to make these delicious Lettuce Wraps. Wash the lettuce leaves ahead of time, dry with paper towels and place in a plastic bag. Refrigerate.

1. Rinse the lettuce leaves. Drain well. Pat dry with paper towels. Place in a plastic bag and keep in the refrigerator until ready to use.
2. In a small bowl stir together 2 Tablespoons sugar and ¼ cup warm water until dissolved. Add the soy sauce, vinegar, ketchup, lime juice, sesame oil and chili paste. Mix well. Set aside.
3. Heat the oil in a wok or a large frying pan over medium/high heat. Stir-fry the pork quickly in the oil breaking the meat up as much as possible. Add the onions, garlic and water chestnuts and continue to stir-fry until the pork is cooked through and the onions are soft. Add the brown sugar, soy sauce, rice wine vinegar. Cook until the liquid has evaporated. A couple of minutes. Serve warm.

*There are many brands of red chili paste. The one I recommend is in most grocery stores - Sambal Oelek Ground Fresh Chili Paste, Huy Fong Foods, Inc.; 8oz. jar.

4. **To Serve: Place the cold, rinsed and dried lettuce leaves on a plate.** Spoon the pork mixture into a dish. Pour the sauce into a small bowl. Let people make their own lettuce wrap. Spoon some meat mixture onto a lettuce leaf. Spoon on some sauce. Spoon on extra red chili paste for more flavor. Fold the lettuce over like a taco and eat. Plan on 3 to 4 lettuce wraps per person if serving for lunch or dinner. Less per person as a side dish. (I don't fill them very full.)

We all love Lettuce Wraps.
This is my delicious, easy version to make for your family.
This is a healthy, quick side or meal. Enjoy! xo

Meatless
STEAMED HONEY GLAZED CARROTS

Serves 2
Time: 10 minutes

Plan Ahead: Cut carrots up and keep in plastic bag.

4 whole fresh carrots, peeled and cut into sticks - not "baby" carrots in plastic bags
Softened butter to taste
Clover honey to taste
Coarse salt

1. Peel the carrots. Cut in half. Cut in half lengthwise, then in half again. You should end up with at least 8 carrot sticks per carrot. (Some carrots are extra thick and you could cut more sticks.)
2. Steam carrots for 10 min., Remove and toss hot carrots with butter and drizzle with honey. Lightly salt. Serve immediately.

*Carrots are one of my most favorite vegetables.
Nothing beats butter and honey drizzled on steamed carrots.
Steaming carrots is the quickest way to cook them. xo*

Meatless
SAUTÉED SPINACH WITH PARMESAN

Serves 2
Time: 5 minutes

Plan Ahead: Buy spinach in bags at the grocery store already cleaned and rinsed.

2 teaspoons olive oil
4 cups fresh spinach
Coarse salt or sea salt
1 Tablespoon fresh Parmesan cheese, finely shredded

In a small fry pan add the olive oil over medium heat. Add the spinach when the oil begins to heat up. Stir-fry 1 to 2 min. The spinach is done when it is wilted but still bright green. Remove from heat. Salt lightly to taste. Sprinkle with finely shredded fresh Parmesan cheese. Serve immediately.

Serve with: beef or lamb.

*I love fresh spinach cooked just this way.
For years I didn't know how to cook fresh spinach that tasted really great. It is this easy and this delicious! xo*

FRESH GREEN BEANS WITH GARLIC & BACON

Serves 4
Time: 30 minutes

***Prepare Ahead:** Cook the bacon and save 1 Tablespoon bacon grease. Rinse the beans, snip the ends off and snap in half. Cook 5 min. in boiling water. Then it takes just 10 min. to put together.*

4 strips bacon, cooked and crumbled
1½ pounds fresh green beans, rinsed, ends snipped, snapped in half, cooked
2 Tablespoons sugar
2 Tablespoons soy sauce
¾ teaspoon coarse salt
1 Tablespoon bacon grease, (optional)
1 Tablespoon olive oil
1 small red onion, sliced thin
5 cloves garlic, minced
Fresh ground black pepper to taste

1. Fry the bacon on top of the stove, or place bacon on a small baking sheet and bake at 425° for 20 min. until crisp. Save 1 Tablespoon bacon grease. Let cool on paper towels. Crumble. Set aside.
2. Fill a large pot with water. Bring to a boil. In the meantime rinse the beans, snip the ends off, then snap in half and add to the boiling water. Boil for 5 min. Drain off all the water, very important. Set aside.
3. In a small bowl mix together sugar, soy sauce and salt. Set aside.
4. In a large frying pan over medium heat add the bacon grease and olive oil. Add the onion and sauté until caramelized, at least 5 min. Add the garlic and stir until you can smell the aroma. Add cooked beans. Stir for 2 min. Add the cooked bacon pieces. Stir. Pour on the sugar mixture. Stir-fry for about 3 more min. Add fresh ground black pepper to taste.

Serve with: Just about anything!

This is the way my Grandma served the fresh beans from her garden. Except she used all bacon grease and no soy sauce. You may finish the beans off with freshly grated Parmesan cheese. You can put fresh Parmesan on just about anything and I do!! ha-ha. Take them to your next potluck! xo

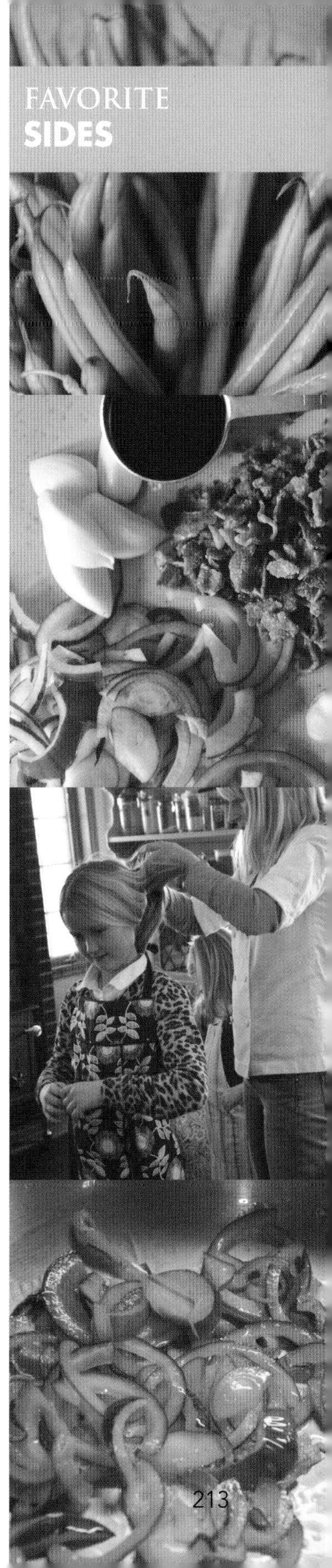

Meatless SOLVANG DANISH RED CABBAGE

Serves 4-6
Time: 2 hours

Plan Ahead: Buy the cabbage already chopped.

- ½ head medium-sized red cabbage
- 1 cup white vinegar
- 1 cup sugar
- 1 teaspoon coarse salt
- 1½ cups water
- 2 small bay leaves
- ¼ teaspoon ground cloves

1. Rinse and core the cabbage. Cut in half. Using a chef's knife cut as thin as possible. Chop into one-inch pieces. A mandolin works well.
2. Place the chopped cabbage into a large saucepan. Stir in vinegar, sugar, salt, water, bay leaves and ground cloves. Bring to a boil, then turn down the heat. Cover and simmer for 1½ to 2 hours or until most of the liquid is gone. Serve immediately.

One of the best Danish dishes is this red cabbage. I love it along side the Frikadeller and mashed potatoes with gravy. Susie makes it the best right there in Solvang, California at the Danish Inn. A real treat. They say Solvang, California is more Danish than Denmark!

CLAM DIP

Makes 3 cups
Time: 5 minutes

Plan Ahead: Dip is best made a couple of hours in advance or up to a day ahead. Cover and refrigerate.

- 1 pkg. 8 oz. cream cheese, room temperature
- 1 cup sour cream
- 1 Tablespoon Worcestershire sauce
- 2 Tablespoons lemon juice, fresh squeezed
- ¼ teaspoon onion powder
- 2 teaspoons garlic salt
- 1 6 oz. can minced clams, save the juice
- 2 to 3 Tablespoons clam juice

In a small to medium size bowl, beat cream cheese and sour cream with an electric mixer or whisk, just until mixed. Stir in Worcestershire, lemon juice, onion powder, garlic salt, clams and juice. Cover and keep in the refrigerator until ready to serve.

Serve with: Potato Chips.

Variation: For a Sour Cream Clam Dip, use 1 cup sour cream in place of the cream cheese.

This is my Mom's Clam Dip that we have been serving at every special occasion since I was a little girl. Mom didn't have a recipe written down. So through the years this is what I have written down for my kids. I still remember when Mother was stirring the dip together asking one of us girls to go "pick a lemon." I took "picking a lemon" for granted. I had no idea how special it was that we were growing lemons in our own backyard! This dip is a tradition for my entire family.

Meatless ASPARAGUS THREE WAYS!

Serves 2
Time: 10 minutes

8 fresh asparagus spears, tough ends snapped off
1 teaspoon olive oil
Coarse salt, to taste
Fresh ground black pepper, to taste
½ teaspoon fresh lemon juice
2 teaspoons unsalted butter, melted
1-2 Tablespoons fresh Parmesan Reggiano Cheese, finely grated (optional)

To Grill:

1. Heat the grill to medium high. Fold a paper towel in fourths and drizzle with olive oil. Go over the grill with the paper towel using your tongs. Place asparagus in a shallow pan, add olive oil, salt and pepper to taste. Make sure the asparagus is coated on all sides. Remove asparagus from pan and place on top of the grill turning often for 6 min., depending on how thick the asparagus is.
2. Mix lemon juice and warm butter together. Remove asparagus to a plate and pour warmed butter mixture over top. Add more salt and pepper if desired. Sprinkle cheese on top. Serve hot.

To Roast:

1. Place asparagus on a baking sheet, drizzle with olive oil - make sure the spears are completely covered in oil. Sprinkle with coarse salt and fresh ground black pepper. Roast for 10 min. at 425°. Remove to a plate.
2. Mix lemon juice and warm butter together. Remove asparagus to a plate and pour warmed butter mixture over top. Add more salt and pepper if desired. Sprinkle cheese on top. Serve hot.

To Pan Boil:

1. Omit the olive oil.
2. Use a fry pan or an omelet pan and fill with about ¼ inch water. Place the asparagus spears in the pan. Turn the heat up to medium high and boil for 6-8 min. or until the asparagus is fork - tender - but still green. Drain well.
3. Put asparagus back into the pan and let cook for 30 seconds to make sure the asparagus is dry. Place on a plate. Salt and pepper to taste. Mix the lemon juice and warm butter together and pour over the asparagus. Sprinkle with the cheese if desired. Serve hot.

Variation: Top with my Pesto Sauce on page 44.

These 3 recipies are quick and delicious!!!

Meatless

BROWN RICE WITH ALMONDS, DRIED BLUEBERRIES AND BALSAMIC VINAIGRETTE

Serves 2 to 3
Time: 45 minutes

Plan Ahead: Prepare the rice and vinaigrette ahead of time. Adding the other ingredients takes 5 minutes!

Vinaigrette:
- 3 Tablespoons balsamic vinegar (I prefer cherry-wood aged available at a quality food store)
- 1 Tablespoon crushed garlic
- 1 Tablespoon brown sugar
- ⅓ cup olive oil
- ¼ teaspoon salt
- ⅛ teaspoon ground black pepper

Rice:
- ½ cup brown rice
- 1¼ cups chicken broth or water
- 1 teaspoon olive oil
- 1 teaspoon butter
- 2 Tablespoons raw almonds, chopped
- 1 Tablespoon white corn, fresh or frozen
- 1 Tablespoon dried blueberries

1. In a small bowl mix together the vinegar, garlic and brown sugar. Slowly whisk in the olive oil. Season with salt and pepper. Set vinaigrette aside.
2. In a small saucepan stir together the rice, chicken broth (or water) and olive oil. Bring to a boil, turn heat down to simmer, cover and cook 40 min., or until the rice is tender. Set aside.
3. In a small fry pan over medium heat, melt the butter. Add almonds and corn. Sauté for about 2 min., stirring constantly. Add cooked rice and blueberries. Stir constantly for another minute. Add 2 teaspoons balsamic vinaigrette. Mix thoroughly. Serve warm.

Serve with: Vegetables, beef, chicken or lamb.

I am always trying new ways to fix rice.
It's especially delicious cooked
this way with nuts and fruit.
The vinaigrette just finishes it off!
You are going to love
this delicious rice creation. xo

Meatless
JASMINE RICE

Serves 4
Time: 25 minutes

2 cups water
2 Tablespoons olive oil
1 teaspoon salt
1 cup Jasmine rice

In a small saucepan bring the water, olive oil and salt to a boil. Add the rice. Stir. Cover and turn the heat down to simmer for 25 min. Serve.
If using a rice cooker, follow instructions.

Often I am hungry for plain rice. This is the recipe I reach for every time. Jasmine rice has a tiny bit of flavor to it that makes it special. Try it out. It will become one of your favorites, and it's gluten free.

Meatless
JASMINE & QUINOA

Serves 4
Time: 25 minutes

2¼ cups water
2 Tablespoons olive oil
1 teaspoon salt
¾ cup Jasmine rice
¼ cup quinoa, red or white

In a small saucepan bring the water, olive oil and salt to a boil. Add the rice and quinoa. Stir. Cover, and turn the heat down to simmer for 25 min. Serve.
If using a rice cooker, follow instructions.

I love this combination. It is healthy and delicious. I started putting the two together and thought, now this tastes good and it's healthy!!

QUINOA

Serves 1
Time: 20 minutes

¼ cup white quinoa
½ cup water
Dash of salt

Bring the quinoa, water and salt to a boil in a small sauce pan. Turn the heat down and simmer for 20 min.

Variation: Put butter and maple syrup over it.

I like plain quinoa. It tastes good to me. It is also gluten free. I feel healthy eating it because it is full of protein. Try it sometime along side something saucy.

Meatless COCONUT BASMATI RICE

Serves 4-6
Time: 30 minutes

1¾ cups water
1 cup white basmati rice
½ cup coconut milk
½ teaspoon turmeric
½ teaspoon salt
1 cinnamon stick
¼ cup dried currants or raisins
3 Tablespoons sugar (optional)

Bring water to a boil. Stir in rice and all remaining ingredients.
Return to boil; cover and reduce heat to low, simmering for about 25 min.
Remove cinnamon stick, stir to fluff the rice and serve.

Serve with: BBQ Chicken page 203. Lamb recipes on pages 30,185,188.

Variations: Leave out the currants or raisins.

*Jenny, thank you for sharing this recipe with me.
I am so in love with this coconut rice. It's not very often that you get a recipe that you can't live without.
This is one of them. xo*

Meatless FRIED POTATO ROUNDS

Serves 2, about 25 potato rounds
Time: 15 minutes

2 medium Russet potatoes, peeled & sliced into ¼ inch rounds
1 cup sunflower oil
Sea salt

Candy thermometer for checking the temperature. Paper towels to dry and drain the potatoes on.

1. Quickly rinse the potatoes - don't soak them with water. Dry with paper towels really well.
2. Pour the oil into a small fry pan. Heat oil to 225°. Use a candy thermometer to check the temperature. Fry potato rounds in two batches - about 12 rounds per batch. Fry 7 to 8 min., turning often with tongs.
3. Lay the potato rounds onto paper towels to drain, or pat off excess grease. Salt lightly. Serve hot.

Serve with: Hamburgers, beef, chicken, fish or sandwiches.

*We eat these little round fries everywhere in Italy.
I love frying with sunflower oil, it seems to change the taste to something special. These great fries are quick and easy to make for you or your family. xo*

SWEET AND SOUR MEATBALLS

Makes About 35 1-inch Meatballs
Time: 40 minutes

Plan Ahead: Make meatballs ahead and re-heat in sauce over low heat on top of the stove.

Meatballs:

- 1½ lbs. hamburger
- ½ onion, minced
- ¾ cup homemade breadcrumbs. Put white or wheat bread into a food processor or blender and blend until you have crumbs.
- ½ teaspoon salt
- ⅛ teaspoon fresh ground pepper
- ¾ teaspoon Worcestershire sauce
- 1 egg, beaten
- ⅓ cup milk

Sauce:

- 1 large green bell pepper, diced
- 1½ cups chicken broth
- 1-13 oz. can pineapple tidbits, drained
- ½ cup cider vinegar
- ¾ cup sugar
- ½ teaspoon salt
- ⅛ teaspoon ground ginger
- 2 Tablespoons soy sauce
- 1 Tablespoon corn starch
- 1½ Tablespoons water
- 1-11 oz. jar Maraschino cherries, drained

Meatballs:
In a medium size bowl mix together the ingredients in order given. Stir with a fork or combine with your hands. Roll into 1" balls and place on a foiled lined baking sheet. Bake uncovered at 350° for 20 to 30 min. Add the meatballs to the sauce after it simmers.

Sauce:

1. In a medium size saucepan place the green pepper, chicken broth, pineapple, vinegar, sugar, salt, ginger and soy sauce. Stir together the cornstarch and water in a small bowl. Whisk the cornstarch mixture into the sauce and bring to a boil. Turn the heat down and simmer for about 15 min.
2. Add the cooked meatballs and drained cherries. Warm through. Thicken with more cornstarch and water if needed. (I prefer the sauce just barely thickened.) Serve warm.

Serve with: Rice, or use as an appetizer.

We crave these meatballs especially at Christmas. Shana makes them all year long for Sunday Dinner and serves them over rice. Mary Kay gave us this recipe 20 years ago and we have been making them every since.

MACARONI SALAD WITH ROTISSERIE CHICKEN

Serves 12 as a side dish
Time: 20 minutes

Plan Ahead: Buy a rotisserie chicken at the market. Make salad hours ahead, cover and refrigerate.

2 cups elbow macaroni, cooked
1½ sticks celery, chopped
1 cup frozen peas
1½ cups cooked rotisserie chicken, chopped
½ cup cubed (¼ x ¼ inch cubes) cheddar cheese
½ teaspoon celery salt
½ teaspoon Bon a Appetite spice mix
Salt
Fresh ground black pepper
1 cup mayonnaise
¼ teaspoon sugar
1½ Tablespoons olive oil
½ teaspoon soy sauce

1. Boil the macaroni according to package directions, about 10 min. Drain. Place in a medium size bowl. Add the celery, peas, chicken, cheese, celery salt, Bon a Appetite, salt and fresh ground black pepper to taste.
2. In a small bowl mix the mayonnaise, sugar, olive oil and soy sauce. Pour the mayonnaise mixture over the macaroni and chicken salad. Stir together. Check for seasoning. Cover and refrigerate for a couple of hours. May be eaten immediately.

Serve with: Steak, other salads, fish. (This Side Salad also stands alone) Liz's Crescent Rolls page 249 or Corn Bread.

Variation: Double the recipe for a large group. Leave out the rotisserie chicken. Replace it with ham, tuna, small canned shrimp or nothing at all. Use small shells in place of macaroni.

*Elaine brings this salad to every family dinner.
She makes it so easy using the rotisserie chicken,
which gives it a nice flavor.
I love how she puts this salad with everything!
Last time we were together there was not a drop left.*

Meatless

FOOD NANNY FRY SAUCE

Makes about ½ cup
Time: 2 minutes

- ⅓ cup mayonnaise
- 2 Tablespoons ketchup
- ⅛ teaspoon ground cayenne pepper, optional

In a small bowl mix the mayonnaise and ketchup together with a spoon. Stir in the cayenne pepper if using. Serve at room temperature.

Serve with: French fried potatoes.

Variations: Try using Miracle Whip in place of mayonnaise. Try using chili sauce or BBQ sauce in place of the ketchup.

I was raised in California. When we visited our Grandparents and cousins in Utah they had a really great sauce that came in a tiny paper cup along side your french fries. It was called "fry sauce." We looked forward to it every summer. This is my version. Most people in Utah cannot eat a french fry without a version of this fry sauce - because it is really good!
xo

Meatless

ROASTED YAM FRIES

Serves 2
Time: 30 minutes

- 1 large yam (about 1 lb.) peeled, cut into ¼ inch strips (like french fries)
- 2 teaspoons olive oil
- Coarse salt

Pre-heat oven to 450°.

1. Peel yam. Rinse. Wipe dry. Cut in half. Cut in half again, lengthwise. Cut into ¼ inch strips like french fries. Lay yam strips on a small baking sheet. Drizzle with olive oil, making sure that each entire yam fry has been covered in oil. Lightly salt. Place the baking sheet on the middle rack in the oven.
2. Bake about 20 min. If you like really crisp fries, roast about 5 more min., but be careful not to burn them. Sprinkle with a little more salt if desired. Serve hot.

Serve with: Sandwiches. Hamburgers. Fried or BBQ Chicken. Fish.

Variation: Use Russet potatoes or sweet potatoes in place of yams. Sprinkle with fresh rosemary.

*I love what you can do with yams and sweet potatoes.
I like to order these in restaurants and dip them
into something yummy,
like my Blue Cheese Dressing on page 264*

CLASSIC CHEESE BALL

Time: 15 minutes

Plan Ahead: Make cheese ball one day ahead. Wrap in plastic and refrigerate. Use left over ham cut with a mandolin to get ultra thin strips.

2 8 oz. packages cream cheese, softened
2 Tablespoons mayonnaise
1 Tablespoon fresh lemon juice
1 bunch green onions
10 slices ultra thin ham or chipped beef, cut into ¼ x ½ inch small strips
1½-2 cups chopped nuts - cashews, almonds or walnuts

1. In a medium bowl mix the softened cream cheese with mayonnaise and lemon juice.
2. Rinse off the onions. Trim the ends. Cut the onions, stem and all into tiny pieces with scissors into the bowl. Stir onions and ham or beef strips into the cream cheese mixture.
   Form into a ball. Roll in the chopped nuts of choice. I prefer cashews. Cover in plastic and refrigerate at least 2 hours before serving.

Tip: This makes enough for a party. Cut recipe in ½ if using just for your family.

Serve with: Favorite crackers.

Jeselyn brings her delicious famous cheese ball to every family party. When you want to take something to a party or family gathering take this! It will be the hit.

BAKED BEANS WITH BACON AND PINEAPPLE

Serves 6
Time: 1 hour

Plan Ahead: Cook the bacon, onion and green pepper 1 day ahead

2 15 oz. cans pork and beans with juice
¼ lb. bacon, diced
½ yellow onion, chopped
½ green bell pepper, chopped
1 cup pineapple tidbits
3 Tablespoons pineapple juice
½ cup brown sugar
½ cup ketchup
1½ teaspoons Worcestershire sauce
1½ teaspoons yellow mustard

1. In a small saucepan sauté the bacon until cooked. Pour off all the grease but 1 teaspoon and drain the bacon on a paper towel. Sauté the onion and bell pepper in the bacon grease until soft.
2. Pour the beans in a bowl, add cooked bacon, sautéed onions and peppers, pineapple and juice, brown sugar, ketchup, Worcestershire sauce and mustard. Stir to combine.
3. Pour the bean mixture into an 8x8 inch-baking dish. Bake at 350° for 45 min. or until hot and bubbly.

Serve with: Especially great with BBQ Hamburgers, Hot Dogs, Steak, Chicken, Food Nanny Chicken Croissant Sandwiches.

Variations: May double or triple this recipe.

*I crave these beans!!! Barbara gave me this recipe.
My entire family thinks these are
the best baked beans in the world.
We love 'um!!!*

Meatless

LINGUINE WITH BUTTER & PARMESAN CHEESE

Serves 4 as a side dish
Time: 15 minutes

1 teaspoon salt
½ pound linguine noodles
1 Tablespoon olive oil
1 Tablespoon unsalted butter
¼ cup pasta water from cooking the linguine
¼ cup Parmesan cheese, grated
Coarse salt to taste
Fresh ground black pepper to taste - I like a lot!

1. Fill a large pot with water. Bring to a rolling boil. Add 1 teaspoon salt and the pasta. Cook 10 min., stirring a couple of times. Drain the pasta. Reserve ¼ cup pasta water.
2. In a medium size saucepan over medium high heat, heat the olive oil until hot. Add the butter. Add the cooked pasta to the saucepan with the hot oil and butter. Stir with tongs. Add ¼ cup hot pasta water. Stir with tongs. Sprinkle with salt and pepper to taste. Continue to mix and coat the pasta with the sauce. Turn off the heat and add the Parmesan cheese. Mix. Serve immediately.

Serve with: Steak, pork, veal, chicken, fish.

Variation: Use fettuccine. Cook 11 min. Cut the recipe in half for 2 people.

*This is my version of one of my all-time favorite side dishes.
A piece of steak, veal, fish or chicken served with this pasta
and fresh Asparagus with Lemon Butter page 215
and Honey Glazed Carrots page 211.
Well, it doesn't get any better than that!
It is quick and SO good!
Another dish they serve at my favorite restaurant! xo*

Meatless

ROASTED BEETS AND BEET GREENS

Serves 4 as a side dish
Time: 1 hour 10 minutes

Plan Ahead: Roast beets and re-heat.

4 medium size fresh beets with greens
Olive oil
Coarse salt
Fresh ground black pepper
Sour cream for garnish, optional
Feta or Blue Cheese, optional

1. Preheat the oven to 375-400°.
2. Rinse beets, scrub lightly. Cut the root off the bottom, discard. Cut off the greens at the top - discard greens if not roasting. Rinse and pat dry beets and beet greens with paper towel. Do not peel the beets, no need.
3. Place the whole beets in a roasting pan. Lay the greens next to the beets. Drizzle the beets and greens generously with olive oil and sprinkle lightly with coarse salt and fresh ground black pepper. Put the lid on and place the pan in the oven on the middle rack. Roast for 1 hour or until the beets are tender when a knife inserts easily. Check the beets half-way through and turn. If roasting the greens, check them to make sure they are not burning. If desired, remove early.
4. Remove the beets and greens to a plate. Pass the sour cream and eat the beets like a baked potato. You can eat the skins or choose to peel the skins back. I like the skins! Eat the greens along side the beets. Save leftovers for another meal.

Serve with: Serve with beef, chicken or pork.

Variation: Slice warm roasted beets ¼ inch thick. Remove skins if desired and lay out on a plate. Sprinkle with olive oil or walnut oil, and feta or blue cheese. Delicious.

My sister, Sue, called me and said "Have you tried roasting beets?" I tried them and fell in love!

Breads

Never underestimate the power of homemade bread. When you want to capture feelings of warmth all you have to do is bake some homemade bread. Any kind.
My Grandmother was the postmistress of the small post office in her town.
One morning a young man, not very well kept, came into the post office just to take a look. A few hours later this same young man knocked on my Grandma's front door. She yelled, "Come in," which he did. As he walked towards her, she recognized him from earlier in the day. She said, "You look hungry, why don't you sit down here and let me give you some homemade bread and chili sauce.
I am just taking it out of the oven." He sat down. He even asked her to fry him an egg.
Years later this same man came into the post office asking for my Grandmother.
Grandma was out that day, but he left a message for her with her daughter.
He said, "I came to your Mother's home to rob her of her cash box and to do whatever it would take to get that money, even if it meant hurting her. I could not, because all I could smell was homemade bread and it took me right back to the memories I had of my own Grandmother who I loved so much." He continued, "I was headed down a wrong path that day and while I sat there and ate that bread I vowed to myself, right then and there, that I would leave that house and turn my life around."
Which he did. He had come that day to thank my Grandma.
A life saved all because of the power of the smell of homemade bread.
Change the life of someone in your home for the better. I have some great recipes here for you to try out on your family. Make some great memories for your kids or grandkids and see what an inspiration you too will become in their lives.

The Food Nanny. xo

FAVORITE BREADS

GERMAN BROWN BREAD

Makes 1 Loaf
Time: 2½ hours

Plan Ahead: Bake bread ahead of time and freeze.

¾ cup warm water, (105-115°) 1¼ teaspoons active dry yeast
2 teaspoon sugar
2 teaspoons clover honey
2 Tablespoons molasses
2 teaspoons unsweetened cocoa powder
2 cups all-purpose flour
½ cup whole-wheat flour
½ teaspoon coarse salt
1½ teaspoons olive oil

1. Pour the water in a small bowl. Add the yeast and sugar. Stir. Let bloom - about 10 min. In a medium size bowl add the honey, molasses, cocoa, flours, salt and oil. Add the yeast mixture and stir together. Turn the dough out onto a counter and form into a ball. If it is too sticky add just a bit of flour.
2. Put a few drops of olive oil into a small bowl, spread it around and place the dough in the bowl. Cover with plastic that has been sprayed with cooking oil. Let dough rise until double, about 1 hour. Form the dough into a loaf. Spray the bread pan generously with cooking oil. Place dough in the greased pan.
3. Let rise until double, 30 to 45 min. and bake at 350° 25 to 30 min. Check the bread by dumping it out just barely and tapping the underneath to see if it sounds hollow. Do not over bake. Cool on a cooling rack.

Serve with: This bread is good for eating with something hearty on a cold winter day! It is delicious.

This bread takes me right back to my Swiss-German ancestry. All my life I have been intrigued with Brown Bread. It is the molasses and the chocolate that does the trick.

ORANGE MUFFIN ROLLS

Makes 24 Rolls
Time: 3 hours

Plan Ahead: Freeze ahead of time, unthaw and bake.

¼ cup warm water, (105-115°)
1 Tablespoon active dry yeast
1 cup milk, scalded
1 Tablespoon sugar
1 teaspoon salt
6 Tablespoons butter, room temperature
2 eggs, beaten
3½-4 cups all-purpose flour

Spread:
1 cup sugar
1 stick butter (½ cup), room temperature
Grated rind of 1 orange

1. Stir the water and yeast together in a small bowl. Let it bloom about 10 min. Scald the milk in the microwave for 1 min. 45 sec. Let cool to lukewarm. In a large bowl add the sugar, salt, butter and eggs. Stir in the milk and yeast mixture. Add 3½ cups flour and beat with a spoon. (If the dough is still too sticky add the last ½ cup flour).
2. Place the dough in a large bowl that has been greased with a little butter.Cover with dishtowel. Let dough rise 1½ hours. Pour out onto counter top (lightly flour if necessary) and roll out to about 2 ft. long and ¼ inch thick.
3. Cream together the ingredients for the spread - sugar, butter and grated orange rind. Spread evenly over the dough. Roll like you would for cinnamon rolls, starting from the short end.
4. Cut the dough in half and cut 12 rolls from each side. Place in generously greased muffin tins, greased with shortening or baking spray.
5. Cover with a dishtowel. Let rise 1 hour 20 min. Place in a preheated 350° oven on the middle rack for 15 to 20 min. or until they start to get light brown on top. Serve warm. Cooled rolls will keep for 2 days in plastic. May freeze.

Serve with: Soup or a hearty dinner.

Variation: May freeze rolls after they are cut. When you want to bake them, thaw frozen rolls for a couple of hours on a greased baking sheet covered with plastic that has been sprayed with baking oil. Bake as directed.

These rolls turn out beautiful made in the muffin tins. They are as delicious as they are beautiful. These will become one of your all-time favorite rolls to make for your family dinners.

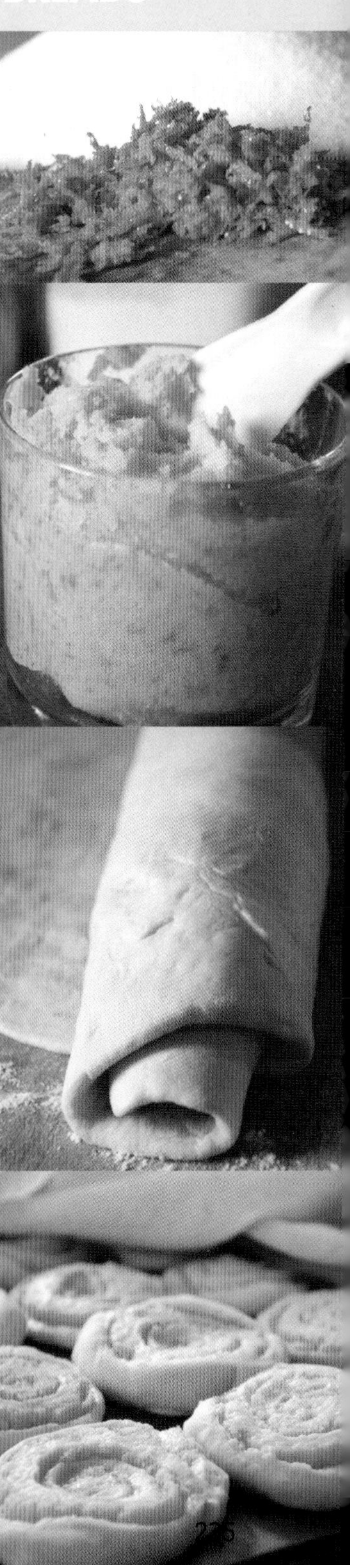

EVERYDAY ARTISAN BREAD

Makes 3 loaves
Time: 5 minutes to prepare.
Keep in refrigerator up to 2 weeks.

- **3 cups warm water, (105-115°)**
- **1½ Tablespoons active dry yeast**
- **1 Tablespoon coarse salt**
- **6 cups all-purpose flour or bread flour, plus flour for dusting**

1. In a large bowl mix the water, yeast and salt. Add the flour and stir together with a wooden spoon until well combined. You will have sticky dough. Add a little more water if it seems dry.
2. In another bowl put a little olive oil, add the dough and turn to coat. Spray plastic wrap with baking oil and cover loosely. Leave out on the counter for 2 hours. After 2 hours put a tight lid on the bowl or wrap the bowl tightly with plastic wrap. Place in refrigerator for up to 2 weeks. You will have enough dough to make 3 grapefruit size balls.
3. Pull out one grapefruit size ball at a time. The dough will be really sticky. Flour the counter. Work some flour into the dough as you manipulate and form the bread into preferred shape, I usually do rounds. The dough will still be sticky.
4. Spray a baking sheet with cooking oil and place the dough on the baking sheet. Turn the oven to 450°. Sprinkle the dough with a little flour and score it about ¼ inch deep with a sharp knife. Make a 3-inch slit crosswise or a 3-inch slanted slit in the middle.
5. When oven is heated, place the baking sheet on the middle rack with 1 cup of water in a shallow pan on the rack below. This helps to create steam and make the bread crusty. Bake for 20-25 min. Cool on baking rack.
6. Serve warm or at room temperature. Keep in a paper bag. Plastic will soften the crust.

Variations: Add 1 Tablespoon Italian seasoning when forming a round. Use for Pizza dough or Focaccia bread. I also bake this bread on my stone or tiles. Let rise on baking sheet and then lift off very carefully and place on stone or tiles.

This is true Artisan bread that can be made at home very easily. Artisan breads have lots of moisture in them which creates a nice crust, open-holed crumb inside, light texture and great flavor. There is no work to this bread and yet you would think you had been letting it rise, punching it down and letting it raise again all day long. This will impress even the best of cooks. Experienced cook or not anyone can make my Artisan bread recipes. Give it a try. This one is super easy.

GREAT GARLIC BREAD

Makes 1 large loaf Italian Bread
Time: 5 minutes

- ½ cup butter, softened at room temperature
- ¼ cup mayonnaise
- 2 cups shredded cheese – a mix of these 3 kinds: Colby/Jack, Parmesan and Asiago

Mix the butter, mayonnaise and cheeses together. Slice a loaf of Italian Bread down the middle so it will open up like a sandwich. Spread the butter and cheese mixture on thick. Broil until bubbly. Serve hot.

Variation: Add grilled thin slices of steak on top of the cheese. Try adding just Colby/Jack and softened cream cheese together along with the butter.

We were enjoying a great steak dinner at home with Scott, Kathy, Mike and Sally. Sally brought out this amazing garlic bread that looked so good you almost wanted to forget about everything else. This is the recipe. It is sinful, but delicious!!

PEASANT WHITE BREAD

Makes 2 loaves
Time: 3 hours

Plan Ahead: Make bread the day before. Wrap in foil and re-heat in 300° oven for 30 min.

- 1½ cups warm water (105-115°) divided
- 4½ teaspoons active dry yeast
- ¼ cup clover honey
- 3 cups all-purpose flour
- 1 Tablespoon coarse salt
- 1 Tablespoon rosemary, dried or fresh (optional)

1. Mix ½ cup warm water, yeast and honey together in a small bowl until it blooms. In a large bowl combine the yeast mixture, 1 cup warm water, flour, salt and rosemary if using. Knead on a lightly floured surface for 3 to 4 min.
2. In another bowl put a little olive oil, add the dough and turn to coat. Cover with a damp dishtowel and let dough rise for one hour. Punch the dough down, cover and let rise again for an hour.
3. Divide the dough in half. Shape like Ciabatta, Italian loaves or Baguettes. Place on a buttered baking sheet. Cover and let rise 20 min.
4. Preheat the oven to 350° and bake for 13 min. on the middle rack and 13 min. on the bottom rack. The loaves are ready when slightly browned and hollow sounding when the bottom is tapped.

Serve with: Anything!

This is one of those breads that is wonderful served right out of the oven with unsalted butter. It is really good! I love the flavor of the rosemary. It is not too much - just right. A really nice homemade artisan bread. Thanks, Lindsey, for sharing. xo

NAAN OR ROTI INDIAN BREAD

Makes about 9
Time: 1 hour 45 minutes

1 Tablespoon active dry yeast
1 cup warm water (105-115°)
1 teaspoon sugar
3½ Tablespoons sugar
1 egg, beaten
3 Tablespoons milk
2 teaspoons coarse salt
½ teaspoon baking soda
4 - 4½ cups all-purpose flour
1 large clove fresh garlic, minced (optional)
Olive oil for frying
Butter for spreading

Expose your family to the different kinds of breads from around the world. xo

1. In a small bowl mix the yeast, water and 1 teaspoon sugar together. Let stand 10 min. until it blooms. In a large bowl stir together the 3½ Tablespoons sugar, egg, milk, salt and soda. Stir in the yeast mixture and the flour to make soft dough.
2. Turn out onto a lightly floured surface and knead for 6 to 8 min. or until smooth. Place the dough in a large bowl coated with olive oil. Cover it with a damp dishtowel. Set dough aside to rise until double, about 1 hour. Punch down and knead in the fresh garlic if using.
3. Pinch off dough about the size of a tennis ball. Roll into a ball, spray a baking sheet with cooking oil and place the balls on it. Let rise until double, about 30 min.
4. Turn a pancake griddle to about 350°. Roll out each piece of dough as thin as you can get it. Should be about 1 foot long. (You won't need any flour to roll the dough out on). Lightly oil the grill with olive oil.
5. Place dough on grill and oil the topside lightly with a rubber brush. Cook for about 2 min. on one side, turn and cook the other side. Turn again if needed. You can cook 3 or more at a time. Continue the process until all the dough is cooked. Serve warm with butter.

Roti recipe: 3 cups whole wheat flour (Indian Brand), ¼ teaspoon salt, ½ teaspoon olive oil, ¾ cup warm water. Make firm dough. Shape into 8 balls.
Roll out in a circle. Bake on a grill, turn over when bubbles. Serve warm with butter.

Variation: Make a wrap out of the Naan with grilled chicken, garlic salt, shredded cheese, chic peas, black, white or red kidney beans and fresh spinach. Sort of make a Taco out of it.

Serve with: Along side soup, salad or any hearty meal.

FOOD NANNY BEST GLUTEN FREE FRENCH BAGUETTES

Makes 2 Baguettes
Time: 1 hour

2¼ cups warm water (105-115°), divided
1½ Tablespoons active dry yeast
2 teaspoons sugar, divided
2 teaspoons coarse salt
3½ cups Gluten Free all-purpose flour*

Gluten Free all-purpose and whole grain flours I have used and recommend:

- ***Premium Gold, Flax & Whole Grain all-purpose flour, Gluten Free. Order on-line.***
- ***William Sonoma – Cup for Cup Gluten Free. (Has dairy in the flour) Available in stores.***
- ***Oh My Gluten Free – you're my everything flour all-purpose flour. Order on-line.***
- ***Grandpa's Kitchen Gluten Free Flour Blend. Order on-line.***

1. In a small bowl combine ½ cup of the water, yeast and 1 teaspoon of the sugar. Stir just to combine and cover over with plastic wrap or a plate. Let the mixture stand about 5 min. or until it blooms and gets bubbly or foamy.
2. In a large mixing bowl beat the flour, salt and the remaining 1 teaspoon of sugar, yeast mixture and 1¾ cups warm water with a wooden spoon until totally combined and smooth, about 1 min.
3. Spray a baguette pan generously with cooking oil. Spoon half of the dough into each side of baguette pan, forming a baguette with the spoon. Cover with plastic wrap sprayed with baking oil and let rise until double about 20 to 30 min.
4. Preheat oven to 450°. Place the baguettes on the middle rack with a pan of water on the lowest rack of the oven to create steam. Bake baguettes for 15 min., brush with butter. (Gluten Free bread flour will not brown without the butter on top. It will also help to make the bread more crisp.) Continue baking for 10 more min. Cool on wire rack.

Variations: Add up to 1 cup more flour and 2 Tablespoons olive oil and knead briefly. Form into loaves. For whole grain use half Gluten Free all-purpose flour and half Gluten Free whole grain flour.

Our friend Brent who has celiac, has tried every gluten free bread out there! He and Rebecca, his wife who bakes for him, say this is the fastest, easiest and most delicious gluten free bread they have eaten.

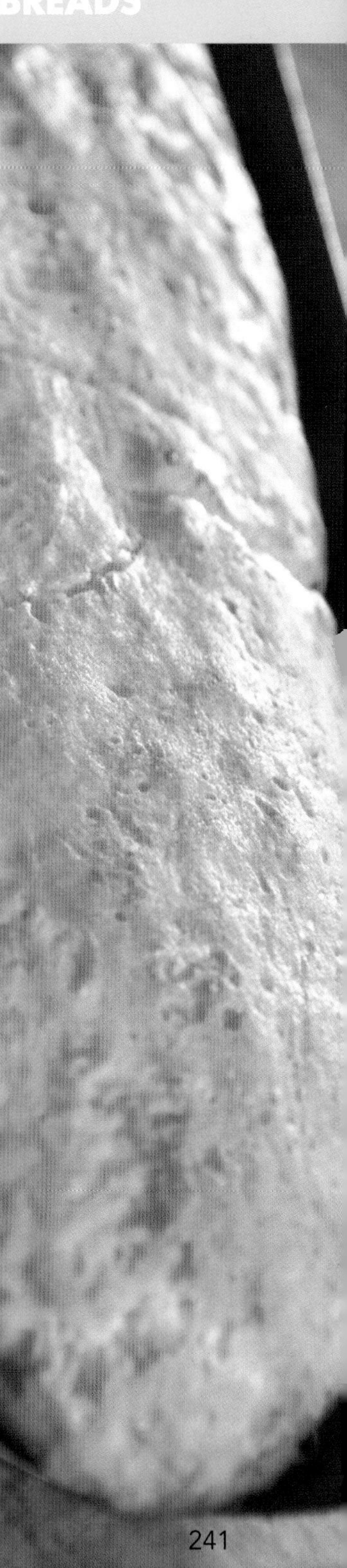

FRENCH BAGUETTES

Makes 2 baguettes
Time: 45 minutes

1½ cups warm (105-115°) water, divided
1½ Tablespoons (2 packets) active dry yeast
2 teaspoons sugar, divided
3¼ cups all-purpose flour
2 teaspoons salt

1. In a small bowl, combine ½ cup water, yeast and 1 teaspoon sugar. Stir just to combine and cover with plastic wrap or a plate. Let the mixture stand about 5 min. or until it blooms a little.
2. In a large mixing bowl or the bowl of a heavy-duty mixer or a food processor, blend the flour, salt, the remaining 1 teaspoon sugar and the yeast mixture. Gradually add water up to the remaining 1 cup and mix until the dough forms a smooth ball that is not too sticky to handle. (If the dough ends up too sticky add a little more flour.) Turn the dough onto a floured surface and knead briefly, until the dough is smooth and elastic.
3. Cut the dough in half and shape the halves into baguettes by folding the dough over once and shaping from the center towards the ends as you roll. Grease a baguette pan (available at kitchen stores) and place the loaves in the pan. Score the loaves down the middle, making a shallow cut, cover with a dishtowel and let dough rise in a warm place about 30 min. or until doubled in bulk.
4. Meanwhile, preheat the oven to 450° and place a shallow pan of water in the bottom of the oven to create steam. Bake the baguettes for 15 min. or until they have a hollow sound when tapped on the bottom. If desired brush the tops with butter halfway through the baking time. For a softer crust, brush with butter when they have finished baking.

Variations: This bread is my most versatile bread ever! I have people who make it for every bread need: hamburger buns, hot dog buns, French bread pizza, sandwiches - the list goes on and on. You can also make this bread whole grain by using half all-purpose flour and half whole wheat, or white spelt, or kamut, even gluten free. Check out my Gluten Free recipe on page 241.

I will not forget the first time we bought a baguette in France. We all savored every bite. More dense than Italian bread, it is wonderful plain or with butter and also makes excellent garlic bread and bruschetta.

BUTTERNUT SQUASH ROLLS

Makes 40
Time: 50 minutes

Plan Ahead. Prepare the dough the night before.

1 cup Butternut squash, peeled, baked and mashed. About ½ Butternut squash equals one cup (Cannot use frozen squash, it is too watery.)
1 cup scalded milk
1½ teaspoons active dry yeast
½ cup warm water (105-110°)
½ cup sugar
1 stick butter (½ cup), room temperature
1 teaspoon coarse salt
5 cups all-purpose flour

1. Cut the squash into pieces. Leave on the rind. Place on a small baking sheet and drizzle with olive oil. Cover with foil and bake 1 hour at 350° in the oven. Cut the rind off the squash. Remove the seeds. Mash with a fork. Set aside.
2. Scald milk in the microwave for 1 min. 45 sec. Cool to warm. Dissolve the yeast in warm water and let bloom 5 to 10 min. Mix the warm milk, sugar, butter and salt in a large bowl. Add the yeast mixture. Combine. Mix in the squash and flour. Spray some plastic wrap with cooking oil and place over the bowl. Let dough rise in the refrigerator overnight.
3. Roll out on lightly floured surface directly out of the refrigerator to ¼ inch thick. Use a 2-inch round biscuit cutter and cut the dough into rounds, or shape into small circles. Fold over and place on a buttered baking sheet. Cover with a dishtowel (not terry cloth) and let raise until double, about 30 min.
4. Bake at 375° on the middle rack for 8 min., move to bottom rack and bake for 8 more min. Serve warm.

Serve with: Anything!!

Variations: May double this recipe to make about 80 rolls. May use Acorn squash.

I learned how to make these rolls when
I was living in NY over 40 years ago.
Jean brought these to every social event we had.
They were a hit then and still are.
You are going to go crazy over these rolls!
My entire family requests them often.
I love how you can sneak something extra healthy in there
for your family and they don't even know it.
These are soft and delicious. xo

HONEY WHITE BREAD

Makes 2 loaves
Time: 1 hour 15 minutes

2½ cups milk
¼ cup butter
⅓ cup honey
2½ teaspoons active dry yeast
1 egg, beaten
2 teaspoons salt
5-6 cups all-purpose flour

1. Heat together the milk, butter and honey in the microwave for about 40 sec.; stir and heat for another 40 sec. Cool liquids down to lukewarm.
2. Pour the milk mixture into a large bowl or in a heavy duty mixer. Add the yeast, egg, salt and enough flour to stir together to make a moderately stiff dough. Knead for about 6 min. by hand or in a bread mixer.
3. Generously grease two bread pans. Form dough into 2 loaves and place in pans. Cover with a dishtowel. Let dough rise until double. Bake at 350° for 30 to 35 min. on the middle rack.

Variations: 2½ teaspoons instant yeast. Try using in my Bread Pudding page 315.

This is a delicious, easy, rich white bread. Julie brought it to me and it has become one of our family's favorites!

FOOD NANNY PARMESAN BREAD STICKS

Makes 30
Time: 1½ hours

2 sticks butter plus 2 Tablespoons, divided
1½ teaspoons garlic salt
2 teaspoons dried oregano
2 teaspoons dried basil
2 teaspoons dried parsley
1 cup Parmesan cheese, grated

1 Recipe Tucson Sun Pizza Dough, may use water or beer. Use four cups all-purpose flour. Follow instructions on page 133 through to step #4

1. Prepare the dough according to the instructions on page 133. When the dough has doubled in bulk in step # 4, punch down. Lightly flour your counter top. Roll the entire amount of dough out to about a 24 inch x 15 inch wide rectangle.
2. Melt one stick of butter in the microwave. Add the garlic salt. Stir. Brush half the dough long ways with about half of the garlic butter mixture. Fold the dough in half, towards you. Then roll the dough loosely away from you. Cut the dough in half. Each half will be cut into 15, ¼ inch wide pieces.
3. Turn the oven to 400°. Grease two baking sheets with butter. Roll each piece on the counter top, (one at a time) into a 6½ inch long rope. Twist the rope and lay on the baking sheet, one inch apart. Push each end down with your finger so the bread stick will stay in place.
4. Once the first baking sheet is full with the first 15 bread sticks, prepare the cheese mixture. Melt 1 stick butter plus 2 tablespoons in a small bowl in the microwave. Add the oregano, basil, parsley and Parmesan cheese. Stir together. Using a spoon, top each bread stick with some of the cheese mixture. Use half of it, save the other half for the next 15 bread sticks. Let rise until almost double. Brush lightly with more of the garlic butter, just before going into the oven to bake. (They will most likely be ready for the oven when you finish rolling the next 15 bread sticks.)
5. Place on the bottom rack of the oven and bake for 12 min. Move to the middle rack and bake for another 12 min. Brush lightly again with the melted garlic butter just before serving. Repeat with the other pan of Bread Sticks. Serve warm or at room temperature.

Serve with: Just about any meal you can think of! I just served them tonight with pasta, salad and fresh vegetables. Best eaten the same day.

Variation: Use my Basic Pizza Dough recipe on page 137.

I have never met a kid or an adult who did not love my breadsticks. You can't just eat one! They are the perfect size, tasty and crunchy.

ARTISAN BEER BREAD

Makes 1 loaf
Time: 8 - 18 hours

Plan Ahead. Start the bread when you get up early in the morning. Bake it for dinner.

Tip: 72° in the kitchen is best for baking bread.

3¼ cups all-purpose flour
¼ teaspoon active dry yeast, or instant yeast
1¼ teaspoons coarse salt
¾ cup warm water (105-115°)
¾ cup beer or (non-alcoholic beer) at room temperature. (¾ cup equals about 6 oz. beer)

Pizza stone, tiles, baking sheet, or 6 to 8 quart cast iron, enamel with lid.

1. In a medium size bowl whisk together flour, yeast and salt. Add water and beer and mix together with a wooden spoon. Spray plastic wrap with cooking oil and place over bowl. Let the dough sit at room temperature 8 hours. The longer the rise the more dense the bread. You can let it rise as much as 18 hours.
2. Flour a work surface with 2 Tablespoons flour and pour dough out onto it. Fold it over a couple of times. Sprinkle the top with about a Tablespoon of flour.
3. Roll off a sheet of plastic wrap 2 feet long. Lay it on the counter. Spray the entire plastic with cooking oil. Sprinkle the middle of the plastic with 2 Tablespoons flour. Place the dough on top of the plastic gently, and quickly fold the sides of the plastic over the dough, one side at a time.
4. Turn the oven to 450°. (If using a pot, put it in the oven, with the lid, and let it get hot. Let dough rise at least 30 min. while the oven is heating.
5. Gently lift the bread over to the oven and drop it from the plastic, upside down onto a pizza stone, tiles, oiled baking sheet or in a hot pot on the lowest rack in the oven. (If using pot, cover with lid, bake 35 to 45 min. or until golden and remove the lid half way through.) Bake at 450° about 20 to 25 min. or until golden brown. Serve warm or cool on rack.

Serve with: Raspberry Butter or Strawberry Butter.

Raspberry Butter
2 sticks butter (1 cup), softened at room temperature
½ cup honey
½ cup raspberry jam (homemade is wonderful)
½ - 1 teaspoon vanilla
In a small bowl mix together butter, honey, jam and vanilla. Spread on bread.

Strawberry Butter
1 stick unsalted butter (½ cup) softened at room temperature
3 Tablespoons strawberry jam (homemade is wonderful)
3 Tablespoons powdered sugar
In a small bowl mix together butter, jam and sugar. Spread on Bread.

This bread is worth all the effort. xo

LIZ'S CRESCENT DINNER ROLLS

Makes: 24 rolls
Time 3-4 hours

2 Tablespoons active dry yeast
¼ cup plus 1 Tablespoon warm (105-115°) water
1 cup milk
3 eggs
½ cup sugar
½ cup canola oil
About 5½ cups all-purpose flour, divided
2 teaspoons salt
Butter

1. In a small bowl combine the yeast and water. Cover and let the mixture bloom about 10 min.
2. Meanwhile, heat the milk in the microwave until just warm, not scalding, 1 min. 45 sec.
3. In a large bowl, beat the eggs, sugar and oil with a whisk. Stir in the milk and yeast mixture. With a wooden spoon stir in 4-5 cups of the flour and salt until combined.
4. Cover with plastic wrap sprayed with cooking oil and let dough rise in a warm place, 2 to 3 hours.
5. Lightly grease a 12 x 18-inch sheet pan and set aside.
6. Punch the sticky dough down and turn it onto a lightly floured surface. Pat it with additional flour if necessary for handling and keep your hands floured.
7. Divide the dough into thirds. Roll one section into a circle about the size of a dinner plate. With a pizza cutter, cut once down the middle, then across, then diagonally (the same way a pizza is cut) to make eight wedges. Roll up each wedge from the wide end toward the point. Place the rolls point side down on the prepared pan. Repeat with the remaining sections. (All rolls should fit on one sheet pan.)
8. Cover with a clean dishtowel and let rise until doubled in bulk, about 15 min.
9. Meanwhile, preheat the oven to 400°. Bake 5 min. on the bottom rack; move to the middle rack and bake 5 min. or until the rolls are light brown. Remove the rolls from the oven and brush the tops with butter.

Tip: Less flour makes for lighter rolls.

The best thing about these rolls is that they are still moist and delicious for 3 days when you keep them sealed in a plastic bag after they are cooled.

LIZ'S CRESCENT DINNER ROLLS VARIATION

Makes: 24 rolls
Time 3-4 hours

I make these every year into little Turkeys for Thanksgiving.

1. Grease the entire muffin tin, not just the muffin hole but the entire thing.

2. Instead of rolling into crescents, place the triangle piece of dough into greased muffin tin.

3. Lay the fat end out onto the muffin tin and use scissors to cut feathers (3 to 5) at the fat end of the crescent.

4. Lay the tiny pointed end out on the muffin tin as well and use a toothpick to poke one hole for an eye at the point of the crescent. The body of the turkey is most of the dough that lays down in the muffin hole.

5. Let rise and bake as directed. Check them to make sure they don't burn by the "feathers". Cover with foil if needed.

These are the cutest little turkeys you have ever seen or eaten!

foodnanny
50 mL

HAMBURGER BUNS - HALF WHITE, HALF WHOLE WHEAT

Makes about 60 hamburger buns or about 150 Sliders or 200 minis
Time: 35 minutes

3½ cups warm (105-115°) water plus 1 Tablespoon
1 cup canola oil
¾ cup sugar
6 Tablespoons active dry yeast
3 eggs, beaten
1 Tablespoon coarse salt
4 cups white whole wheat flour or white spelt
6¼ cups all-purpose flour or bread flour

1. In a large bowl mix the water, oil, sugar and yeast. Let sit until it blooms, about 10 to 15 min. Add the beaten eggs, salt and flour. Stir together.
2. If doing by hand, turn the dough out onto lightly floured surface and knead until smooth about 5 min. Adding more white flour if needed until the dough does not stick to the surface. May use a heavy duty mixer. When the dough comes away from the sides of the bowl you have enough flour. Knead for 5 min.
3. Preheat the oven to 425°. Roll the dough out ½ inch thick on a lightly floured surface. Shape the dough into different size buns as desired. (For regular hamburger buns I use a wide mouth canning jar lid, or a biscuit cutter also works nicely.)
4. Spray baking sheets with cooking spay and place the buns about 2 inches apart. Cover with a dishtowel and let dough rise for 15 min. Bake 5 min. on the bottom rack, then 5 min. on the middle rack. Let cool on a wire rack. Store in plastic bags until ready to use or freeze for up to 3 months.

Variations: Mini-sliders 1½ inch round: Bake 4 min. on middle shelf and 4 min. on bottom shelf. Sliders 2 ½ inches round: Bake 5 min. middle shelf, 2 to 3 min. bottom shelf. Use all white flour or all whole wheat flour.

*These are wonderful hamburger buns.
I love to make them with White Whole Wheat flour.
There is nothing like a great hamburger made with homemade buns! These freeze so well.
You can make them days ahead, thaw and warm in the oven or on the grill for perfect buns! xo*

Salads

Nothing excites me more than to present to you my new Salads and Sandwiches.
This is the way I like to eat and live. I love to serve these salads as main dishes for dinner. I work them into my meal plan so I can make sure to have the ingredients on hand when I need them. I use these Salads and Sandwiches for special occasions, such as luncheons. Or, eating with a special friend or family member at lunchtime.
I use them in the summertime when we are grilling.
I use them as side dishes. I choose them for any night of the week.
So much of what I have for you in this chapter is good clean eating.
We can and should get all the nutrition our body needs through what we eat daily.
Great salads can be a big part of that.
Some of my most favorite ingredients in a salad are arugula, spinach, quinoa, orzo, blue cheese dressing, olive oil and balsamic vinegar, nuts, fruit, veggies of all kinds, couscous, you get the idea.
You can make a salad these days out of most any grain or any fruit or vegetable.
In fact, the salads that I love the most are just good healthy ingredients with only a little dressing. I prefer the lighter dressings.

The Food Nanny

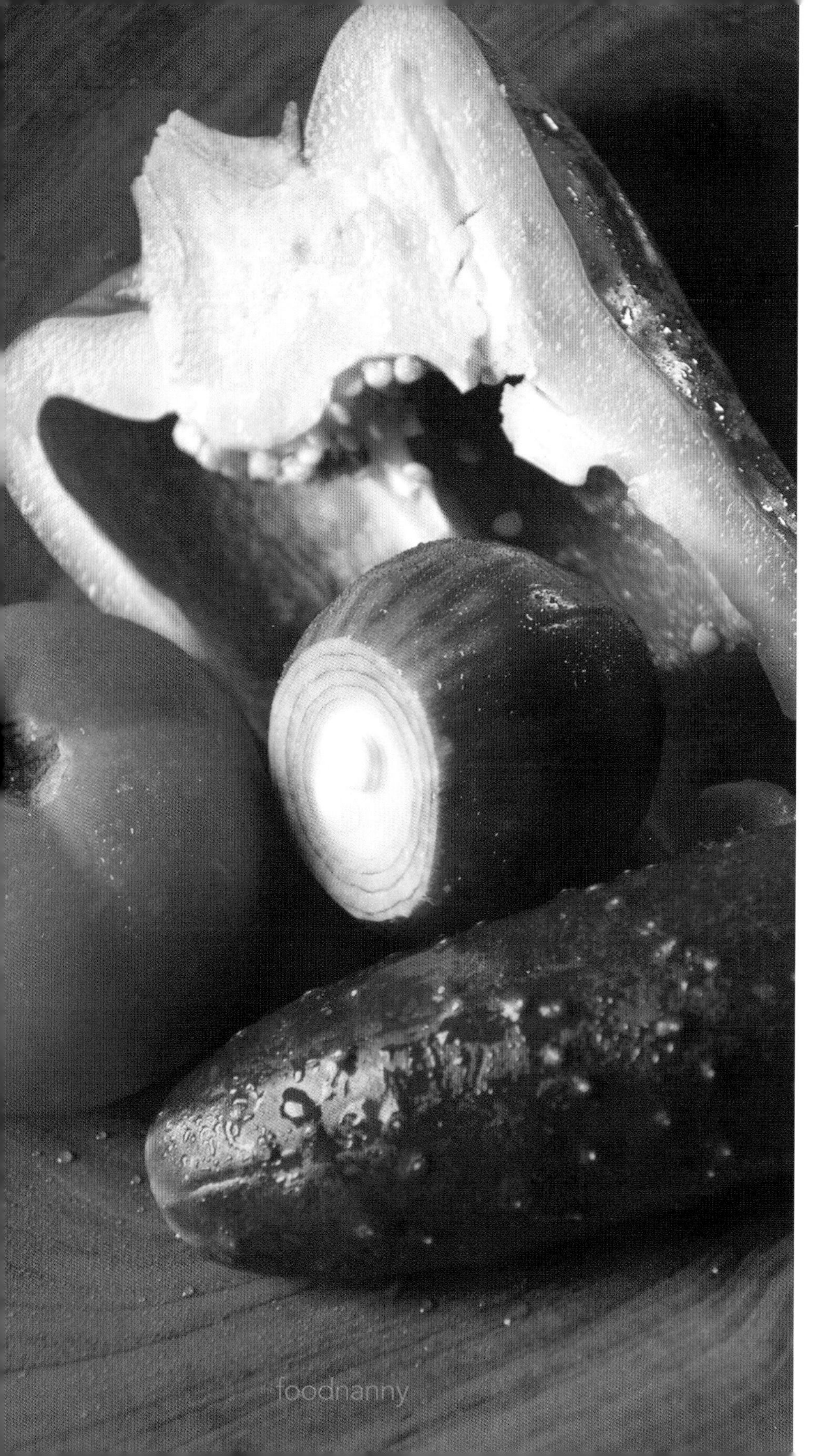

EVERYDAY SALADS

ATHENS GREEK SALAD

Serves 4
Time: 10 minutes

1 large tomato, sliced into 4 wedges
1 cucumber, peeled and cut into ½ in. pieces
1 small red onion, sliced thin
½ green Bell pepper cut into small strips
Kalamato olives to taste, about 10
2 Tablespoons capers
Greek oregano fresh or dried, to sprinkle on
Sea salt/coarse salt, to taste
White pepper to taste
Big slice of Feta cheese (sheep or cow) - about 1in. thick and 3 in. long
¼ cup olive oil

1. Select a medium size bowl to make this salad in…I like a shallow bowl for this salad.
2. Cut the tomato in half lengthwise, then in half again to make 4 pieces. Place in bowl. Peel the cucumber and cut into ½ in. pieces, place in bowl. Slice the red onion and green bell pepper, place in bowl. Add olives. Sprinkle on the capers, oregano, salt and white pepper.
3. Lay the Feta on top of the vegetables. Drizzle generously with olive oil and serve immediately.

Serve with: Artisan Bread page 236, Peasant White Bread page 237, French Baguettes page 242. Serve this salad along side most any meal, Yamista on page 194.

I learned how to make this original Greek salad in Athens from some of the best Chefs. The best part of the salad is dipping your bread into the last of the olive oil and spices left in the bottom of the bowl.

TWO BASIC SALADS

Serves 4
Time: 2 minutes

Salad #1:
3 fresh Roma or heirloom tomatoes, chopped
2 2-inch balls Buffalo Mozzarella Cheese, cut up
Olive oil, to taste
Coarse salt, to taste
4 large fresh basil leaves, torn

Salad #2:
3 fresh Roma or heirloom tomatoes, chopped
½ head Butter lettuce, torn
Olive oil, to taste
Fresh lemon juice, to taste
Apple cider vinegar, to taste

In a medium sized bowl mix all the ingredients together, for salad #1 or salad #2.

I learned how to make these simple delicious salads in Italy.
There is nothing better than wonderful tomatoes.
The Italian tomatoes have a very thin skin and are delicious.
Garden tomatoes are the best yet!
Heirloom tomato varieties have great taste if you can find them.
Look for them at your local Farmer's Market. xo

BROCCOLI SALAD WITH BACON

Serves 4
Time: 2 minutes

Plan Ahead: Make salad up to 24 hours ahead.

1 Broccoli head (4 cups), fresh cleaned broccoli flowerets, no stem, small dice
½ cup red onion, minced
¾ cup raisins
12 bacon slices, cooked and crumbled pieces
1 cup mayonnaise
2 Tablespoons cider vinegar
¼ cup sugar

1. In a medium sized bowl mix the diced broccoli (diced broccoli, small is key), onion, raisins and crumbled bacon pieces.
2. In a small bowl mix the mayonnaise with the vinegar and sugar. Pour over the salad. Mix.
3. Cover and place in refrigerator for at least 2 hours or overnight before serving.

Serve with: This can be served with most meals as a vegetable.

I was speaking in Louisiana and Linda shared her recipe with me.
This is the BEST Broccoli Salad ever! xo

WARM ORZO SALAD WITH CHICKEN

Serves 2 as a Main Dish
Time: 20 minutes

Dressing:
3 Tablespoons olive oil
3 Tablespoons fresh lemon juice
¾ teaspoon salt
Fresh ground black pepper

Pasta:
¾ cup Orzo pasta, cooked

Sautéed Chicken:
1 boneless/skinless chicken breast, chopped
2 teaspoons olive oil
2 teaspoons unsalted butter

Other Ingredients:
3 Tablespoons shallot or red onion, chopped
3 Tablespoons fresh dill, chopped
3 Tablespoons fresh parsley, chopped
6 grape tomatoes cut in half lengthwise
¼ cup Feta cheese, crumbled
½ cup Pine nuts or toasted almonds, optional
1½ cups baby arugula

1. In a small bowl whisk together the olive oil, fresh lemon juice, salt and fresh ground black pepper. Set aside.
2. Cook the Orzo according to package directions. Drain. Keep warm. Set aside.
3. Wipe off the chicken with a wet paper towel. Chop. Sauté the chopped chicken in the olive oil and butter until cooked through about 4 min. Keep warm. Set aside.
4. In a medium size bowl add: cooked Orzo, onion, dill, parsley, tomatoes, cheese, and nuts if using. Mix in the warm chicken and arugula. Toss with the dressing and serve immediately.

Serve with: Warm Nann bread page 239, Peasant White Bread page 237.

Variations: Instead of chicken, use ½ lb. raw shrimp, cleaned, tails removed, diced. Place diced shrimp on a baking sheet and drizzle with olive oil and fresh lemon juice. Sprinkle with coarse salt and fresh ground black pepper. Bake at 350°on the middle oven rack for 5 to 6 min. Add (optional) dried cherries or cranberries.

This is one of my all time favorite salads!
This salad is a meal. I love it.
It is so healthy and tastes so good.
It was hard to create the recipe because there isn't one!
Nellie, who is a great cook, showed me how she just throws in this and that. I am so excited to share this original recipe that I have been working on for a while.
It is fabulous.

FOOD NANNY SIGNATURE SALAD

Serves 4-6 as a Main Dish
Time: 15 minutes

Plan Ahead: Rinse arugula, spinach and romaine ahead of time. Store separately. Keep cold. Chop the vegetables ahead of time and keep cold separately. Chop nuts and keep separate as well. Prepare grapes ahead of time.

3 cups arugula or mixed greens
3 cups spinach
3 cups romaine, rinsed and chopped
Coarse salt
Fresh ground black pepper
Ground ginger
¼ cup EACH - red, green and yellow Bell peppers, diced
¼ cup cocktail peanuts (roasted and salted), whole
¼ cup walnuts, chopped
⅓ cup cashews, chopped
⅓ cup golden raisins
½ cup green or red grapes, cut in half
1 crisp apple, skin on, diced
Honey
Juice of 1 fresh lemon
Olive oil

1. On a medium size platter or a medium size shallow bowl, spread out the arugula. Lightly sprinkle with coarse salt, fresh ground black pepper, and dried ginger. Sprinkle on the diced bell peppers. Drizzle with honey. This is the first of 3 layers.
2. Spread out the spinach. Lightly sprinkle with coarse salt, fresh ground black pepper and ground ginger. Sprinkle on the nuts. Drizzle with honey.
3. Spread out the romaine. Lightly sprinkle with coarse salt fresh ground black pepper and ground ginger. Sprinkle on the raisins, grapes and apple. Drizzle with honey.
4. Drizzle with lemon juice and olive oil. Serve immediately.

Serve with: Warm Nann bread page 239, Artisan Beer Bread page 247.

Variations: The key to this salad is the 3 different kinds of lettuce and the nuts. Use what you have on hand. Butter lettuce is a nice substitute. Pecans and pistachios are a nice variation as well. Add chopped cilantro and mint to the greens for more flavor, if desired. If using carrots cut in half, steam, then dice. Add diced kiwi, tomato or avocado.

I ate a salad years ago in the Philippines while visiting Rick and Nancy. It was the most memorable salad I had ever eaten. You can change around the greens, veggies, fruits and nuts to your taste. Experiment with it. This is a meal in itself!

WARM QUINOA SALAD WITH CASHEWS

Serves 1 as a Main Dish
Time: 25 minutes

- ½ cup Red Quinoa, cooked
- 2 Tablespoons olive oil
- 1 Tablespoon butter
- ⅓ cup red onion, minced
- 1 clove garlic, minced
- Coarse salt
- Fresh ground black pepper
- 3 Sun-dried tomato halves, minced
- 3 Tablespoons dried currents, (buy a small quantity at a quality food store) or golden raisins
- ⅓ cup chopped cashews
- 1 cup baby arugula
- 1 Tablespoon balsamic vinegar
- 1 Tablespoon honey

1. Rinse quinoa. In a small saucepan add 1 cup water and quinoa. Bring to a boil over medium high heat and boil until the water is gone, about 15 min. Remove from heat. Cover. Let sit for 5 min.
2. In a medium size saucepan over low heat, add olive oil and butter. Add onions and garlic and caramelize for 10 min. Season with coarse salt and fresh ground black pepper. Add sun-dried tomatoes, currents or raisins and cashews. Sauté for 1 min. Add the arugula. Sauté for 1 min. Add cooked quinoa. Mix. Remove from stove.
3. Mix the balsamic vinegar and honey. Pour over the quinoa mixture. Warm through for 30 sec. on low heat. Serve.

Serve with: Warm French Baguettes page 242 or Beer Bread page 247.

Variations: Add toasted pine nuts. Add Feta cheese.

My friend Cynthia and I die for warm Quinoa Salad. We are soul mates. Here is my rendition. It is really great!

THE WEDGE WITH HOMEMADE BLUE CHEESE DRESSING

Serves 4 as a Main Dish or Side Salad
Time: 20 minutes

Plan Ahead: Make the dressing 3 days ahead. Cook the bacon and boil the eggs ahead, if using.

1 head Iceberg lettuce core removed, rinsed and drained. Wrap in plastic and chill until ready to use.
½ cup Blue Cheese crumbles
4-5 Tablespoons buttermilk
2½ Tablespoons mayonnaise
2 Tablespoons sour cream
½ teaspoon white wine vinegar or apple cider vinegar
¼ teaspoon sugar
½ teaspoon garlic powder
Coarse salt
Fresh ground black pepper
¼ lb. bacon, cooked and diced (optional)
3 hard boiled eggs, chopped (optional)

1. On a small plate mash the Blue Cheese crumbles and buttermilk together with a fork. Place the Blue Cheese mixture in a small bowl and add mayonnaise, sour cream, vinegar, sugar, garlic powder, salt and fresh ground black pepper to taste. Mix with the fork until smooth. Cover and refrigerate for up to 3 days.
2. Cook the bacon, drain and dice. Set aside. Boil the eggs, peel and dice. Set aside.
3. Cut the lettuce in half. Then half again. You will have 4 quarters. Cut the quarters in half. You will have 8 wedges. If you are making a meal out of this salad you will want to give each person 2 wedges. Place the wedge on a plate and spoon the Blue Cheese dressing generously over top. If desired, sprinkle on diced bacon and egg. Add more ground black pepper to taste. Serve immediately.

Serve with: Liz's Crescent Dinner Rolls page 249. French Baguettes page 242, Peasant White Bread page 237 or Beer Bread on page 247. Serve this salad along side veggies, chicken, beef or lamb.

Variation: If I am making this salad as a main meal, I add the bacon and egg. You may need to double the dressing as well. If I am serving it as a side dish I usually serve this salad without the bacon and egg.

*When I am feeling like Blue Cheese I go straight to this salad.
I was raised on Homemade Blue Cheese Dressing,
even before Ranch dressing was a common household name.
Dad and Mom used to take us girls to
a special restaurant called "Freddie's" just to order
their Blue Cheese Salad in the 1950's and 60's.
This salad was memorable then and still is.
I love it.*

SPINACH SALAD WITH SWISS CHEESE, BACON AND MUSHROOMS

Serves 10-12
Time: 10 minutes if you plan ahead.

Plan Ahead: Marinate the onions 8 hours. They will keep for 3 days. Make dressing up to 3 days ahead. Cook the bacon.

2 cups cider vinegar
2 cups sugar
1 small red onion, peeled, sliced thin
1 9-10 oz. package fresh spinach leaves
1 9-10 oz. package fresh romaine lettuce
½ lb. Swiss cheese, grated
⅓ lb. bacon, cooked and crumbled
⅓ cup mushrooms, sliced very thin
⅔ cup cottage cheese (add at the last minute)

Dressing:
¼ cup sugar
½ cup apple cider vinegar
1 Tablespoon olive oil
1 teaspoon salt
½ teaspoon dry mustard
1 Tablespoon poppy seeds

1. Mix the vinegar and sugar together in a medium size bowl. Add sliced onions. Cover. Marinate in the refrigerator up to 8 hours. Drain and throw away the liquid.
2. In a large bowl mix both kinds of lettuce, Swiss cheese, bacon and mushrooms. (Can keep in the refrigerator up to 1 day.)
3. When ready to serve, add the drained onions and cottage cheese.
4. In a small bowl whisk together the sugar, vinegar, olive oil, salt, dry mustard and poppy seeds. Pour over the salad. Mix thoroughly.

Serve with: Liz's Crescent Dinner Rolls page 249. Take this to a picnic or serve with dinner 3 nights in a row. Just don't mix in the onions, cottage cheese or dressing until just before serving.

Elizabeth, who has been a dear friend of mine for over 30 years, shared this recipe with me. Everyone loves this salad.
Elizabeth has a farmhouse in my little town.
Her flower and vegetable gardens have made her famous.
Elizabeth turned 91 years old this year.
Thanks for your exemplary life! xo

STRAWBERRY DAYS SALAD

Serves 6
Time: 15 minutes

Plan Ahead: Prepare the almonds one day ahead. Make the dressing one day ahead.

Dressing:
- **¼ cup red wine vinegar**
- **¼ teaspoon dry mustard**
- **½ teaspoon salt**
- **2½ Tablespoons sugar**
- **¼ cup strawberry jam**
- **⅓ cup olive oil**

Sugared Almonds:
- **½ cup sliced raw almonds**
- **2 Tablespoons sugar**

Salad:
- **5 cups Romaine lettuce, chopped**
- **1 cup baby arugula**
- **¼ cup red onion, little strips**
- **1 cup fresh strawberries, sliced**
- **¼ cup fresh Parmesan cheese, grated**
- **½ tomato chopped, or 6 grape tomatoes, halved**

Dressing:
Prepare the dressing in a small bowl. Whisk together the vinegar, dry mustard, salt, sugar, jam and olive oil. Keep in the refrigerator for up to one day.

Sugared Almonds:
Stir the almonds and sugar together in a small saucepan over low heat. When the sugar is melted and the almonds begin to barely turn brown, (about 5 min.), the almonds are ready. Put the almonds on foil to cool. Store in a plastic bag when cool.

Salad:
Mix the romaine, arugula, red onion, strawberries, Parmesan cheese and tomatoes together. Mix in the sugared almonds. Pour on the dressing. Mix.

Serve with: Almost anything!

*This salad is a keeper!
We enjoy it all year long.
It is one of our favorites!!*

CORN SALAD

Serves 4-6
Time: 15 minutes

- 2 fresh, uncooked cobs of corn. Cut corn off cob with a sharp knife
- 1 can black beans, drained and rinsed
- 1 Tablespoon cilantro, chopped
- ½ cup red onion or sweet onion, chopped
- ¼ cup each Red and Green Bell pepper, chopped
- 2 fresh garlic cloves, crushed
- ¼ cup olive oil
- 3 Tablespoons apple cider vinegar

In a medium size bowl add the fresh corn, beans, cilantro, onion, red and green peppers, garlic, oil and vinegar. Mix. Serve at room temperature.

Serve with: This is a side dish to be served mostly in the summertime when the fresh corn is on. It goes nicely with any meal off the grill.

Variations: Add chopped, cooked chicken for a main dish.

This is a fabulous tasting salad and one of Sally's favorites. And it's good for you too! xo

CHIOGGIA BEETS WITH RASPBERRY MINT VINAIGRETTE

Serves 4
Time: 40 minutes

- 1 lb. Chioggia* beets
- 3 Tablespoons scallions, sliced thin
- 2 to 2½ Tablespoons raspberry vinegar
- 2 teaspoons fresh lemon juice
- 2 Tablespoons fresh mint, chopped
- 1 Tablespoon orange zest, finely grated
- ½ teaspoon coarse salt
- ½ teaspoon fresh ground black pepper
- ¼ cup olive oil

1. In a 2 quart saucepan, cover beets with 1 inch water and simmer until tender, about 25 min. Drain water and let cool until beets can be handled. Slip off and discard the skins. Cut the beets into thin slices, about ¼ inch.
2. While beets cook, stir together remaining ingredients, except oil. Add oil in a slow stream, stirring until combined. Add warm beets and toss to combine. Add salt to taste if desired. Serve warm or chilled.

Serve with: As a side salad or a cold vegetable with any meal.

*Chioggia beets are sometimes called candy-cane beets because of their red and white stripes. They are delicious to eat and beautiful to serve.

Ann created this recipe to use her home grown Chioggia beets. They love it.

COUSCOUS SALAD WITH APRICOTS, DATES, AND PINE NUTS

Serves 6
Time: 30 minutes

Plan Ahead: Prepare the couscous ahead of time.

- 1 box Pine Nut Couscous (or any of their other flavors)
- ½ cup pitted dates, chopped
- ½ cup dried apricots, chopped
- ½ cup raisins
- ¼ cup red onion, diced
- 1 can mandarin oranges, drain and reserve juice
- 2 Tablespoons olive oil
- 2 Tablespoons cider vinegar
- ½ teaspoon sugar
- 2 Tablespoons fresh ginger, grated
- Coarse salt, to taste

1. Prepare the couscous according to directions. Let cool.
2. Add dates, apricots, raisins, onion and mandarin oranges.
3. With a fork, mix juice from oranges, olive oil, vinegar, sugar, fresh ginger and salt in a small bowl.
4. You might not need to use all the dressing. Add dressing a little at a time to couscous mixture and toss until lightly coated, but not soggy.

Serve with: Grilled Chicken page 159 or Grilled Chicken Sandwiches page 277.

Variation: Substitute 1 large orange: grate the peel; squeeze and save the juice, instead of using the mandarin oranges. If you don't use Pine Nut Couscous, add ½ cup pine nuts.

Ann, my editor, made this salad for me years ago and I am still dreaming about that day. She made it as a side dish for one of her kid's weddings. It is wonderful! Couscous is a nice option. It is also a nice salad to take to a gathering like I have many times.

APPLE, DRIED CHERRY AND WALNUT SALAD

Serves 4
Time: 10 minutes

Plan Ahead: Toast the walnuts. Prepare the dressing one-day ahead.

- ¼ cup mayonnaise
- ¼ cup pure maple syrup
- 3 Tablespoons white wine or sherry vinegar
- 2 teaspoons sugar
- ½ cup olive oil
- ½ cup walnuts, toasted and chopped
- 1 5 oz. bag mixed baby greens or Romaine, about 10 leaves
- 2 small apples, skin on, diced or cut into matchstick size strips
- ½ cup tart dried cherries, or dried cranberries

1. In a small bowl whisk together the mayonnaise, maple syrup, vinegar, sugar and oil. Store in the refrigerator until ready to use.
2. Toast the walnuts in the oven at 350° for 10 min.
3. In a medium size salad bowl add the lettuce, apples, dried cranberries or cherries, and walnuts. Toss with enough dressing to coat.

Serve with: Honey White Bread page 245. I love this salad with a turkey or ham dinner.

This is a good Go-To salad of mine. Very easy. Keep the ingredients around and you can make it up in no time!

Sandwiches

I love my Sandwiches. They are tasty and nutritious.
They will bring more variety into your meal plan. Isn't that what a meal plan really is? It's the variety that keeps us interested in cooking.
It's the variety that makes dinnertime fun for the entire family.
It keeps us coming back night after night excited to spend time together.
If we make a meal plan, we can afford to eat the foods we love and crave.
When at the grocery store armed with a grocery list, we don't buy unneeded food.
We buy the food that is on our list so that nothing goes to waste.
We don't buy impulse foods that will never be eaten.
That is the beauty of my meal plan. It's also fun to try new foods.
You can do this on a consistent basis when you work a new recipe into your plan.
This forces us to get out of our comfort zone and to try and eat greener,
which means healthier. Take good care of yourself first, Mom,
so that you can be there for those who need you.
It is our responsibility as the "nurturer" in the home to present good
wholesome food to our families on a daily basis.
I hope some of these recipes will inspire you to create that at your dinner table. xo

The Food Nanny

SANDWICHES FOR DINNER

Meatless

GRILLED FOOT LONG TURKEY AND BACON SANDWICH WITH FRESH MOZZARELLA CHEESE

Serves 4
Time: 20 minutes

Plan Ahead: Buy the Ciabatta bread, freeze. Make Food Nanny Italian Bread ahead. Freeze.

1 fresh foot-long loaf Ciabatta bread or Italian bread. (These 2 kinds of bread are wide and so this makes a great sandwich to share.)
Olive oil
Balsamic vinegar
Dijon mustard
¼ pound fresh Mozzarella cheese, sliced thin
¾ pound oven roasted deli turkey, sliced thin
Red onion, sliced thin (optional)
¾ pound bacon, cooked
2 tomatoes, sliced thin
2 avocados, sliced thin
Coarse salt
Fresh ground black pepper
Mayonnaise
Fresh spinach or fresh arugula (as desired)

This sandwich makes a beautiful presentation. It is as delicious as it looks. Evelyn shared this with me years ago. Lisa takes this sandwich to friends who are not feeling well. Grill, then wrap in foil and deliver warm. You are going to be making this sandwich often!

1. Cut the long loaf of bread down one side. Open it up like a sandwich. You have 2 halves. On the bottom half drizzle generously with olive oil, then drizzle with the vinegar. Spread on the Dijon mustard to taste. Lay the cheese evenly over the mustard.
2. Place the turkey on top of the cheese, add onion (if using). Arrange the bacon slices on top of the turkey. Place the tomatoes next, then the avocados. Salt and pepper to taste. Top with spinach or arugula sprigs.
3. Drizzle the top piece of bread with the olive oil and vinegar, then spread on a little more mustard and mayonnaise (if desired).
4. Put the lid on to the sandwich and push down. (Be careful not to over-fill the sandwich, as it will be too hard to keep together when turning). Turn the sandwich over and butter the bottom side.
5. Pre-heat the grill to medium heat. Place the sandwich, bottom side down, on the grill and butter the top. (It is easiest to turn the sandwich over very quickly with a pancake spatula and your fingers.)
6. Grill each side for about 10 min., or until you see the cheese start to melt. If you have an iron press, to flatten a sandwich, put that on top of the sandwich to help flatten it. (Be careful not to burn the bread.)
7. Use a spatula to slide the sandwich onto a platter. Place the sandwich on a breadboard, slice and serve.

Serve with: Your choice of chips, salad or fresh fruit.

Variation: When using my Italian Bread, pick out some of the bread on the bottom half so the sandwich filling will sit down inside the bread better and it will be easier to grill. You can also place the sandwich on a baking sheet and bake it at 300° for 15 to 20 min. Add Jalapeno Cranberry Freezer Jam Spread page 285.

Meatless OPEN FACE WHOLE WHEAT WITH GARDEN TOMATOES AND ARUGULA

Serves 1
Time: 2 minutes

1 slice whole wheat sandwich bread
Mayonnaise for spreading
1 medium garden tomato, sliced thin
Coarse salt
Fresh ground black pepper
1 cup baby arugula
Olive oil (peppery, basil or garlic flavor oil is best)
Knife and fork (to eat it)

Spread one slice whole wheat bread with plenty of mayonnaise. Place the sliced tomatoes on top of the bread. Sprinkle with salt and pepper. Pile the baby arugula high. Sprinkle with good olive oil of choice. Serve. You will need to eat this sandwich with a fork and a knife. Enjoy!

Serve with: Chips of choice.

Variation: Make a sandwich of sliced fresh garden tomatoes with mayonnaise and salt and pepper. Eat and enjoy!

In the summertime, especially when we have great tomatoes, this is my sandwich of choice. There is nothing like summer tomatoes with mayonnaise, arugula and olive oil. Yum!! xo

Meatless ROMANO-CRUSTED GRILLED CHEESE

Makes 2 Sandwiches
Time: 10 minutes

1 cup finely shaved (use a microplane grater) Romano cheese
Butter for spreading
4 slices white sandwich bread
2 very thin slices Gruyere cheese
2 very thin slices Colby/Jack cheese
Dijon mustard for spreading
¼ apricot jam
1 cup baby arugula

1. Grate the Romano cheese really fine. Butter each piece of bread on one side. Press ¼ cup of the grated cheese into the butter. (It sticks perfectly). These are the outside pieces of bread that will be grilled.
2. On the opposite side of the bread, lay a thin slice of the Gruyere Cheese, then a thin slice of Colby/Jack cheese. Spread on some mustard. On the other opposite piece of bread, spread on some apricot jam. Add the arugula. Bring the two pieces together to form a sandwich with the butter and cheese on the outsides. Repeat.
3. Heat a pan to medium heat. Place the sandwiches in the pan and grill until the cheese is melted on the inside and the outside is golden brown. Serve immediately.

Serve with: Chips of choice.

Variation: Use colby/jack shredded cheese and spread on mayonnaise and top with minced yellow onion. Butter the bread and grill. This was my Grandma's version of a kicked up Grilled Cheese. I loved it!

Gruyere cheese, jam and arugula are three of my favorite foods. The flavors of the 3 different kinds of cheeses come together really well. It has a tiny bit of sweet flavor to it with the jam. Try my creation! It is fast, easy and delicious.

HERB CRUSTED GRILLED CHICKEN SANDWICH

Serves 4
Time: 15 minutes

8 chicken tenders
2 Tablespoons fresh or dried rosemary
2 Tablespoons fresh or dried sage
1 Tablespoon fresh or dried thyme
10 cloves fresh garlic, crushed
Coarse salt, to taste
Fresh ground black pepper, to taste
4 French rolls - 6 inches long or French Bread-sliced
Butter for spreading
Mayonnaise
Dijon mustard (optional)
Sliced tomatoes
Arugula or spinach (optional)

1. Wipe off the tenders with a wet paper towel. Set aside. Combine the rosemary, sage, thyme, garlic, salt and pepper in a small bowl. Mix. Rub the seasoning into the chicken pieces.
2. Heat the grill up to medium high. Fold a paper towel in a square and drizzle it with olive oil. Using your tongs go over the grate to oil it so the chicken won't stick. Place the chicken on the grill and cook about 4 min. per side. (I like mine to be a little burned, crusty). Baste with olive oil once or twice. Take off the grill and cover to keep warm.
3. Butter the rolls and grill them until the butter melts and the buns are lightly toasted. Place 2 pieces of chicken on per roll, spread on some mayonnaise, mustard (optional) and top with sliced tomato, salt and pepper and arugula. Smash the bun down a little so the sandwich will stay together. Serve warm.

Serve with: Chips of choice. Baked Beans page 226, Raw veggies and dip. Fresh Fruit.

Variations: Use Munster or Provolone cheese to add more flavor. Grill the French rolls on a pancake grill in the house. Use my French Baguettes on page 242.

Dave, our neighbor, is famous for these sandwiches. He started making them when he was in dental school. He would put his tiny hibachi grill just outside their patio door and grill these sandwiches for his darling new wife. Dave is still grilling for his family and friends with his famous recipe. You're going to love 'um!! xo

atless

FOOD NANNY GRILLED PEANUT BUTTER AND JELLY SANDWICH

Makes 1 Sandwich
Time: 5 minutes

2 pieces white or whole wheat sandwich bread
Peanut butter (I prefer crunchy)
Jelly or jam (I prefer Blackberry jam)
Unsalted butter

1. Spread one piece of bread with peanut butter. Spread on the jelly or jam of choice. Top with the other piece.
2. To grill, butter the outside of each bread slice. Place the sandwich on a pancake griddle; or a small 8-inch frying pan on top of the stove over medium heat. Grill both sides until the peanut butter is melted and the bread is just barely golden brown. Serve immediately.

Serve with: Milk and chips of choice.

Variation: Use any kind of jelly or jam. Try using Almond butter if you can't have peanut butter.

This is my comfort food whenever I am tired or hungry for something easy, gooey, delicious and only takes 2 seconds. When I am so tired I can't move, this is what I want. I even crave it when I am not tired, especially for lunch! I raised my kids on PB&J for lunch. One day I started grilling them. This is my most favorite sandwich in the entire world. If you have not had one, you have missed out on so much goodness. I promise you, you will be making these for the rest of your life.

CHICKEN PHILLY

Serves 4
Time: 20 minutes

***Plan Ahead:* Prepare the chicken ahead of time. Cover. Keep warm.**

1 Tablespoon unsalted butter
1 Tablespoon olive oil
⅓ cup yellow onion, diced
1 pound boneless/skinless chicken breasts, diced
1½ Tablespoons garlic powder or 3 Tablespoons fresh garlic, minced
¼ cup chicken broth
8 ounces, bottled Cherry Peppers, diced
1 Tablespoon Cherry Pepper juice from bottle
Coarse salt
Fresh ground black pepper
4 Soft French or Hoagie Rolls about 6 inches long, buttered
Butter for spreading
4 slices Provolone cheese
¼ head iceberg lettuce, shredded
1 Tomato, chopped
Olive oil

1. In a medium side fry pan over low heat melt the butter with the olive oil. Add the onion, chicken, garlic powder or fresh garlic, chicken broth, cherry peppers, cherry pepper juice, coarse salt and fresh ground black pepper to taste. Sauté, stirring often and breaking up the chicken as fine as possible until the chicken is cooked and most of the liquid is gone. (You don't want the chicken to dry out) About 8 to 10 min. Take off the heat, cover and set aside.
2. Open the roll, butter it and lay the cheese on. Broil the roll until the cheese is mostly melted and the bun is warm, not crunchy.
3. Spoon on the chicken mixture, sprinkle with lettuce and tomato. Drizzle with a little olive oil and season with salt and pepper. Serve warm.

Serve with: Your choice of chips.

Variation: Use my French Baguette page 242 for the bun.

Whenever I visit Colin and Katie they take me straight to get this Chicken Philly at a tiny little Deli near their home. It is wonderful! This is my version of that sandwich that calls me time and time again.

PECAN CRUSTED FRIED GREEN TOMATO SANDWICH

Serves 2
Time: 20 minutes

Plan Ahead: Fry the tomatoes ahead and keep warm. Prepare the sauce ahead and keep in the refrigerator.

Aioli sauce:
- ½ red bell pepper, roasted
- 2 garlic cloves, whole
- ⅓ cup mayonnaise
- 2 Tablespoons olive oil
- Salt and pepper to taste

Sandwich:
- 2 pieces bacon, cooked
- ¼ cup Panko bread crumbs
- ⅓ cup pecans, chopped fine
- ¼ teaspoon garlic powder
- ¼ teaspoon salt
- ¼ teaspoon pepper
- ¼ teaspoon Tony Cachere's Creole Seasoning (optional) or ¼ teaspoon paprika
- 1 heirloom green tomato, or green garden tomato, sliced ¼ inch thick
- 2 egg whites
- 2 Tablespoons olive oil
- 1 teaspoon unsalted butter
- 4 pieces ¼-inch thick sour dough bread, (white or multi grain)
- Butter for bread
- 2 oz. Goat Cheese
- Arugula (optional)

1. Roast half a red bell pepper under the broiler until blackened turning often about 5-7 min. Place the pepper in a plastic bag for 10 min. and then peel off the skin.
2. Put the skinned red pepper in a food processor or blender and add garlic cloves, mayonnaise and olive oil. Blend until smooth. Add salt and pepper to taste. Set aside.
3. Cook the bacon. Set aside.
4. In a pie plate mix the panko, pecans, garlic powder, salt, pepper and Tony Cachere's or paprika. Turn on the broiler.
5. Slice the tomato into 4 slices. Beat the egg whites with a fork and dip each tomato in the whites and then in the panko/nut mixture. Set aside.
6. In a medium size sauce pan over low heat fry the tomatoes in olive oil and unsalted butter. Fry until golden brown, about 2 min. per side. Set aside.
7. Butter sour dough bread. Divide the goat cheese over 2 slices of bread. Place the 4 pieces of bread and cheese under the broiler and when the cheese and butter begin to warm, remove.
8. Top one slice of bread with red bell pepper Aioli sauce. Place the Fried Green Tomatoes on top of the warm cheese, and then a bacon slice. Top with arugula if desired. Top with remaining piece of warm buttered bread. Cut in half. Serve immediately.

Serve with: Chips of choice.

Variation: Try using a crossiant in place of the sour dough bread. Use my French Baguette on page 242.

Jenny and I went to the "Carolina Inn" and ordered Fried Green Tomato Sandwiches when I was visiting her in North Carolina doing a Food Nanny Presentation. She had never eaten one. We so enjoyed our memorable sandwiches. This is my version of a perfect Fried Green Tomato Sandwich with a kick! This sandwich is seriously delicious. This one is for you Jenny!!!

Meatless VEGGIE SANDWICHES GRILLED-OR-NOT-GRILLED

Makes 2 Sandwiches
Time: 15 minutes

Plan ahead: Mix the mayonnaise, sour cream and mustard together. Have your veggies cut and ready to place on the sandwiches before you get started.

¼ cup mayonnaise
2 Tablespoons sour cream
¼ teaspoon Dijon mustard
4 slices - ¼ inch thick *Food Nanny Italian Bread*, Whole Wheat or store bought Artisan Bread
Whole Berry Cranberry sauce for spreading (optional)
2 slices Swiss cheese
6 thin slices cucumbers, skin on
4 thin slices tomatoes, skin on
½ avocado sliced, divided
Coarse salt
Fresh ground black pepper
1 cup spinach leaves

1. Mix the mayonnaise, sour cream and mustard together. Spread on both sides of the bread. Spread on some cranberry sauce if using. Place one slice of cheese on one side of the bread.
2. Add the cucumbers, tomatoes, avocado, salt, pepper and spinach leaves. Place the other half of the bread on top and smash it down a little bit so the sandwich will stay together. (It is best to use soft bread for this sandwich so it will hold together nicely). Serve, if not grilling.
3. If grilling, heat a pancake griddle or pan to 350°. Butter one side of the bread and place it down on the grill. Butter the other side of the bread and grill both sides to a golden brown. (I use my iron press to smash down the sandwich a little.)

Serve with: Chips of choice.

Variation: Use my Cranberry Jam on page 285. Sprinkle with olive oil and balsamic vinegar.

This is my first real sandwich creation. We have been making these sandwiches for years. My girls and daughters-in-law and I especially eat them a lot! We make them when we get together for lunch or have friends for lunch. They are so delicious!

Meatless WARM PITA MUSHROOM MELT

Serves 2
Time: 15 minutes

Plan Ahead: Make the dressing ahead of time. Slice the mushrooms, grate the cheese.

- **2 7-inch rounds of Pita bread**
- **2 teaspoons olive oil**
- **2 teaspoons unsalted butter**
- **2 cups sliced (¼ inch) white mushrooms**
- **⅔ cup mozzarella cheese, grated**
- **½ to 1 Tablespoon Italian dressing (store bought)**

1. In a medium size frying pan over low heat, sauté the mushrooms in the olive oil and butter about 3 min. Salt lightly. Add the mozzarella cheese just until it melts. Set aside.
2. Warm each Pita in a small frying pan over medium heat about 2 min. per side with a few drops of olive oil. Cover. Turn so both sides are warm. Divide the mushrooms and cheese between the 2 Pitas.
3. Pour ½ to 1 Tablespoon of the dressing on to each mushroom melt. Fold over. Serve immediately.

Serve with: Chips of choice. Basic Salad on page 258, Strawberry Days Salad on page 267 or Couscous Salad on page 269.

Variation: Use my French Baguette on page 242 for this sandwich.

This is one of my all time favorite sandwiches. It is easy and so delicious. Low in calorie and tasty! Great for Vegetarians. Eat this on Wednesday for a nice easy meal, or serve it for lunch to your friends. xo

Meatless JALAPENO CRANBERRY FREEZER JAM SPREAD

Makes 9-12 Half Pints
Time: 20 minutes

3 cups (about 1½ lbs.) fresh cranberries rinsed, ground
3 cups apples (about 5 medium) any kind, cored, skins removed, ground
2½ -3 Jalapeno peppers, seeds removed, ground
1 1.75 oz. package Fruit Pectin (I use Sure Jell or MC)
8½ cups sugar
9-12 half pint containers, glass or plastic with lids

1. Grind the fruit and peppers in a food processor to make 6 cups. Pour into a large pan, add the pectin, stir and bring to a boil.
2. Add sugar, stirring well and bring to a full boil again. Pour the hot sauce in jars or plastic tubs. I have used both. Put the lids on and let sit out on the counter over night. Freeze. Will keep for months.

Serve with: Use on Turkey Sandwiches page 275 or Veggie Sandwiches page 283.

Variation: Omit jalapeno; or, use more Jalapeno for more kick.

Carol brought this delicious spread to us one Christmas. I asked her for the recipe and she shared it with us. I added jalapeno to it. We can't live without it on our Turkey Sandwiches especially! If you are a cranberry, apple, jalapeno lover you are going to love this sandwich spread. It is really sweet, but I love sweet. xo

MONTE CRISTO

Makes 2 sandwiches
Time: 20 minutes

Food Nanny Favorite Pancakes – Dry Mix
⅔ cup all-purpose flour
¼ cup whole wheat flour
2 Tablespoons sugar
2 teaspoons baking powder
½ teaspoon salt

Mix flour, whole wheat flour, sugar, baking powder and salt in a bowl. Remove ¾ cup mix to make the batter for the sandwiches. Store the remaining mix in an airtight container.

Monte Cristo Sandwich:
¾ cup Food Nanny Favorite Pancake Dry Mix
1 egg
¾ cup milk or water

Mix ingredients in a 9 inch pie pan. It will be thinner than it would be for pancakes.

4 slices whole grain or white bread
2-4 slices mild or sharp cheddar, garlic cheddar, or pepper jack cheese
4-6 slices deli ham, turkey or chicken, your choice
Mayonnaise and mustard, optional, to taste

Powdered sugar
Raspberry jam

1. Prepare the sandwich by lightly spreading mayonnaise and mustard on both inside pieces of bread.
2. Place 1 slice of cheese, (2, if the slices are very thin) and 2-3 slices of meat on each sandwich. Place the second piece of bread on top, mayo inside.
3. Preheat a 10-12 inch frying pan on medium high. Add 1 Tablespoon canola oil.
4. Carefully take each whole sandwich and place it in the prepared batter. Turn the sandwiches over and make sure the sides are also dipped in the batter. Place in the heated frying pan. (This part is messy!) Watch the sandwiches carefully so as not to burn, but check inside to see that the cheese is melting and the batter is cooking. With a large spatula, turn the sandwich over to brown the other side.
5. Remove finished sandwich to individual plate. Sprinkle top with powdered sugar. Add 2 Tablespoons raspberry jam on top of the powdered sugar. Serve immediately. Eat with a knife and fork.

Serve with: Bacon or breakfast sausage. Fruit in season – strawberries, raspberries, grapefruit, orange slices.

Tip: This sandwich is messy transferring to the frying pan - but it's worth it!!

*Ann, my editor makes these delicious sandwiches all the time.
I like to order them when they are on the menu in a restaurant.
If you haven't tried a Monte Cristo you are in for a treat!
These are fun to serve company as well.*

Desserts We Love

While filming an episode of The Food Nanny, I was in a home where the 14-year old boy said this to me: "I just want to smell something 'sweet' coming from our kitchen."
I asked his cute mom if that could be possible.
She answered, "Yes, as long as he eats plenty of other good, nutritional foods."
This young man was starving for homemade cookies, cakes or pies.
He just wanted to smell and taste something that made him happy.
That is what homemade desserts do for us. These foods make us happy!
When people pass by a bakery and get a whiff of those luscious smells, they are instantly in a better mood. So if baking sweet treats once in a while makes us happier, it's worth it! Homemade food or dessert says "I love you."
Of course, we cannot live on sweets alone. Fresh vegetables, fresh fruits and whole grains are what keeps our bodies healthy and going throughout the day.
But a little bit of "sweetness" makes life richer and more enjoyable.
My desserts are "sweet" inspirations that will bring smiles from ear to ear.
Now that's worth baking for!
So turn on your ovens and get baking some homemade goodies for those you love!!!!!

The Food Nanny. xo

DESSERTS WE LOVE

CRAZY-GOOD FRUIT TART

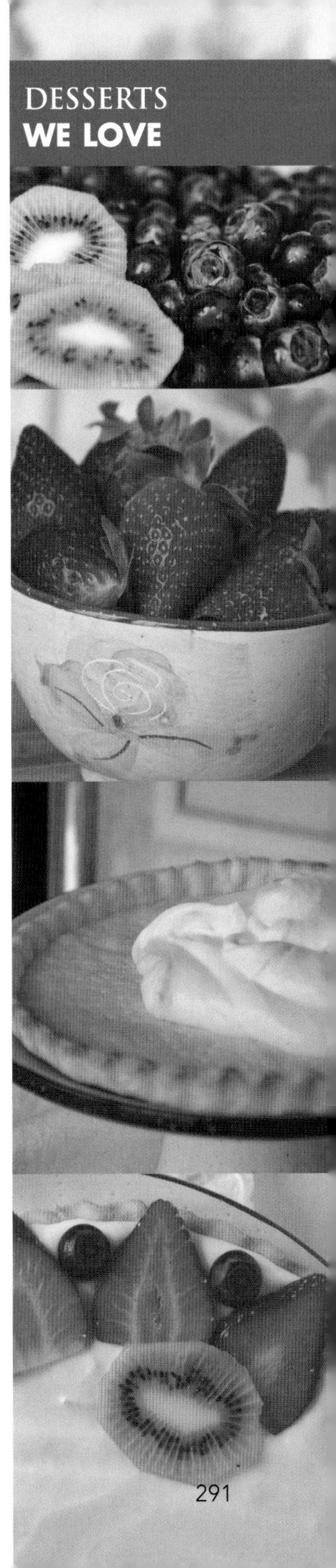

Serves 8
Time: 1 hour

Plan Ahead: Make crust a day ahead, then the prep. is 20 min.

You will need an 11x1 inch *round* tart pan with a re-movable bottom. This dessert is worth purchasing the pan. You will also use it with my Victorian Chocolate Tart page 309.

Crust
½ cup butter at room temperature
⅓ cup sugar
1¼ cups all-purpose flour
2 Tablespoons milk
2 teaspoons almond extract

Cream Cheese topping
3 oz. cream cheese, softened
½ cup powdered sugar
2 teaspoons almond extract
1 cup heavy whipping cream
2½ cups of your choice of fresh fruit, cleaned and rinsed. May use all one kind of fruit. Thinly sliced strawberries, kiwi, or whole blueberries, raspberries or blackberries.

1. Preheat oven to 400°.
2. Mix the softened butter, sugar, flour, milk and almond extract with mixer or food processor until it comes together. Spray tart pan lightly with vegetable oil.
3. Spread the soft dough inside and up the sides of the entire tart pan with your fingers.
4. Bake in the oven on the middle rack at 400° for 8 to 10 min. or until light brown around the top. Let cool in pan.
5. When cool enough to handle, push the bottom of the tart pan out of the ring. Slide onto a cooling rack. Let the tart cool completely. Carefully slide the tart onto a serving dish.
6. While the tart cools, make the cream cheese topping. With an electric hand mixer, mix the softened cream cheese, powdered sugar, extract and cream until thick and creamy. Spread evenly over top the cooled crust.
7. Prepare the fruit of choice and decorate the tart. A nice way is to do one row around in one kind of fruit, one in another, etc. Whatever combination you like or all the same fruit.
8. Serve immediately or cover with plastic wrap and chill up to 6 hours.

I would put this recipe up against any dessert. This is crazy good!!! Thank you, Lisa, for sharing it with us. This is one of my favorite desserts ever!! Serve this at casual dinners or for the most special occasion.

BANANA CAKE WITH CREAM CHEESE FROSTING

Serves 16
Time: 30 minutes

Plan Ahead: Cake has to cool, be frosted, and refrigerated for 3 hours before serving

Cake:

½ cup (1 stick) butter, softened
1½ cups sugar
2 large eggs
1 cup sour cream
2 cups all-purpose flour
1 teaspoon baking soda
1 teaspoon salt
2 bananas, mashed with a fork

Frosting:

8 oz. cream cheese, softened
½ cup (1 stick) butter, softened
2 teaspoons vanilla
3½ cups powdered sugar
1½ cup chopped walnuts (optional)

Cake:

1. Move the oven rack to the middle of the oven. Preheat oven to 350°.
2. Mix everything in order given. Spray a jelly roll pan (15x11 inch) with baking oil or use the baking spray with flour added.
3. Pour in the batter and evenly spread with a spatula. Bake for 18 to 20 min. Cool for 45 min. Frost.

Frosting:

4. In a small bowl combine cream cheese, butter, vanilla and powdered sugar. Mix well with an electric mixer or beaters. Stir in nuts if using. Spread on top of cake.
5. Refrigerate for 3 hours before serving.

Variations: Use two 9-inch round cake pans.

This cake is easy, moist and so delicious! A Go-To cake. Thank you, Tamara!

GRANDMA EVA'S SPUD-NUTS (DONUTS)

Makes 3 dozen donuts
Time: 2½ hours

Plan Ahead: Prepare mashed potatoes ahead of time. Prepare glaze ahead.

Donuts:

½ cup mashed potatoes, not instant. Use 2 medium size Russet potatoes. Save the potato water.
½ cup potato water
2 Tablespoons active dry yeast dissolved in ¼ cup warm water
½ cup shortening
½ cup sugar
2 large eggs
3 to 4 cups all-purpose flour
5 cups sunflower oil or shortening for frying. More as needed.

Glaze:

4 cups powdered sugar
½ cup hot water
1 teaspoon vanilla
⅛ teaspoon salt

1. Peel the potatoes, cut into nickel size chunks. Place potatoes in a small sauce pan and cover with water by 2 inches. Bring to a boil, turn down the heat to low and cook the potatoes until tender, about 13 min. Drain the water off the potatoes and save ½ cup potato water. Set aside.
2. Mash the potatoes. (With a fork, or a potato masher). Do not add any liquid or seasoning to the potatoes. Let cool. Set aside.
3. Stir the yeast into ¼ cup warm water in a small bowl. Cover and let rise until foamy, about 10 min.
4. With an electric mixer, in a medium size bowl cream together the shortening, sugar and 2 eggs. Add the yeast mixture, cooled mashed potatoes and the potato water. Stir until combined. Stir in the flour one cup at a time. Make a moderately stiff dough.
5. Put a drizzle of olive oil in a large bowl and add the mixed dough. Cover with a dish towel. Let rise until double in bulk. About 1 hour and 15 min.

Prepare the glaze:

6. In a small, deep bowl mix together the powdered sugar, hot water, vanilla and salt until smooth. Set aside. The deep bowl is easier for dipping the donuts.
7. Roll dough out onto a lightly floured surface to ¼ inch thick. Cut with donut cutter. Set the donuts aside on the counter as you cut all the dough. Gather unused dough and roll out again until all the donuts are cut.
8. Using a skillet or an electric fry pan, fill it ½ full with sunflower oil or shortening. Heat to 350°. Oil is ready when you can fry a piece of bread in it quickly and it browns nicely.
9. When you have cut all the donuts they will be ready to fry. Fry a few donuts at a time quickly until golden brown on both sides. (Turning with 2 dinner forks or tongs). Remove immediately to paper towels to let drain for just a minute.
10. Hold the donut with your fingers and dip in the glaze and place on a cooling rack with wax paper underneath to catch the extra icing that you can re-use. When the glaze has dripped off remove donuts to a platter. Serve warm for best taste. Can re-heat in the microwave.

I loved watching my Grandmother make spud-nuts in her darling kitchen with pink counter tops!
They are a labor of love.
She used to make hundreds of these donuts and donate them to the town bake sale on the 24th of July.
My Grandma was my rock.

THE QUEEN OF CHOCOLATE CUPCAKES

Makes 21 cupcakes
Time: 45 minutes

Plan Ahead: You will need a 1M tip and frosting bag to make the frosting "bakery beautiful." If not, frost like you would normally with a knife. You will also need 21 cupcake papers. You can freeze these cupcakes up to 1 week ahead of time and frost while still frozen.

- **1 Devils Food cake mix**
- **4 eggs**
- **1 5.9 oz. (large) package instant chocolate pudding mix**
- **¾ cup canola oil**
- **¾ cup boiling water**
- **8 oz. sour cream**
- **1½ cups semi-sweet chocolate chips**

Butter Cream Frosting:

- **2 sticks (1 cup) butter at room temperature**
- **1 teaspoon vanilla**
- **4 cups powdered sugar**
- **1 teaspoon milk**

1. Place the rack in the middle position of the oven. Preheat the oven to 325°.
2. In a large bowl combine the cake mix and eggs. Add the chocolate pudding, oil and hot water, mix. Add sour cream, mix. Stir in the chocolate chips.
3. Pour individual cupcake papers ¾ full. Bake at 325° for 15 to 25 min. or until they spring back when touched. It is very important not to over cook these cupcakes. Remove from oven and let the cupcakes cool in the freezer. These can be frozen ahead of time and frosted frozen if desired.

Butter Cream Frosting:

1. In a small bowl mix the softened butter, vanilla, powdered sugar and milk with an electric hand-held beater until smooth. (Keep mixing, it will all come together).
2. Fill a pastry bag with frosting and a 1M tip. Starting from a little bit inside the outside edge, holding the bag up straight over the cupcake, begin to make a circle and continue with the circle until the cupcake has the desired amount of frosting. (You want to see that the cupcake is chocolate, so not to cover the entire top.) This is enough frosting to frost 21 cupcakes.

This is the best recipe for cupcakes I have ever eaten – thanks to Kathy and Tara. My wonderful butter cream frosting that Patrice shared with me is a perfect match. What's not to love! xo

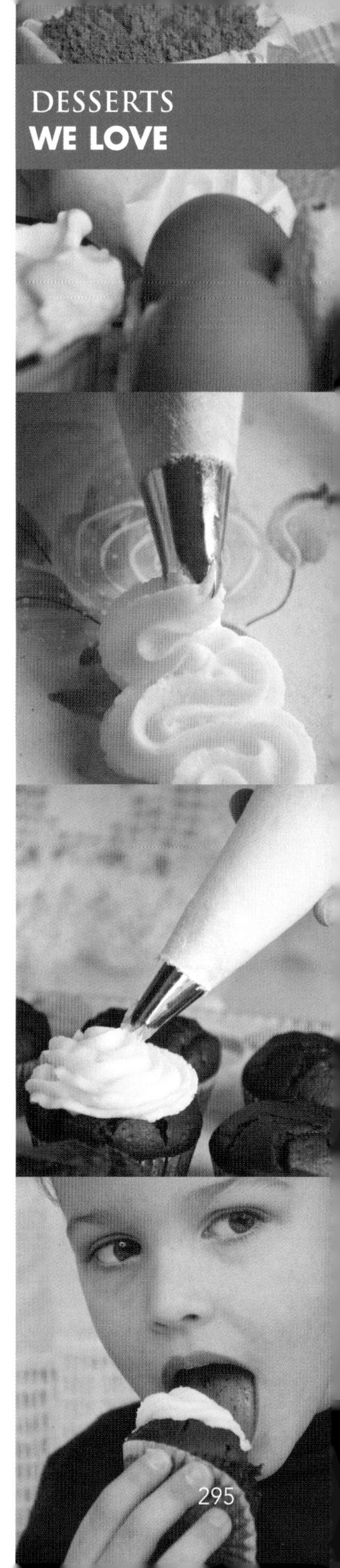

DARK SECRETS

Makes 30 cookies
Time: 20 minutes

- 1 cup (2 sticks) salted butter, softened at room temperature
- ¾ cup sugar
- 1 teaspoon almond extract
- ½ teaspoon vanilla extract
- 2 cups all-purpose flour
- 1 cup pecans, finely chopped
- 1 package dark chocolate kisses, unwrapped

Powdered sugar

1. Move oven rack to the middle of the oven. Preheat the oven to 375°.
2. With an electric mixer in a medium size bowl, cream together butter, sugar, almond and vanilla extracts for 2 min. Add flour and nuts. Blend well. Cover and chill if desired at this point.
3. Measure a tablespoon of dough and shape around a kiss to cover it completely. Roll into a ball and place on an ungreased cookie sheet.
4. Bake at 375° for 12 min. until set but not browned. Roll or sprinkle in powdered sugar. Cool.

These cookies are best eaten the same day. When cool, if desired, place in a plastic baggie and freeze. I love them straight out of the freezer.

Variation: Make these cookies without the chocolate kisses.
Use a tablespoon of dough and roll in a ball and bake for 10-12 min.
Roll warm cookies in powdered sugar. Cool. Freeze if desired.

These cookies are just like Mexican Wedding cookies or Russian Tea Cakes only with a chocolate kiss added in. Thanks, Sally for coming up with the idea to put the dark kisses in the middle.

DARK CHOCOLATE FROSTING

Time: 10 minutes

Frosts one 9x13 inch cake or two 9 inch cake rounds.

- 4 cups powdered sugar
- ⅔ cup unsweetened cocoa powder
- ¼ teaspoon coarse salt
- 1 cup unsalted butter, at room temperature
- 1 Tablespoon vanilla
- 2 Tablespoons dark corn syrup
- ⅓ cup heavy cream

1. Stir powdered sugar, cocoa and salt together in a medium bowl.
2. In another bowl, cream the butter until light and fluffy with an electric mixer for 3 min. Beat in the vanilla and corn syrup. Beat in the sugar mixture, one cup at a time.
3. Blend in the cream. Whip on high speed for 2 more minutes. Add more cream if necessary to spread easily.

Serve on: Best on chocolate, yellow, or white cake.

This is the best dark chocolate frosting in the world. Put it on any boxed cake and you will have a winner!!

CHOCOLATE GANACHE CAKE

Serves 12
Time: 25 minutes

Plan Ahead: Chill at least 5 hours before serving. Make cake 1 day ahead.

1 Devils Food cake mix, NOT with pudding in it
16 oz. (2 cups) sour cream
4 large eggs
1 small package, 3.9 oz. chocolate instant pudding mix
½ cup canola oil
½ cup water
¾ cup semi-sweet chocolate chips

Ganache
2 cups semi sweet chocolate chips
¾ cup heavy cream
⅛ teaspoon cinnamon
1 teaspoon vanilla

1. With a rack in the middle position, preheat the oven to 350°. Very generously grease and flour two 9-inch cake pans. (Use the new cooking spray with flour in it.)
2. In a large bowl, mix the cake mix, sour cream, eggs, pudding, oil and water all together until well blended. Add the chocolate chips. Do not over mix.
3. Pour into cake pans. Bake at 350° for 25 min. or until a toothpick inserted comes out with just a hint of moist cake on it. Remove cake immediately and let sit for 5 min.
4. Turn cake out onto a cake platter very carefully, still warm, and pour half the Ganache over top the first layer. Place the second layer on top and pour on the rest of the Ganache and let it flow down the sides. Place in the refrigerator. Cake should chill for at least 5 hours before serving. Can make a day ahead.

Ganache

5. Put the chocolate chips in a microwavable bowl. Add the cream. Heat until almost melted, stirring a few times as it is melting; go slowly so you will not burn the chocolate. Use a small whisk to blend the chips with the cream. Once smooth, add cinnamon and vanilla. Spread on the layers.

Serve with: Fresh raspberries, whipped cream or chopped semi-sweet chocolate as a garnish.

Variations: Can use a 10-inch spring form pan. Bake at 350° for 45 min. Can use a bundt pan. Bake 350° for 60 plus min. Cover the cake with foil the last 15 min.

Mindy, my co-worker at Sur la Table, shared this fabulous recipe with me. It is honestly one of the best cakes I have ever eaten. It tastes as good as any top-tier restaurant cake. I like using good quality chocolate chips to make a fabulous presentation. xo

ALMOND CAKE WITH FRESH ROSEMARY CREAM

Serves 10
Time: 50 minutes

Plan Ahead: Bake cake the day before. Make Rosemary Syrup the day before. You will need one 9-inch cake pan or one 9-inch spring form pan.

Almond Cake:

¾ cup (1¼ sticks) unsalted butter 1½ cups sugar
2 large eggs
½ teaspoon coarse salt
1 teaspoon vanilla
2 teaspoons almond extract
2 cups all-purpose flour

Topping:

1 Tablespoon sugar
¾ cup sliced raw almonds

Fresh Rosemary Syrup:

½ cup sugar
½ cup water
2 stems fresh rosemary, 3 inches long

Fresh Rosemary Cream:

½ cup heavy cream, whipped stiff
2½ Tablespoons cooled rosemary syrup

Almond Cake, Topping

1. Place the baking rack in the middle of the oven. Preheat the oven to 350°.
2. Grease bottom and sides of pan with cooking oil spray. Cut parchment paper or wax paper to fit the bottom of a 9 inch cake pan, place in pan. (If using a spring form pan no need to cut paper.) Spray with cooking oil again.
3. Melt the butter and pour in a large bowl. Stir in the sugar and eggs and beat until creamy-2 min. Add the salt, vanilla, almond extract and flour. Stir until combined.
4. Spread the batter in the pan. Mix the sugar and almonds together in a small bowl and sprinkle over top the cake.
5. Bake for 35-40 min. or until a wooden skewer comes out with just a bit of moist cake on it. Let cool 5 min. on a cooling rack. Invert. Cool. Can serve as-is without rosemary cream.

Fresh Rosemary Syrup

6. In a small sauce pan bring ½ cup sugar and ½ cup water to a boil. Stir until the sugar is dissolved. Add the fresh rosemary stems. Boil for 2 min. Turn off the heat and cover. Let steep for an hour or so. Cool. Remove rosemary.

Fresh Rosemary Cream

7. In a medium size bowl whip the cream to stiff peaks with an electric mixer on high. Add in cooled 2½ Tablespoons Rosemary Syrup. Mix with a spoon.
8. Cut a piece of cake; place on a saucer and spoon 2 Tablespoons Rosemary Cream along side the Almond Cake. Serve.

This is one of my favorite all time cakes. Judy shared this recipe with me. After tasting fresh Rosemary Ice Cream, I decided to try my version of Rosemary Cream which I made especially for this cake.

GINGERSNAPS WITH VANILLA CHIPS FROSTING

Makes About 5 dozen cookies
Time: 40 Minutes

Plan Ahead: Make cookies and freeze them. Thaw just before serving.

2 cups sugar
1½ cups canola oil
¼ cup (½ stick) butter, softened
2 large eggs
½ cup molasses, mild flavor
4 cups all-purpose flour (for high altitude add 2 Tablespoons more flour)
4 teaspoons baking soda
2 teaspoons ground cinnamon
1 Tablespoon ground ginger
1 teaspoon salt
½ cup sugar for rolling the cookies in

3 - 11 oz. bags vanilla chips or white classic
1 Tablespoon shortening

1. In a medium size bowl combine sugar, oil, butter and eggs, one at a time. Mix for 2 min. Stir in the molasses. In a separate bowl, combine the flour, baking soda, cinnamon, ginger and salt. Gradually add into the wet ingredients until well mixed in.
2. Put ½ cup sugar in a pie plate. Shape the dough into balls using a tablespoon and roll in sugar. Bake at 350° for 9 to 11 min. Cool completely.
3. Melt 3 bags vanilla or white classic chips in a double boiler. (Can melt in the microwave: go slow, stirring after every 30 seconds.) Add shortening. Stir until smooth. Pour the chocolate into a small, deep bowl. Dip half of the cookie into the melted vanilla chips and cool on waxed paper.

Joni, these cookies are for you!
Every single person that tastes these cookies wants the recipe.
Eat these cookies slowly because you will want to enjoy every bite!! Thank you, Nancy!

GRAHAM STREUSEL CAKE

Serves 12
Time: 45 minutes

Plan Ahead: Make the cake a day ahead. Cover with plastic wrap when cool.

2 cups graham crackers, crushed (1 individual package)
¾ cup walnuts or pecans, chopped
¾ cup brown sugar
¾ cup melted butter

1 yellow butter cake mix, mixed as directed on the pkg.
2 Tablespoons sour cream
1 cup powdered sugar
1 Tablespoon plus 2 teaspoons milk
½ teaspoon vanilla extract

1. Place the rack in the middle position of the oven. Preheat oven to 350°.
2. In a small bowl mix the crackers, chopped nuts, brown sugar and melted butter together. Set aside.
3. In a medium size bowl mix the cake mix as directed on package, adding in 2 Tablespoons sour cream.
4. Spray a 9x13 inch baking pan with cooking oil. Pour ½ of the cake batter into the bottom of the pan. Sprinkle half the streusel on top of the cake batter. Repeat.
5. Bake for 35 min. or until a wooden skewer comes out almost clean. (A bit of soft crumb on the skewer is good).
6. Mix the powdered sugar, milk and vanilla in a small bowl until smooth. Drizzle over top warm cake. Serve.

Variation: Use Cinnamon Graham Crackers.

This is my favorite "Coffee Cake". It is everything you dream about in a coffee cake, super moist and delicious. For some reason the graham crackers make it. Thank you Kathy. Enjoy!

PECAN BARS

Serves 16 Bars
Time: 1 hour

Crust:
2 cups all-purpose flour
½ cup powdered sugar
1 cup butter (2 sticks), softened

Pecan Filling:
⅓ cup butter, softened
½ cup brown sugar
1 cup light corn syrup
3 eggs, slightly beaten
1¼ teaspoons vanilla
⅛ teaspoon salt
1 cup pecans, chopped

Crust
Blend the flour, powdered sugar and butter in a medium size bowl. Spray a 9x13 inch baking dish with cooking oil. Spread the crust mixture evenly into the bottom of the dish with your fingers. Set aside.

Pecan Filling - can also be used in a pie crust (Page 312)
1. Stir the butter until soft. Slowly add the brown sugar. Mix in the corn syrup, eggs, vanilla and salt. Stir in the pecans. Pour onto the crust.
2. Bake at 350° for 40 to 50 min. - or until the filling is set. You may need to cover with foil the last 10 min. if it starts to get too brown on top. Cut into squares when cool.

Debbie brought these to a Christmas party. You won't be disappointed. They are fabulous with my Pecan Fillng. xo

GOOEY HOT FUDGE SUNDAES

Makes 1¼ cups
Time: 15 minutes

Plan Ahead: Make days ahead and re-heat in the microwave.

¾ cup semi-sweet or bittersweet chocolate chips
1 14 ounce can sweetened condensed milk

1. In a double boiler over low heat melt the chocolate with the milk. Stir with a whisk until smooth and glossy 3 to 5 min.
2. Serve immediately over vanilla ice cream. Add nuts and a cherry if desired. Keep in the refrigerator for up to 1 month.

Variations: Top the Sundae with my Caramel Popcorn page 319, sliced bananas or brownies to your sundae.

Evan takes this hot fudge to family and friends at Christmas time. He ties a red ribbon on each jar and adds an ice-cream scoop or a package of nuts to go with it. Everyone gets hungry for a Hot Fudge Sundae. Who doesn't love hot fudge?

CHEWY GRANOLA COOKIES

Makes 30 cookies
Time: 30 minutes

¾ cup sugar
1 cup brown sugar
1 cup (2 sticks) butter, softened
1 teaspoon vanilla
2 eggs
2 cups all-purpose flour
1 teaspoon baking soda
½ teaspoon salt
½ teaspoon baking powder
2 cups rolled oats
1 cup coconut
1 cup chocolate chips
1 cup dried cranberries
2 cups corn flakes (not crushed)

1. Position the rack in the middle of the oven. Preheat oven to 350°.
2. In a large bowl, with an electric mixer, beat together sugar, brown sugar and butter until light and fluffy. Add vanilla and eggs continuing to beat well.
3. In a separate bowl add flour, baking soda, baking powder and salt. Blend well and add to the dough mixture. Stir in oats, coconut, chocolate chips, dried cranberries and corn flakes.
4. Spoon onto ungreased cookie sheet and bake at 350° for 10 to 12 min. until lightly browned. Remove to cooling racks.

Variations: Can use bran flakes in place of corn flakes. Use dried apples or golden raisins in place of dried cranberries. If you bake these cookies too long, they are crispy and not as flavorful. (However I love crispy.) If just right, they are chewy and good to the last cookie. Freeze. Take them out one by one to eat like we do.

Elaine shared this recipe with us. She is a great cook. Everything she brings us is wonderful. We make them often to share with family and friends as well.

STRAWBERRIES AND CREAM CAKE

Serves 16
Time: 1 hour

***Plan Ahead: Make cakes a day ahead of time or freeze and frost when ready.* You will need two 9-inch cake pans.**

- **1 15.25 ounce box white cake mix**
- **1 cup all-purpose flour**
- **1 cup sugar**
- **½ teaspoon coarse salt**
- **1⅓ cups water, room temperature**
- **1 cup sour cream**
- **2 Tablespoons coconut oil**
- **1 teaspoon vanilla extract**
- **1 teaspoon almond extract**
- **4 large eggs whites**

Fresh Strawberry Frosting:

- **3-4 fresh strawberries, cleaned and rinsed**
- **⅓ cup butter, room temperature**
- **4 oz. (½ cup) cream cheese room temperature**
- **½ teaspoon vanilla**
- **¼ teaspoon almond extract**
- **4 cups powdered sugar**

1. Place oven rack in the middle of your oven. Preheat the oven to 325°.
2. Spray two 9-inch round cake pans with cooking oil. Cut parchment paper or wax paper to the size of the bottom of the cake pan. (I place my cake pan on top of the paper and draw a circle around the pan, then cut and place the paper inside the pan.) Spray again.
3. In a large mixing bowl, add cake mix, flour, sugar, salt and stir together. Add water, sour cream, coconut oil, vanilla and almond extracts, and stir until combined. Add 4 egg whites – one at a time, stirring after each one until the ingredients are thoroughly mixed.
4. Divide the batter evenly between the 2 pans which will each be ¾ full. Place in the middle rack of your oven and bake for 35 to 38 min. or until a wooden skewer comes out clean.
5. Immediately when the baked cakes are taken out of the oven, put 2 paper towels together and push the raised surfaces down till even with, or a teeny bit lower than, the edge of the pan. Make sure the levels are smooth and uniform. Push them down firm enough to ensure that the cake stays where you push it and that it doesn't spring back up.
6. After hot cakes are pushed down, invert them onto cooling racks. Remove the paper. Place the hot pans back over the layers and let them cool with the pans on the cake to keep the moisture and steam in.
7. Frost when cool.

Fresh Strawberry Frosting

8. Process berries in your food processor or blender until smooth. Strain the puree. Discard the seeds. You should end up with 2-3 Tablespoons of puree.
9. Beat the butter, cream cheese, vanilla and almond extract together with an electric mixer. Add puree. Gradually add the powdered sugar and mix until smooth at medium speed.
10. Spread evenly over the 2 layers and sides of cake. Place frosted cake in the refrigerator. Serve cold.

Variations: May use raspberries in place of strawberries. If you use a strawberry cake mix use 4 whole eggs. Use raspberry extract in place of almond.

Paula showed me how to make really dense cakes. I had no idea at the time that you literally pushed the cakes down while still hot to create this effect. I think this recipe of mine is fabulous tasting and an elegant dessert. xo

AMERICA'S BEST SUGAR COOKIES

Makes 4 dozen
Time: 2 hours

Sugar Cookies
1½ cups (3 sticks) salted butter softened at room temperature, not in the microwave
2 cups sugar
4 eggs
1 teaspoon vanilla extract
2 teaspoons baking powder
5 cups all-purpose flour
Powdered sugar for dusting the counter and rolling pin

Cream Cheese Frosting:
½ cup (1 stick) salted butter softened at room temperature
8 oz. cream cheese softened at room temperature
2 teaspoons vanilla extract
4-5 cups powdered sugar

These are the most delicious, soft sugar cookies out there! They make a beautiful presentation anytime of the year. Shannon shared the recipe with us and we feel so lucky to be able to share them with our friends and family. I cannot wait for you to try them. xo

1. With a hand mixer on low, cream the softened butter and sugar together until it is smooth and fluffy. Add the eggs one at a time to the butter mixture still beating on low speed. Add vanilla. Gradually add the flour and baking powder. Make sure that all the flour is mixed into the dough.
2. Gather the dough together and wrap in plastic wrap. Chill the dough for 1-2 hours to stiffen up the dough. (Very important step.) When the dough has been chilled for the allotted time, preheat your oven to 400°.
3. Divide the dough into thirds. Generously sprinkle powdered sugar (not flour) onto a clean counter top and begin rolling the dough with a rolling pin. Roll one third at a time. Make sure to add some powdered sugar to your rolling pin and to the top of the dough to prevent it from sticking. (Keep adding a little powdered sugar as needed throughout this process.)
4. Roll the dough to ½ inch thick. Use cookie cutters to cut out desired shapes and set them on an ungreased cookie sheet. Make sure there is at least 1 inch between each cookie.
5. Position the rack in the middle of the oven. Preheat oven to 400°. Bake for 6 to 8 min. depending on the size of your cookies. If you have extra large cookies they will need to cook for 8 min. DO NOT over bake. They may not look done, but they are. Let them cool a bit before removing them from the pan.
6. Chill in the refrigerator before frosting or serving. This helps the cookies to be moist and delicious.

Cream Cheese Frosting

7. In a small bowl with an electric hand-held mixer, mix butter and cream cheese until soft. Add vanilla. Beat until light and fluffy. Add powder sugar, one cup at a time. (I use 4½ cups.) Beat until smooth. Add your favorite food coloring if desired.

PUMPKIN CHOCOLATE CHIP COOKIES WITH MAPLE CREAM FROSTING

Makes 24-30 large cookies
Time: 30 minutes

Cookies:

1 cup (2 sticks) butter, softened
1 cup brown sugar
1 cup sugar
4 eggs
3 cups solid pack pumpkin
1 teaspoon lemon extract
5 cups all-purpose flour
1½ teaspoons baking soda
4 teaspoons baking powder
1 teaspoon salt
2 teaspoons cinnamon
1 teaspoon nutmeg
2 to 3 cups chocolate chips

Maple Cream Frosting:

½ cup butter (1 stick), softened
3¼ cups powdered sugar
4 Tablespoons cream
2 teaspoons maple flavoring

Cookies

1. Preheat the oven to 350°.
2. In a large bowl with an electric mixer, mix the butter, sugars, eggs, pumpkin and lemon extract. Mix on low speed for 3 min.
3. In another bowl mix the flour, baking soda, baking powder, salt, cinnamon and nutmeg. Add this to the wet ingredients a little bit at a time until all mixed together. Stir in the chocolate chips.
4. Spray a baking sheet with cooking oil. Drop the cookies onto the baking sheet with a tablespoon. Bake at 350° 12 to 15 min. Cool on a cooling rack. Frost with Maple Cream Frosting.

Maple Cream Frosting

1. Cream the butter in a medium size bowl with an electric mixer.
Add sugar gradually. Mix well.
2. Add cream and flavoring. Cream well. Spread on top of cooled cookies.

Every Fall I get hungry for pumpkin desserts. In my last book I shared with you my favorite delicious Pumpkin Chocolate Chip Bread. I am a maple "nut" so of course these would be my favorite pumpkin cookie. I hope you will love them as much as we do.

VICTORIAN CHOCOLATE TART

Serves 10
Time: 40 minutes

Plan Ahead: Make tart and then place in refrigerator for 4 hours before serving. Or prepare one day ahead. You will need an 11x1 inch round tart pan with a removable bottom. This dessert is worth purchasing the pan. You will use the pan again with my Crazy Good Fruit Tart page 291.

Tart Crust:
Makes enough for 2 tart crusts (Freeze half the dough or bake both and freeze one for later)
2½ cups all-purpose flour
1 teaspoon sugar
⅛ teaspoon salt
1 cup (2 sticks) chilled butter, cut into small pieces
¼ to ¾ cups ice water

Victorian Chocolate:
Makes enough to fill 1 chocolate tart
1 cup (8 oz.) good quality semi-sweet chocolate chips
⅓ cup sugar
2 cups heavy cream
Sea salt to taste (optional)

Tart Crust

1. Place rack in the middle of the oven. Preheat oven to 400°.
2. In a medium size bowl mix the flour, sugar and salt together. Slice the cold butter into small pieces and put in with the flour mixture. With a pastry blender work the butter and flour mixture together. (Or you can use your fingers.) When you have the consistency of coarse crumbs slowly add in the ice water, 3 Tablespoons at a time. Stir with a spoon and when the dough holds together nicely without being wet or sticky you have enough water. Divide the dough in half. (If not using all the dough you can wrap one half in plastic wrap and then again in foil to freeze).
3. Turn the dough out onto a lightly floured surface. Roll the dough into a 12 inch round, using a little more flour if needed. Place the dough into the tart pan, fitting it into place, folding down any extra dough into the sides of the pan.
4. Place a regular pie pan on top of the crust (it will help the crust to stay in place) and bake at 400° for 25 min. Remove the pie pan just over half way through the baking time.
5. Remove from oven and let cool on a cooling rack. Remove the bottom of the tart pan. Set the tart aside to cool until ready to fill with the chocolate. Wrap and freeze at this point if not filling. Bake the next tart if doing so.

Victorian Chocolate

6. In a medium size sauce pan melt the chocolate with the sugar over low to medium heat. Stir until smooth. Add the cream and continue to stir over medium heat until it begins to thicken, 5 to 8 minutes. (Should be the consistency of heavy cream.) This chocolate will thicken up as it cools.
7. Take off the heat and let cool down. Stir a couple of times while cooling.
8. When your tart is cool and the chocolate has cooled but not set, fill the tart with the chocolate. Place in the refrigerator for at least 4 hours, preferably overnight. Sprinkle LIGHTLY with sea salt before serving.

Variation: Can serve with a dab of whipped cream or Crème Fraîche on the side.

This is the most incredible Chocolate Tart you have ever eaten. It compares with the very best that I have tasted in France. If you are a chocolate lover, this recipe is for you. No need to spend extra on expensive chocolate chips. The Sea Salt compliments this recipe just perfectly. xo

ZUCCHINI BROWNIES

Makes 16 brownies
Time: 1 hour

Plan Ahead: Make the frosting in advance.

2 cups all-purpose flour
1¾ cups sugar
¾ teaspoon salt
1½ teaspoon baking powder
¼ cup cocoa powder
½ cup canola or coconut oil
2 teaspoons vanilla
2 cups grated zucchini
1 cup chopped walnuts (optional)

Chocolate Frosting
¼ cup (½ stick) unsalted butter, softened
⅓ cup cocoa powder
1½ cups powdered sugar
3 Tablespoons milk
½ teaspoon vanilla
Dash of salt

1. Place oven rack in the middle of the oven. Preheat the oven to 350°.
2. In a medium size bowl mix the flour, sugar, salt, baking powder and cocoa powder together with a wooden spoon. Stir in the oil, vanilla and zucchini until completely mixed. Add the nuts if using.
3. Pour into a 9x13 inch greased baking pan. Bake for 35 to 40 min. Brownies are done when just a little bit of moist brownie adheres to the toothpick. You don't want the toothpick to be completely dry.
4. Remove from oven and let cool on a wire rack. Frost with Chocolate Frosting if desired.

Chocolate Frosting

5. In a small bowl or food processor combine butter, cocoa, sugar, milk, vanilla and dash of salt. Stir until smooth.
6. Spread on top of cooled brownies. Cut into squares.

In the summertime especially when our zucchini is growing like a weed and we don't know what to do with all of it, I make these brownies. Elisabeth shared this recipe with me and I think I made them 10 times the first summer I had the recipe.

FOOD NANNY PIE CRUST

Recipes for 1 or 2 pie crusts
Time: 5 minutes

Double Crust Pie:
2½ cups all-purpose flour
1 teaspoon salt
¾ cup shortening
¼ cup (½ stick) chilled butter, cut in small pieces
¼ cup to ¾ cup ice-cold water

Single Baked or Unbaked Crust Pie:
1¼ cups all-purpose flour
½ teaspoon salt
¼ plus 2 tablespoons shortening
2 Tablespoons chilled butter, cut into small pieces
¼ cup to ½ cup ice-cold water

1. Stir the flour and salt together in a large bowl. Cut in the shortening and butter with a pastry blender or two knives until the mixture resembles coarse crumbs. Sprinkle with ice water, 3 Tablespoons at a time and stir with a fork to moisten the dough.
2. Gather the dough into a ball with your hands. Divide the dough in half. Place the bowl over the half that you are not rolling out so it doesn't get dried out. Roll out one half of the dough 1/8 inch thick on a lightly floured surface and fit it into a 9-inch pie plate. Trim bottom crust even with rim of the pie plate. (This is the point where you would put the prepared filling into the pie shell.)
3. Roll out the next crust and lay on top of the filled pie and trim ½ to 1 inch beyond edge; fold under and flute edge by pressing dough with forefinger against wedge made of finger and thumb of other hand. Cut slits in top.

Use the same recipe instructions as above. Trim the crust ½ to 1 inch beyond edge; fold under and flute edge by pressing dough with forefinger against wedge made of finger and thumb of other hand. If you are going to fill it with a filling that needs to be baked, like pumpkin, fill the crust and bake it according to pie recipe directions.

If you are filling it with a filling that does not need to be baked, like a prepared pudding or fresh fruit, then the crust must be baked before it is filled. Prick sides and bottom with a fork. Bake the crust at 450° for 10 to 12 min. or until light brown.

Tip: Make pie crusts ahead and freeze them. Freeze unbaked bottom pie crusts in the pie pan; or stack the rolled-out dough with waxed paper in between them. Place them in larger freezer bags and pull out 1 or 2 as needed.

My pie crust recipe is flaky and delicious and turns out every time. I have noticed that making a great pie crust varies from region to region. Some require less water in the dough and others require much more water. The key is to have the right amount of water so you can roll it out easily. As soon as the dough sticks together nicely, without being too wet, your dough is ready to roll out. You can do it. There is nothing like a homemade pie with homemade crust.

FOOD NANNY ANY BERRY PIE

Serves 8
Time: 1 hour

Plan Ahead: Purchase fresh berries in season on sale. Make pies ahead and freeze.

- 1 Double Crust Pie Crust page 312
- 4 cups any kind of fresh berries - blackberry, raspberry, blueberry, elderberry, mixed or all one kind
- ¾ cup sugar
- 2 Tablespoons fresh lemon juice
- ¼ teaspoon salt
- 2 Tablespoons all-purpose flour
- 2 Tablespoons unsalted butter, cold
- Milk
- Sugar

1. Prepare the Pie Crust from page 312. Preheat the oven to 400°.
2. Measure 4 cups fresh berries. Rinse and make sure all the water has drained off them. Place berries in a medium size bowl. Add the sugar, lemon juice, salt and flour. Mix with a spoon being very careful not to break up the berries. Pour into the pie crust. Dot berry mixture with cold butter.
3. Place the top crust on. Seal. Make some slits in the crust for the steam to escape. I make a curve down the middle with some slits coming off the curve and then a small one just like it on each side. You can make one hole in the middle if you prefer. Brush lightly - I prefer the rubber brushes - the entire top of the pie with milk. Using your fingers or a small spoon sprinkle on some sugar.
4. Place the pie into the oven and bake for 40 min. Halfway through you may choose to cover the crust edges with foil or simply place a pie crust protector over top so the crust edges do not get over done.
5. Serve warm with vanilla ice cream or milk.

Variations: For fresh Peach Pie, eliminate the lemon juice and add ¼ teaspoon cinnamon, ¼ teaspoon nutmeg and ½ teaspoon vanilla extract.

Freeze Pies: Make up pies with fresh berries or peaches and freeze them. Wrap carefully in plastic wrap and then again in foil. To bake, remove plastic wrap and foil. Place frozen pies in the oven at 400° for 60 min.

At certain times of the year all I want is a piece of warm Berry Pie. This is my go-to Berry Pie recipe that I made up years ago. My favorite way to eat it is putting a piece of pie in a bowl and pouring milk over it. My favorite is blackberry, then raspberry. When the berries are in season, that is when they taste the best! Try making your own pie crust, it makes all the difference in the world.

BREAD PUDDING WITH CARAMEL SAUCE

Serves 6 to 8
Time: 3 hours

Plan Ahead: Bake the Bread Pudding and Caramel sauce ahead of time and warm in the oven or microwave when ready to serve.

Bread Pudding:
2 cups milk
4 eggs
½ cup sugar
1 teaspoon vanilla
¼ teaspoon salt
3½ cups Sweet Hawaiian Bread, Hawaiian Rolls or Egg Bread, cut into 1-inch cubes
¾ teaspoon ground cinnamon
¾ teaspoon ground nutmeg

Caramel Sauce:
¾ cup packed brown sugar
½ cup butter
½ cup heavy cream
1 quart vanilla ice cream (optional)
2 bananas, sliced (optional)

Bread Pudding
1. In medium bowl whisk together milk, eggs, sugar, vanilla and salt.
2. Slice bread into 1 inch cubes. Place cubes of bread into a buttered 8x8 inch-baking pan. Pour milk mixture over the bread and let soak 15 min. Press bread down into liquid. Sprinkle with cinnamon and nutmeg.
3. Bake at 250° for 2½ hours. Cut warm bread pudding into squares or scoop out with a spoon and serve in individual bowls or on a plate. Pour the caramel sauce over the bread pudding.

Caramel Sauce
4. Combine the brown sugar, butter and cream in a heavy saucepan and cook over medium heat until butter melts, stirring occasionally. Reduce the heat and simmer 15 min., stirring occasionally. Serve warm over bread pudding or serve the bread pudding with a scoop of vanilla ice cream and sliced bananas and warm caramel sauce on top.

Variations: Add dried Cranberries to your bread pudding. Instead of the bananas, sprinkle with pine nuts or chopped pecans over the caramel sauce.

*I love serving this dessert with vanilla ice cream and bananas.
The caramel sauce is dreamy.
You will love my variations! xo*

ANYTIME FRUIT SALAD

Serves: 4-6
Time: 30 minutes

2 teaspoons coarse salt
2 cups apples, sliced, salted, then minced
2 cups watermelon, seeds removed, minced
2 cups fresh pineapple, minced
1 cup grapes minced (red or green)
1 cup mango minced
1½ cups fresh squeezed orange juice
2 Tablespoons sugar, (optional)

One of my most favorite desserts is fruit salad poured over vanilla ice cream. Or just plain fruit salad. This fruit salad is so great because you get a sampling of all the fruits in one bite. I learned how to make this in Bangkok from SuNan. This is how they do it in Thailand. This is to die for!!

1. Fill a medium size bowl with water. Add 2 teaspoons coarse salt. Stir. Wash, core and slice the apples with skins on. Put the sliced apples into the salted water as you slice them. (This keeps the apples from turning brown). Let the apples soak in the water 10 min. Drain. Rinse the apples with clean water, drain well. Mince. Place in a medium size bowl.
2. Slice the watermelon into thin slices. Remove the black seeds. Mince. Place in the bowl with the apples.
3. Remove the pineapple skin, slice, rinse with water, then mince. Place in the bowl.
4. Wash off the grapes. If the grapes are large, mince. If the grapes are small cut in half, then half again. Place in bowl.
5. Peel the mango. Slice and mince. Place in bowl.
6. Squeeze the oranges and make the juice. Pour over the fruit and mix. If the juice is sweet no need to add the sugar. If the juice is sour mix 2 Tablespoons sugar with 1 Tablespoon boiling water and add to the juice.
7. Mix all the fruit together with the juice, cover with plastic wrap and keep in the refrigerator up to 4 days.

Serve with: Ice cream. Put a scoop of vanilla ice cream in a bowl and pour the fruit salad over top. This is great served at breakfast, lunch or dinner.

Variation: Use strawberries in place of mango.

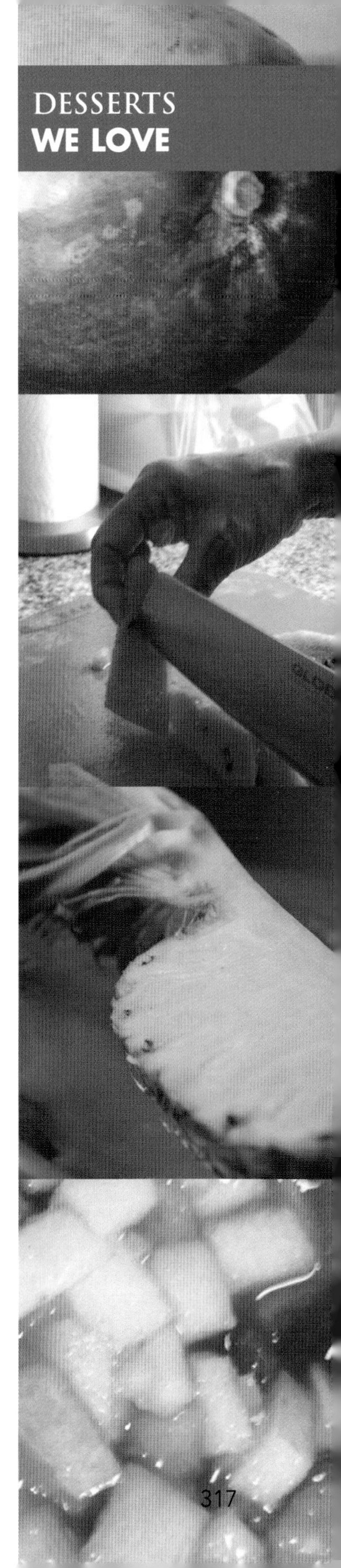

CARAMEL POPCORN

Serves 12
Time: 20 minutes

Plan Ahead: You will need a candy thermometer.

1 cup pecans, whole
1 cup raw almonds, whole
10 -12 cups popped popcorn
3 sticks butter (1½ cups)
1½ cups sugar
½ cup light corn syrup
½ teaspoon cream of tarter
½ teaspoon baking soda
1 teaspoon vanilla extract
Salt to taste

1. Preheat the oven to 300°.
2. Measure the pecans and almonds onto a baking sheet. Roast in the oven at 300° for 5 to 10 min. Remove and set aside.
3. Pop the corn. I use my air popper. You may use any method. It takes me 2 batches of air-popped corn to get 10-12 cups popcorn. Place the popped corn and nuts in your largest bowl. Set aside.
4. In a heavy 2 quart saucepan over low to medium heat add the butter, sugar, corn syrup and cream of tarter. Stir with a wooden spoon until the mixture reaches 240° - soft ball stage, about 10-15 min. Use your candy thermometer to check the temperature from time to time or leave your thermometer in the pan as you stir. Remove from heat.
5. Add baking soda and vanilla - which will foam up a little. Stir. Pour this hot mixture over top the popcorn and nuts and mix thoroughly. Salt as desired.
6. Lightly spray a large baking sheet with oil. Pour the caramel popcorn on and spread it out to cool. Store in plastic bags. Enjoy!

Variations: Take out the nuts.

I love this caramel popcorn!
It is the best! It has just the right
amount of sweet and salty.
Raquel gives it to us every Christmas.
She is famous for it.
You will be too!

750
KIRKLAND
stretch-tite
750
stretch-tite
KIRKLAND

TIPS

- Sprinkle meat with flour in the pan while it's browning, to save time and clean up.
- Spray plastic wrap with cooking spay to cover rising dough.
- Make yourself a bouquet garni (which is fresh herbs) to enhance soups and sauces.
- To help speed up the foaming or (blooming) process of yeast cover with a small plate.
- To flatten meat, pound between two plastic storage bags.
- Add a mix of flour and cornmeal to your pizza peel to make transferring the dough to oven easier.
- Instead of washing chicken in the sink, try wiping it with a wet paper towel to keep bacteria out of your sink.
- Create your own dry mixes for pancakes or cookies to save time.
- Stop eating so much processed food. Process your own food.
- Be smart about using your freezer. Double a soup or sauce recipe and freeze until the next week.
- Substitute pomegranate, apple juice or sparkling grape juice for wine.
- Get a Pressure Cooker. If you really want to save time get a Pressure cooker. It not only cooks fast, but holds in a lot of the vitamins and nutrients...Pressure cooking is a good thing. The electric ones are super great !
- Avoid purchasing pre-prepared, frozen foods, and make them yourself, at home.
- Buy local whenever you can. The fewer miles from farm to table the better.
- Cover celery with aluminum foil. Place in the refrigerator. It will last up to 2 weeks and be crisp.
- When slicing fresh mozzarella cheese put in the freezer for awhile first, then slice really thin.
- Do not store tomatoes, potatoes, fresh garlic, onions or shallots in the refrigerator.
- Eat three to four hours before bedtime to give your body time to digest your meal.
- Use Balsamic Vinegar on Strawberries, Ice Cream and Salad.
- Use powdered sugar in place of flour when rolling out holiday cookies for crispier, sweeter treats.
- Save orange and lemon peels in plastic bags in the freezer to be put in the blender for flavoring cakes, cookies or breads.

STAY
GRADE AA

"A LITTLE MORE HELP"

Cut up raw veggies and place them in separate plastic bags. Refrigerate. When the kids are hungry take a few veggies out of each bag and place on a plate. Dip into Ranch or blue cheese dressing or our favorite dipping sauce. Use vegetables such as broccoli, cauliflower, carrots, cucumbers, celery, red, green, yellow and orange bell peppers.

Picky Eaters:
I am often asked the question what to do about picky eaters. My first answer to that is get them involved in the planning. Have them choose at least one meal of the week. Go through my recipes with them and have them make a choice. Then have another member of the family make a choice. Let them see that if we respect the food choices of others they will also respect their food choice. I have a rule for picky eaters. They are required to at least taste what is prepared and placed on the table. I always make sure that if I know for sure there is someone who will dislike a dish that I have chosen for that night, that there will be plenty of other items that I know he or she will eat. Such as bread, potatoes, rice, noodles, fruit, vegetables, or greens. This is a nice way to keep everyone content and happy.

HOW TO BAKE CHICKEN WHEN YOU DON'T KNOW HOW

Time: 2 hours, including roasting time
1 4-5 lb. whole roasting chicken
Prepare roast chicken.

1. Remove package containing neck and liver etc. from the cavity. Rinse cavity thoroughly with cold water. Pat chicken dry.
2. Place on a rack in a roasting pan. Tent the chicken lightly with foil to prevent spattering the oven.
3. Roast at 425° (20 – 25 min. per pound). It is done when a meat thermometer placed into the center of the thigh muscle reads 180°.
4. Remove from oven and let rest about 15 min. before carving.
5. Carve the bird completely: remove breast skin. Slice off legs, thighs, wings. Slice breast meat for serving. Remove all the meat from the carcass while it is warm. You will have plenty of meat to use for other meals. Additionally, you may keep the carcass to use for making fresh chicken soup or freeze it to use later.

CONVERSATION STARTERS

What is your favorite thing to do each season of the year?
What do you think kids know that adults don't?
Have you ever been really scared of something? Why?
When you are a parent, how will you discipline your children?
What is your favorite vacation? Your dream vacation?
How much did things cost when you were a child?
Whose place do you like to visit the most?
Who is your favorite Disney character? Any Character?
Are you afraid of doing anything?
Who is the craziest in our family?
What is your oldest memory?
Describe the birth of each of your children.
How old were your parents when they got married?
What is your favorite activity? Sporting event?
How do you feel you fit into the family?
What are your talents? Your weaknesses?
What one thing is the most prized by you?
What do your friends like best about you?
What was the craziest or most embarrassing thing that has happened to you?
What would the world be like if everyone were the same?
What is one thing, for sure, that you want to do?
What is one thing that you would change about your school?
What foreign language would you like to learn?
What foreign country would you like to visit?
What name would you choose for yourself?
Do you know which side of the plate the fork goes on? The knife? The spoon?
Do you know your Mom's Birthday? Dad's Birthday?
What year were your Grandparents born?
Did your Mom and Dad have a black and white TV in their home?
What is your most favorite food?
Who is the best cook in our family?
How many times did you tell someone you loved them today?

INDEX

MONDAY
COMFORT FOOD 19

TUESDAY
ITALIAN NIGHT 41

WEDNESDAY
FMB NIGHT 67

THURSDAY
MEXICAN NIGHT

FRIDAY
PIZZA NIGHT

SATURDAY
GRILL NIGHT

SUNDAY
TRADITIONS

FAVORITE **SIDES** 207

FAVORITE **BREADS** 231

EVERYDAY **SALADS** 255

SANDWICHES **FOR DINNER** 273

DESSERTS **WE LOVE** 289

Meatless

Make yourself a copy.........

thefoodnanny

NANNY PLAN

mm/dd/yy - mm/dd/yy

MON	TUES	WED	THURS	FRI	SAT	SUN
THEME	THEME	THEME	THEME	THEME	THEME	THEME

MON	TUES	WED	THURS	FRI	SAT	SUN
THEME	THEME	THEME	THEME	THEME	THEME	THEME

NOTES:

Liz Edmunds

THEFOODNANNY.COM

........and start today!!!

thefoodnanny

SHOPPING LIST

mm/dd/yy - mm/dd/yy

PRODUCE	FISH/MEAT	CANNED GOODS	DAIRY	FROZEN	OTHER GROCERIES

For years Pati Palmer had been telling me about a wonderful girl in Italy that I needed to pair up with. She said that we had the same energy and she felt that we would work very well together on new Food Nanny projects. Michelle and I met and instantly felt a connection.
She has lived in Pistoia, Italy, in the heart of Tuscany for the past 25 years.
We came together on this book project and worked very hard together. We have made a great team along with Mara and Ann. Michelle and I knew right away that we wanted to go into business together ultimately selling Vita Casalinga: handmade ceramics from Italy.
Those beautiful ceramics are used in all our photographs throughout the book. Michelle's first Showroom for retail, wholesale and custom design, is located in Healdsburg, California.
Michelle, as my design director, designed and did all the photography, cooked my recipes and did the food styling. She is truly gifted. Mara Spangaro is not only gifted as our graphic designer but assisted Michelle through every step of the book. These girls really brought the Italian style that added warmth and depth to our book. Ann Luther, Editor, and fabulous cook herself, worked long hard hours with me editing recipes. She kept me going! Ann has also been a great friend and support to me for the past 40 years. Together, Michelle, Mara, Ann and I worked many hours to bring this book to the high level of our expectations. I love these women and would like to thank them publicly and most sincerely for their contributions.
I would especially like to thank my family, extended family and many friends for their continued support and fabulous recipes that they have shared with me throughout the years.

The Food Nanny xo

ACKNOWLEDGEMENTS

I want to thank my husband Steve, my children and their mates and my grandchildren for their forever support and love.

NANNY PLAN
DINNER FOR THE WEEKS:
SUN
MON
TUES
WED
THURS
FRI
SAT
SUN
MON
TUES
WED
THURS
FRI
SAT
NOTES:

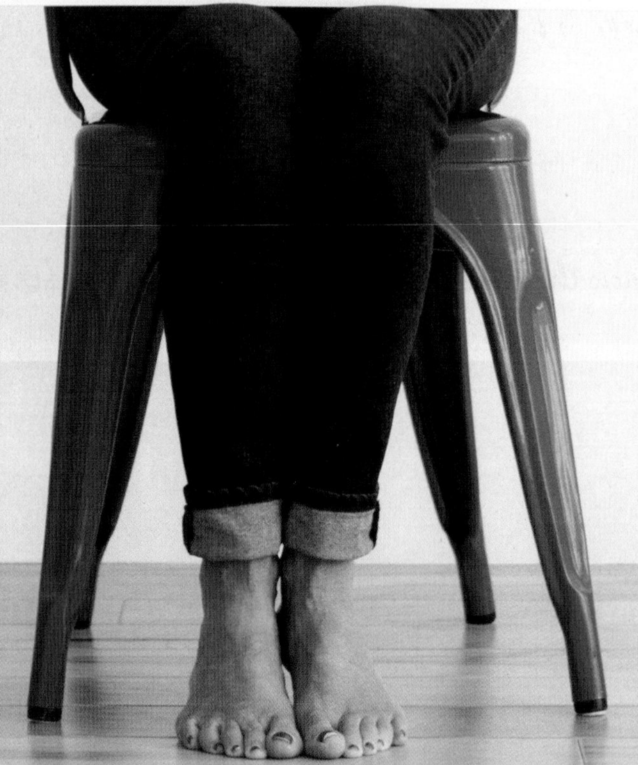

"EVERYONE LOVES THE VARIETY OF FOOD THAT MY MEAL PLAN OFFERS"

Now that you have come to the end of the book, you have not come to the end of your challenges and opportunities to make great food for your family.
In my 2 books, I have over 400 excellent recipes to choose from.
My food is not gourmet food, just good, hot, healthy food – served with plenty of vegetables and eaten with portion control.
I have included my famous "Nanny Plan" and "Shopping List" to make preparation less stressful and easier for you. The hardest part about dinner is trying to decide what to cook.
Waiting until 4 p.m. to decide what to cook is too late.
That is where my "Theme Nights" will help. Even if you are cooking for yourself, you deserve a meaningful dinnertime. In my 2 books I have tried to motivate those who don't want to cook anymore, and teach those of you who don't know how to cook, that cooking is essential in creating a strong family.
World wide, I have observed that dinnertime is the most natural setting for your family to sort out and talk over their day.
To look each other in the eye. To learn the art of conversation.
You cook for who is home. Cook and they will come home!
I know that applying my meal plan can work for your family as it did for mine for the past 30 plus years.
xo The Food Nanny

Liz Edmunds

LIZ EDMUNDS